What Your Colleagues Are

"As Harper points out, writing is a superpower of the twenty-first century. If we want our children to flourish long term, we must teach them to write. I am grateful that in this book I'm given a host of fresh ideas for getting my students writing purposefully and often. I'll keep this one very close to my planning desk."

—Dave Stuart Jr., author
These 6 Things

"You will want to have a full stack of sticky notes when you open up this book. It is full of practical strategies that will add not only purpose across your academic days, but also play, laughter, and fun. Combining humor and wisdom, Harper weaves in lessons and reminders about the different ways people write across platforms and genres. She moves from solid rationale to practical tactics, providing differentiation through modifications and extensions. With a predictable format, this book encompasses higher-order thinking, expanding possibilities for engagement and expression for all learners. You will use up your sticky notes marking the pages you'll want to bring to life in your classroom."

—Melanie Meehan, author
Every Child Can Write and *The Responsive Writing Teacher*

"From quick writing strategies to summarizing techniques to vocabulary building to digital writing invitations, *Write On & Write Now* provides practical yet savvy strategies for any teacher who wants to increase student writing volume without sacrificing space in an already crowded curriculum."

—Andy Schoenborn, co-author
Creating Confident Writers: For High School, College, and Life

"Rebecca Harper's book *Write On & Write Now: Grades 6–12 37 Strategies for Authentic Daily Writing in Every Content Area* is a gift to students and teachers in ELA and content classes. What Harper does will surely resonate with teachers: She offers writing suggestions that can easily be integrated into units of study across the curriculum. She's organized the chapters around daily writing students should and can do: writing summaries, learning academic vocabulary, and digital writing—writing to share text evidence. Practical writing experiences combined with detailed directions and expectations for teachers will ensure that students will be writing daily in every subject and developing an ease with thinking on paper. In the last chapter, Harper builds teachers' self-confidence by addressing, in great detail, common questions such as How do I engage and motivate all students? How can I find the time in my schedule? What if necessary resources aren't available? Teachers will appreciate Harper's authentic voice and experience as well as the Appendix that provides teacher tips for specific writing suggestions. This book is sure to become a resource teachers continually turn to again and again!"

—Laura Robb, author
Guided Practice for Reading Growth and *Read, Talk, Write*

"Content-area teachers are asked to incorporate writing as a regular, often daily, practice. While that is obviously a good idea, what does such writing look like—and how much time will it take out of an already jam-packed curriculum? Harper clearly pondered those questions and then created quick and accessible ways to help teachers find the answers. Grab this book, take a look at the "Write Now & Write On" strategies on the first few pages, turn to the corresponding chapters, and watch your students happily (no kidding!) begin writing."

—**ReLeah Lent, author**
Disciplinary Literacy in Action and *This is Disciplinary Literacy*

Write Now & Write On, Grades 6-12

For my children—Amelia, Macy Belle, and Vin:

Amelia—Strong women like you run in this family, but remember, even Atlas shrugged. When the weight of the world becomes too great, lean on those who love you most.

Macy Belle—The world knew we needed you. Keep marching to that beat that only you can hear; your song is so much better than the music everyone else already plays.

Vin—Remember, I may not be the last woman you'll love, but I was the first.

You are, and will always be, my three greatest accomplishments.

I will love you forever. No matter what.

But if you put me in Shady Pines, I'll come back to haunt you.☺

Love,

Mom

XXOO

Write Now & Write On, Grades 6–12

37 Strategies for Authentic Daily Writing in Every Content Area

Rebecca G. Harper

CORWIN Literacy

FOR INFORMATION:

Corwin

A SAGE Company

2455 Teller Road

Thousand Oaks, California 91320

(800) 233-9936

www.corwin.com

SAGE Publications Ltd.

1 Oliver's Yard

55 City Road

London EC1Y 1SP

United Kingdom

SAGE Publications India Pvt. Ltd.

B 1/I 1 Mohan Cooperative Industrial Area

Mathura Road, New Delhi 110 044

India

SAGE Publications Asia-Pacific Pte. Ltd.

18 Cross Street #10-10/11/12

China Square Central

Singapore 048423

President: Mike Soules

Associate Vice
President and Editorial Director: Monica Eckman

Senior Acquisitions Editor: Tori Bachman

Associate Content Development Editor: Sharon Wu

Editorial Assistant: Nancy Chung

Project Editor: Amy Schroller

Copy Editor: Diane DiMura

Typesetter: C&M Digitals (P) Ltd.

Proofreader: Larry Baker

Cover Designer: Scott Van Atta

Marketing Manager: Margaret O'Connor

Printed in the United States of America

ISBN 9781544398556

This book is printed on acid-free paper.

SUSTAINABLE FORESTRY INITIATIVE
Certified Chain of Custody
Promoting Sustainable Forestry
www.sfiprogram.org
SFI-01268

21 22 23 24 25 10 9 8 7 6 5 4 3 2 1

CONTENTS

ACKNOWLEDGMENTS

Writing this book would never have been possible without the support, encouragement, and help from some very special people who know me, and yet still love me.

My family certainly deserves a lot of the gratitude. Thank you to my husband, Will, and children, Amelia, Macy Belle, and Vin, who tolerate, and make fun of, I might add, my constant examination of all things literacy in this great wide world. Thank you for loving a woman who can be hard to love, because I sure do love you. To my mother-in-law, Deborah, who picks the kids up, takes them to swim and karate, and does anything else I ever need her to do with no questions asked, thank you. To Mom, Dad, and my stepmom, Kathy, I miss the three of you every single time I open my eyes. Here's hoping I have made you proud. I love you all.

Thank you to my boomerang department chair, Dr. E. Wayne Lord, who is probably one of the two people at work who really "get" me. Thank you for helping me spread my wings at work this year and for leaving me alone and letting me just be me.

Thank you to all of my Augusta University Writing Project peeps. You are the absolute BEST and brightest part of my job and I love every single one of you. A special thanks to those who assisted directly with this book:

Sacha Curtis

Carissa Keels

Alysha Mooney

Ashley Noble

Kirsten Pitock

Katie Strickland

Leigh Willmann

Other awesome people have provided me with writing examples and samples:

Melissa Delman

Donna Dugan

Jessica Horne

Lark Jones

Alicia Stephenson

Cindy Taylor

Rae Leigh Warner

Thank you to all the students who provided writing samples for this book:

Violet Childers

Patrick Fields

Will Fields

Hannah "Gunslinger" Gunsallus

Amelia Harper

Macy Belle Harper

Vin Harper

Gina Hofstetter

Lauren Hofstetter

Colette Kearney

Esther Marks

Emma Velie

People in this world who I just love:

Nicole Cain

Darby Finley

Ashley Holland

Robert Jackson

Dr. Karen Wish

And to all the people who still ask me if I am a hairdresser, thank you. It makes me smile. Seriously. Every. Single. Time.

With a full and grateful heart,

Publisher's Acknowledgments

Corwin gratefully acknowledges the contributions of the following reviewers:

Lynn Angus Ramos
Curriculum and Instruction Coordinator,
K–12 English Language Arts
DeKalb County School District
Decatur, GA

Marsha Voigt
Literacy Consultant and Author
Elgin, IL

WRITE NOW & WRITE ON STRATEGIES AT A GLANCE

Strategy	Page	Brief Description	Chapter	Skill(s) Supported	Student Resource Available?
Attack or Defend Writing	33	Students are given a quote and then write a brief argument for or against the issue/topic from the quote.	2: Parachute Writing	Argument writing	No
Brochure Summaries	87	Students write summaries of a text to create a brochure through the use of brief written statements, persuasive writing, and images.	3: Summarizing	Summarization Key details Comprehension Visualization	No
Close Reading Images	185	Students closely evaluate an image related to a concept or topic being studied to gather evidence for a specific purpose.	6: Just the Facts	Evaluation Close reading	No
Commercials	92	Students use persuasive writing to create and perform their own commercials to support the summarization of a text or a concept/unit of study.	3: Summarizing	Summarization Key details Comprehension Oral presentation	No
Continuum Debate 2.0	202	Students use text evidence to craft an argument on a specific concept or topic and then participate in an oral debate against a classmate.	6: Just the Facts	Finding and evaluating text evidence Arguments and claims Oral debate	No

(Continued)

(Continued)

Strategy	Page	Brief Description	Chapter	Skill(s) Supported	Student Resource Available?
Drop Drafts	20	Students informally respond to a question or prompt and then discard the writing.	2: Parachute Writing	Quick writing Reflection	No
Evidence Tug-of-War Activator Strategy	175	Students compare the quantity of evidence from two separate texts.	6: Just the Facts	Finding textual evidence	No
Figure This	51	Students use figurative language to explain their understanding of a specific concept, topic, or idea.	2: Parachute Writing	Quick write Summarization Comparison	Yes (page 51) (optional)
Hashtag Summaries	163	Students create a hashtag to summarize a piece of text or concepts studied and then defend their work.	5: Digital Worlds	Summarization Justification of response	No
Instagram Ideas	140	Students create an Instagram post using visuals and text related to the concept or idea they are studying.	5: Digital Worlds	Visualization Summarization	No
List, Pin, Label, Share	168	Students create a list of words they know related to a specific concept or topic, then they group the words together and create a collage-style board to visually display the word relationships.	5: Digital Worlds	Activating prior knowledge Academic vocabulary	No
Mix and Match	179	Students use colored paint strips to pull text evidence related to a specific prompt from multiple sources.	6: Just the Facts	Finding textual evidence Evaluation of multiple sources	No
Murder Mysteries	198	Students use a crime scene scenario to evaluate text evidence and make conclusions to solve the crime/mystery.	6: Just the Facts	Finding and evaluating text evidence Summarization Drawing conclusions	Yes (page 253) (optional)
Neighborhood Map	45	Students draw a neighborhood map of places that are important to them, orally explaining while they draw.	2: Parachute Writing	Visualization Oral presentation	No

Strategy	Page	Brief Description	Chapter	Skill(s) Supported	Student Resource Available?
Obituaries	96	Students use the style of an obituary to summarize a piece of text, concept, or unit of study.	3: Summarizing	Summarization Key details Comprehension	No
Paint Strip Partners	210	Students use paint strips to write a detailed description of a process, sequence, or protocol as a result of a concept or topic being studied.	6: Just the Facts	Summarization Synthesis	Yes (page 235) (optional)
Pictorial Definitions	111	Students create visual pictures or images to represent the definition of key vocabulary terms.	4: Academic Vocabulary	Comprehension Vocabulary development Imagery	No
Picture Collage Content	153	Students create their own Picture Collage around a specific concept or topic using images, graphics, and words.	5: Digital Worlds	Visualization Summarization Design	No
Pinterest Paragraphs	145	Students create their own Pinterest boards around a specific concept or topic using images, words, and written text.	5: Digital Worlds	Visualization Classification of information Summarization	No
Pizza Slice Summary	63	Students use the sections of an inverted triangle to narrow the amount of information in their summaries, getting down to only the most important main idea(s) at the tip of the triangle.	3: Summarizing	Summarization Main idea Comprehension	Yes (page 230) (optional)
Quick Writes	24	Students informally respond to a question or prompt to springboard into a lesson or at a key point in the lesson.	2: Parachute Writing	Quick writing Synthesis of information	No
Ransom Note Writing	121	Students cut out terms from magazines and newspapers to create a collage of words to support a key academic topic, concept, or unit of study.	4: Academic Vocabulary	Vocabulary development Imagery	No

(Continued)

(Continued)

Strategy	Page	Brief Description	Chapter	Skill(s) Supported	Student Resource Available?
Sketch to Stretch	19	Students informally draw what they "see" in their heads while a text or selection of text is being read.	2: Parachute Writing	Visualization Comprehension	No
Summary Memes	83	Students write a brief summary of the text by creating a meme.	3: Summarizing	Summarization Key details Comprehension Visualization	No
Summary Sentence Sweeps	67	Students categorize details from the text as Important, Not Important, and Don't Know, in order to write a summary of the content.	3: Summarizing	Summarization Key details Comprehension	No
Survival Words	108	Students use a Likert scale rating system to self-assess their vocabulary knowledge of key terms that are essential for understanding prior to reading a text or learning about a concept or unit of study.	4: Academic Vocabulary	Activating prior knowledge Vocabulary development	Yes (page 231)
Text Mapping	190	Students lay out an entire text on a sheet of chart paper to examine, evaluate, annotate, and gather evidence from the text based on specific requirements set by the teacher.	6: Just the Facts	Evaluation Finding textual evidence Close reading Text annotation	Yes
Say What?	40	Students gather specific evidence/arguments on both sides of an issue/topic.	2: Parachute Writing	Quick writing Arguments and claims using evidence	Yes (optional)
Three-Panel Summaries	76	Students create summaries of a text by incorporating key details onto a trifold sheet of paper, adding visuals or images to each portion of written text.	3: Summarizing	Summarization Key details Comprehension Visualization	No

Strategy	Page	Brief Description	Chapter	Skill(s) Supported	Student Resource Available?
Tweet the Text	158	Students create tweets in response to a series of images or text excerpts to summarize or respond to the content.	5: Digital Worlds	Summarization Quick Writing	No
Two Truths and a Lie	207	Students use text evidence to write two truths and a lie in response to a text that they read, and then they present their work to their peers to have them guess which one is the lie.	6: Just the Facts	Finding text evidence Summarization Evaluation	Yes (page 234) (optional)
Word Sort	125	Students sort and classify a group of vocabulary words from a text or unit of study and justify their work.	4: Academic Vocabulary	Vocabulary development Justification of response	No
Word Splash	130	Students make connections between two words from a list related to a text, concept, or unit of study, and then justify their responses.	4: Academic Vocabulary	Vocabulary development Activating prior knowledge	No
What's Missing Activator Strategy	177	Students learn about the quality of text evidence through the use of puzzles.	6: Just the Facts	Finding quality text evidence	No
What's the Word?	177	Students use academic vocabulary to complete sentence frames around a topic, text, or unit of study, and justify their responses.	4: Academic Vocabulary	Vocabulary development Argument/ Justification	No
Write Around the Text	195	Students respond to a text excerpt to evaluate, examine, and annotate based on specific requirements set by the teacher.	6: Just the Facts	Evaluation Finding textual evidence Close reading Text annotation	No
Written Conversations	54	Students take turns writing a conversation back and forth on a selected concept or topic.	2: Parachute Writing	Quick writing Review Synthesis of information	No

Chapter

1

WHY
WRITE NOW?

· ·

"My students just can't write."

"These kids aren't writing anymore."

"They don't write."

"Grammar? They have no idea."

"Social media has ruined writing."

Do any of these statements sound familiar? Regardless of the location, age, demographics, or grade, students today are viewed as having less than adequate writing skills and limited experience with writing tasks and engagements. Yet this isn't a new trend in education. Writing skills, according to news articles and research reports, have been on the decline for a number of years (Bloomberg News, 2012; Dieterich, 1977; Westin, 2013). In fact, in 2018, students received an average score of 536 on the evidence-based reading and writing portion of the SAT (National Center for Education; www.nces.ed.gov). Similarly, the National Assessment of Educational Progress (NAEP) notes that in 2011, only 27 percent of eighth- and twelfth-grade students scored at or above proficient on the writing portion of the NAEP (National Center for Education Statistics, 2011). Plus, in that same year, 20 percent of eighth graders and 21 percent of twelfth graders scored "below basic," meaning that they are not able to perform at grade level or minimum standards with regard to writing.

Now let's consider the *why* behind this decline in writing skills. If you read a recent study of U.S. middle schools conducted by Education Trust (Santelises, 2015) you'll discover that only about 38 percent of the assignments were aligned with grade-appropriate standards. Also, several of the assignments analyzed in this study focused on basic skills and level-one knowledge or recall questions. In addition, few assignments required students to write brief responses, and even fewer required extended,

CHAPTER 1
Why Write Now?

CHAPTER 2
Parachute Writing

CHAPTER 3
Sum It All Up

CHAPTER 4
All the Right Words

CHAPTER 5
Digital Worlds

CHAPTER 6
Just the Facts

CHAPTER 7
Expecting the
Unexpected

multiparagraph responses. This limited engagement and exposure severely impact a student's ability to compose a response. A lack of experience with writing creates students with weak writing abilities simply because they haven't had enough practice doing it. And while some blame technology on these deficits, it's fairly easy to see that students are proficient in informal and underdeveloped writing (those most likely seen on social media); it's the formal and extended responses with rich academic vocabulary that many students find difficult because those are often not the ones they are practicing in their personal lives.

Despite what some individuals blame on technology—communications of today that include texting, blogging, social media, and web posting—the notion that students aren't writing as well as they used to is no new revelation. Teachers have been lamenting for some time, long before our kids carried smartphones, that students simply do not have the writing skills necessary to effectively communicate across disciplines (Graham & Perin, 2006; Pope, 2005; Sheils, 1975). In fact, many teachers note that what writing students do is frequently racked with problems and lacks a basic understanding of the fundamentals of writing. In addition, some teachers state that their students aren't writing at all, thus causing deficiencies due to lack of experience.

Stop & Think

What types of writing do your students struggle with? What types of writing do they enjoy? In what ways do they excel in writing?

Yet today's world demands competency in the skill of writing. According to the National Writing Project, writing skills are among the most important skills needed in order to be successful and label it as a gateway for students' inclusion in a participatory democratic society. Being able to write, and write well, serves as a means to communicate thoughts and ideas, opens doors for people, and eliminates gates often put into place due to cultural and social differences and socioeconomic inequities. Most careers require individuals to possess at least rudimentary writing skills, and many entail the need for a job-specific writing skill set. In fact, according to the National Commission on Writing for America's Families, Schools, and Colleges (2004), writing is referred to as a "threshold skill" for advancement and employment in the workplace. Plus, poor writing has been blamed for corporate lawsuits, taxpayer dollars for remedial writing courses, and loss of internet and retail business due to spelling and grammatical errors (Cullen, 2020; Pope, 2005). There really is no way around the fact that today's students simply need to know how to write for a variety of purposes and audiences.

This should come as no surprise to educators because we are charged with integrating College and Career Readiness standards that emphasize the multifaceted nature of writing and the need to demonstrate competency in composition for a variety of purposes across the content areas, including composition needed for a variety of careers. However, Conley (2005) found, in his study that addressed the skills gap between high school seniors and the literacy expectations of university work, that the students who frequently made As and Bs in high school were not necessarily ready for the sophisticated literacy demands of university coursework. In fact, in a later study, he suggested that the one factor that could increase a high school student's future success rate in college was to increase the quality and amount of writing they were expected to produce (Conley, 2007).

Stop & Think

Writing Lingo—Terms to know

- Genre—the category of the writing. Different genres have varying components, styles, or forms. Some examples of genre include personal narrative, biography, or poetry.
- Audience—Who will read the piece?
- Purpose—the "why" of the writing. This is the reason for writing or the objective of the piece.

The reality is that people write for any number of reasons and on a daily basis. Unfortunately, they aren't always aware of just *how* much they are writing. Part of this can be attributed to the fact that much of what we write daily is what I would call "writing to live." It's the writing that we do that gets us through our day and helps us function in today's society. While most people aren't writing novels, they are sending texts, writing to-do lists, posting on social media, punching up their résumés, and sending emails to colleagues. This kind of writing involves shifting from topic to topic, developing clear purposes for writing, and considering the audience, all while taking part in the daily writing we do.

Just for a minute, consider what you wrote today. Did you send an email? Text? Post something online? Fill out a form? You might be surprised at how much you write daily, and I bet your students would be too. Drawing attention to the vast amounts

CHAPTER 1
Why Write Now?

CHAPTER 2
Parachute Writing

CHAPTER 3
Sum It All Up

CHAPTER 4
All the Right Words

CHAPTER 5
Digital Worlds

CHAPTER 6
Just the Facts

CHAPTER 7
Expecting the Unexpected

CHAPTER 1
Why Write Now?

CHAPTER 2
Parachute Writing

CHAPTER 3
Sum It All Up

CHAPTER 4
All the Right Words

CHAPTER 5
Digital Worlds

CHAPTER 6
Just the Facts

CHAPTER 7
Expecting the
Unexpected

of writing students do on their own can help cast the net wider so that they begin to consider themselves writers as well.

Daily Writing Evolution . . . or Revolution?

While most educators are well aware of the *need* for students to write well, many charge that students are not writing as much as they did in the past. Students are no longer writing letters and mailing them to friends and family, fewer are writing printed stories, and even fewer are fluent at basic grammar exercises and engagements.

Despite these claims, however, upon examination, we'd notice that students are indeed taking part in a number of writing engagements and are writing more than students in the past. How? Think about how social media has changed the way we write. People now can instantly post their thoughts and ideas about myriad subjects at the click of a button. Now, granted, these thoughts and ideas aren't always fully developed and are often anecdotal in nature. In fact, social media has quickly become the place where individuals record their thoughts, reactions, and personal moments throughout a day or week, and is a prime venue to capture underdeveloped writing, responses to activities, and opinions on just about anything. As many of our schools shifted to online or hybrid modes because of the pandemic, students found additional ways to connect with their classmates through writing. Chat features on Zoom and Microsoft Teams, Google documents, and other web-based programs offered students yet another opportunity for writing.

Plus, fluency with social media communication modes and chat applications—which are largely compositional in nature—is starting earlier and earlier as more young people are beginning to utilize technological tools to communicate in personal settings as well as academic ones. This hit home with me right after our daughters each received an iPod Touch for Christmas. I came home, checked their "phones," and was floored at the number of texts our oldest daughter had. Instead of calling my husband, though, I sent him this text (see left).

Part of the appeal of this type of informal writing and responding is its instantaneous nature. It's not necessarily about people fully developing ideas, but more about them responding to their environment, reflecting on events of their lives, and blowing off steam. This instantaneous nature and knee-jerk response posts are often the reasons why some posts end up getting some young people in trouble. Because of the "live" nature of social media, some individuals don't fully process or think about the impact of their words and social media presence. In addition, most social media posts aren't really revised. If anything, you might see that a tweet or post has been deleted if it has been deemed offensive or taken out of context. Yet this instantaneous nature lends itself to pointed class and life lessons through the critical examination of posts, discussions regarding the importance of processing time or wait time, and the permanence of words.

Zinsser (2001) points out that today's information age, with its use of high-tech paraphernalia, is writing based. Texts, emails, and social media posts all have a specific writing craft with a subset of tools, that, like any other tool, must be used correctly. Social media, in particular, has forced change in written communication. And our students are not only part of this evolving world—they are often forging ahead. For example, this is the generation that has grown up with the symbol # meaning hashtag and not another way to say a number, or, to go even further back, the pound button on the telephone. Hashtag just became part of my own personal lexicon a few years ago; I had to *learn* what the word meant as an adult. But it will be part of the core vocabulary of my children and students, as they have grown up experiencing *hashtag* in an organic manner. They lived the emergent definition of the word, which grew out of necessity, out of functionality, and is now permanent. (In fact, just the other day, I listened to an automated menu for a government office and the recording stated, "To hear this menu again, please press the pound or hashtag key." Now there is an example of how much social media has changed the way we live.) Writing in the information age has its own unique set of parameters, vocabulary, and nuances, all of which our students are creating, learning, and reinventing daily.

Even adults who have seen the progression of technology and its effect on our writing are using these so-called new digital literacies as we read and write in our lives. In many ways, digital literacies are helping us "rewrite" our own lives as we learn how to integrate these new literacies into our existing ones. For many students, these literacies are the ones they became proficient in first; there was no substitution or replacement. They have been some of the first modes of written expression available to our students. In essence, it's all they have ever known. Think about the video of the toddler that went viral as her parents recorded her trying to swipe a magazine like an iPad, and kindergartners taking part in Zoom classes while typing in answers to a teacher's prompt.

This same type of phenomenon plays out in the classroom all the time. Recently, a middle school teacher friend of mine was explaining how sometimes when assigning homework, she only wants the students to complete certain numbers, so she will write something like, "Page 17, #7–12." Unfortunately, her students interpreted it differently and asked, "Hey, what's hashtag 7–12 mean?"

 **Stop & Think**

Think about the word *viral*. Prior to the coronavirus pandemic, how many of your students would have thought of *viral* as something that was related only to the internet?

Honor Many Different Kinds of Writing

These are the kinds of exchanges that might be easy to discredit or brush off, with the thought that they are not useful for teaching. However, these real-world types of

CHAPTER 1
Why Write Now?

CHAPTER 2
Parachute Writing

CHAPTER 3
Sum It All Up

CHAPTER 4
All the Right Words

CHAPTER 5
Digital Worlds

CHAPTER 6
Just the Facts

CHAPTER 7
Expecting the Unexpected

CHAPTER 1
Why Write Now?

CHAPTER 2
Parachute Writing

CHAPTER 3
Sum It All Up

CHAPTER 4
All the Right Words

CHAPTER 5
Digital Worlds

CHAPTER 6
Just the Facts

CHAPTER 7
Expecting the Unexpected

writing are just what students need to see that there can be a bridge between the personal writing they are doing on their own and their academic, school-driven writing engagements. In many instances, students fail to see the connection between what they are learning in school and how it relates to their personal lives. How many times do teachers hear the words, "Why do we have to learn this?" or "When am I going to use this?" It isn't always asked simply because students are unmotivated to learn or simply don't want to learn, but instead, because they don't fully understand the *why* behind the instruction.

Here is an example of everyday writing. This is Lark Nation, a weekly sports email column written by Lark Jones, the former mayor of North Augusta, South Carolina. Each week, Lark sends out his play-by-play of the football lineup for the week to a list of fans on an email list. Lark Nation is another example of nonacademic writing people do that does have a specific audience and purpose.

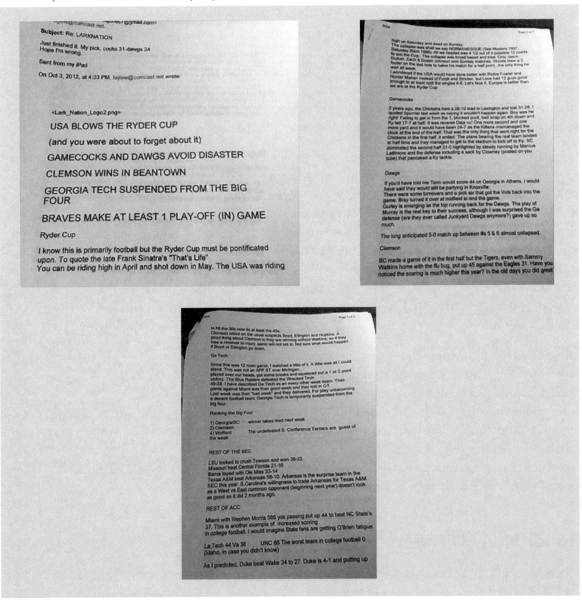

Students need to see that writers are not just those who write novels and plays but are also people who post on Facebook, send texts, and use Instagram. Writers are people who write lists to keep them on track, use note-taking strategies to help them prepare tests, or write lyrics to songs, screenplays, and blogs. They also write ads to sell items online, profiles on dating apps, and workout sets for the gym. It's difficult really to find someone who isn't a writer. Showing students the wide-encompassing definition of a writer can help them see that they already possess many of the skills needed to complete academic-based writing tasks. And bridging their informal writing—like what they're already doing on social media and with technology in school—to the more formal, academic writing required by standards and in college and careers can provide that foundation. As noted earlier, the biggest impediment to improving students' academic writing is volume and practice—so doesn't it make sense to increase writing volume by harnessing into school settings the everyday writing students are already doing?

The Reading and Writing Connection

Reading and writing are so intertwined it is impossible to divorce the two. By teaching writing, you are teaching reading and vice versa. Both serve as important components in successful comprehension and communication of ideas and thoughts. In fact, many of the strategies explored in this book will teach components of both skills. When writing, I am retrieving a number of substantial reading skills that help make sentence construction possible. Similarly, when reading, I am attending to the structure of the piece I am reading, making mental notes about the author's craft and style, and storing new words in my vocabulary repository.

The Call to Write Throughout the Day

There's no arguing that writing is a valuable skill, one that is marketable and demanded in a variety of career, home, and academic settings. It is clear that students need to possess a number of composition skills in their repertoire and this should be done in a pervasive and persistent manner. In other words, students should be writing daily, and they should be writing a lot, both inside and outside of school. Plus, they need to be taught how to write better. Both ELA and content classrooms are where much of this daily writing should be happening.

Stop & Think

What holds you back from incorporating writing daily in the classroom? What challenges make daily writing difficult?

Yet one major issue that often comes up is *how* the teaching and implementation of effective writing instruction play out in the classroom. In some cases, especially in the middle and secondary settings, teaching writing is viewed as the English Language Arts (ELA) teacher's job. Because many non-ELA teachers have not had professional development or courses in the teaching of writing, they are often unsure of how to do it. Whenever I present professional development workshops or teach a class on content literacy, many of the middle and secondary content teachers have the same concern: How are they going to teach one more skill in their already overcrowded curriculum, chock full of standards that are difficult for students to learn anyway?

CHAPTER 1
Why Write Now?

CHAPTER 2
Parachute Writing

CHAPTER 3
Sum It All Up

CHAPTER 4
All the Right Words

CHAPTER 5
Digital Worlds

CHAPTER 6
Just the Facts

CHAPTER 7
Expecting the Unexpected

CHAPTER 1
Why Write Now?

CHAPTER 2
Parachute Writing

CHAPTER 3
Sum It All Up

CHAPTER 4
All the Right Words

CHAPTER 5
Digital Worlds

CHAPTER 6
Just the Facts

CHAPTER 7
Expecting the
Unexpected

⟫⟫ Notebooks as a Teaching Tool

Here's an easy idea. Many content teachers utilize notebooks as a teaching tool. Think about using science notebooks for logging observations about scientific processes, math notebooks for recording formulas, real-world math examples, and models, and interactive notebooks for English language learners.

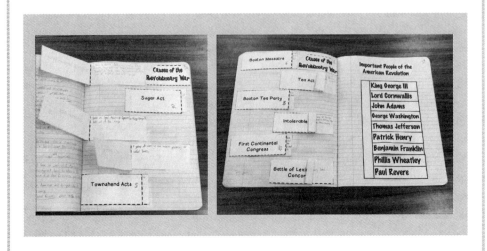

Remember though, we've known for a while that writing doesn't just help students prove they read something or know something; it also generates new thinking (Langer & Applebee, 1987). Plus, Graham and Perin (2007) found that writing in content classes assists students in generating new ideas and thinking, improves their critical thinking skills, and helps them retain new content knowledge.

Knowing there are benefits to a strategy or practice, but not understanding the best way to leverage it in the classroom isn't helpful. It's like knowing that weight training is effective for building muscles, but you don't know which exercises help build what muscles or how to perform them. You end up with over-trained biceps and undertrained rotator cuffs, or you get injured because you train with poor form. For content literacy implementation to be effective, the strategy and content must work in tandem with each other. Teachers need opportunities to determine which engagements work best with their content and they need to see how one engagement looks in a math classroom and then how it looks in another content area, like history, for example.

Sadly, some districts try "one size fits all" training, meaning they attempt to teach the material in the same manner to all grade levels. This doesn't take into consideration that middle school and high school are *so* different from elementary school. The concerns, climate, daily routines, schedule, you name it. Everything is different, so when districts swoop in and develop training programs that don't take this into consideration, they often are ineffective. Additionally, for many teachers, when new initiatives such as a content area literacy emphasis come down the pike, many don't feel like they can add one more thing to their plate. Plus, content literacy instruction can't be delivered in the same manner that literacy strategies for ELA teachers are. Because the purpose, content, and structure are all different, the professional learning for content literacy must be as well.

Real content literacy implementation isn't a quick fix program or a scripted program that you teach with fidelity. Instead, it requires careful consideration of the content that is being taught as well as reflection and critical examination. To effectively teach literacy components in and around other content areas, one must have an intimate knowledge of the standards and a strategic lesson focus.

It has become evident to me, as I have worked with schools across the country, that there is some confusion in our profession about what it means to teach literacy concepts within content classrooms. Here's what I suggest: Know your content and your standards intimately, but also know your students along with their experiences and backgrounds. This will aid in the construction of engagements that are purposeful and meaningful and that make sense for both the content and the group of students in your classes. Choose a variety of writing strategies that will help students process and understand the content that is being delivered in their subject-specific classes. This will help kids realize that writing in content classrooms actually can help them "get" the material and see that there are many different types of writing. Plus, when teachers actively and strategically integrate writing that is reflective of the real world, students are more likely to see the relevance and the big picture.

This is where the win occurs: when students are able to see how what they are already doing in their personal writing and reading lives is related to what is expected in their school lives. This is showing students true literacy. Literacy has a transformative power and is not just a technical skill but the foundation for individual agency and power (Freire & Macedo, 1987).

Much of the writing that is conducted across the school day should be messy. It should look rough. In fact, when I conduct professional development on the subject, I include a picture of me in middle school. Why? Because it is ugly and I explain that this is what most writing in content classes should look like; it should look like me in seventh grade: ugly!

However, something that on the outside looks like trash can represent hours of thinking and planning. This is key: In order to increase the volume of writing our students are doing, the writing that is done daily is not meant to be polished. Instead, it simply serves as a vehicle for making sense of the material, processing the dense content, or reflecting on a subject. That type of writing is powerful.

How do I know? Because I live it. Yet there is *one* particular experience with writing that truly made me see how powerful the messy process of writing is.

When my mother was diagnosed with inoperable brain cancer in 2016, I began the task of writing her eulogy. Not on paper, but in my head. For almost four months, I drafted this document in my head whenever I had time and ideas. In the hospital while she slept. On a plane to speak at a literacy conference in Arkansas. In the car line waiting to pick up my kids. At night when I could not sleep. However, it was not until the day after she died and the night before her funeral that I actually put pen to paper. The images below are some of the documents used to deliver my mother's eulogy at her funeral in December of 2016. If you notice, it looks messy. Haphazard. Unorganized. Yet these images represent almost four months of deliberate planning. Drafting and revision. Rewrites that existed only in my head, but aided substantially in the final, yet not so final product.

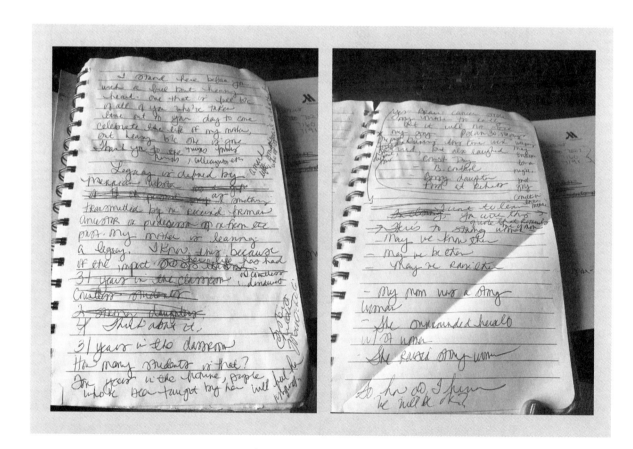

Writing my mother's eulogy taught me a number of things about writing that I want ELA and content teachers to convey to our students:

- Most writing is messy.

- Pre-writing does not have to be written.

CHAPTER 1
Why Write Now?

CHAPTER 2
Parachute Writing

CHAPTER 3
Sum It All Up

CHAPTER 4
All the Right Words

CHAPTER 5
Digital Worlds

CHAPTER 6
Just the Facts

CHAPTER 7
Expecting the Unexpected

CHAPTER 1
Why Write Now?

CHAPTER 2
Parachute Writing

CHAPTER 3
Sum It All Up

CHAPTER 4
All the Right Words

CHAPTER 5
Digital Worlds

CHAPTER 6
Just the Facts

CHAPTER 7
Expecting the
Unexpected

- Revision is ongoing.

- Research writing needs to be relevant.

Most Writing Is Messy

The writing that most of us do on a daily basis is less than perfect and lives a drafty existence. In other words, most of what we write in our daily lives never becomes published and polished. Instead, it functions mainly as a means to inform, communicate, understand, explain, and process a variety of pieces of information. In the content classroom, this tenet is especially important. For one, it gives students the freedom to write without the pressure of making certain that every piece of writing they complete is publishable quality. In fact, 90 percent of what students write in their classrooms should fit the above descriptors, but they should be doing these types of writings DAILY. (Some possible strategies that will be highlighted in later chapters are drop drafts, five-minute drops, and quick writes.) Practicing writing for a variety of purposes gives students opportunities to improve these basic skills and aids students when they do complete writing tasks that need to be more polished and presentable. Consequently, because so much of the writing that students should be doing in the classroom will be less than perfect, the amount of formal grading that teachers should do when it comes to writing decreases. Instead, qualitative feedback on papers with a specific focus could yield better results from students since many writers focus on a letter grade and either ignore the comments if the grade were satisfactory, or shut down completely if the grade is poor.

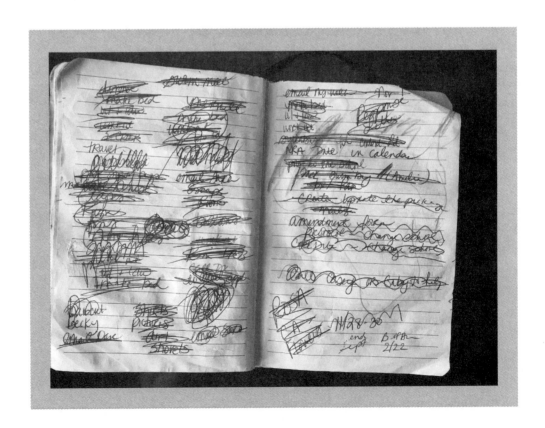

Pre-Writing Does Not Have to Be Written

One mistake I made early on as a writing teacher was requiring students to submit a graphic organizer or another form of written pre-writing as proof that they planned out their writing piece. While the written pre-writing task did aid some students in the construction of their composition, I found that some students haphazardly filled in the obligatory organizer at the end of the writing task so they would not lose points for omitting this portion of the assignment. This is not the true purpose of pre-writing or planning. Some tasks require more planning than others. In fact, for some writing engagements, little planning may be needed before the student is ready to begin the drafting phase, whereas, for others, a substantial amount of planning is warranted. Plus, planning and pre-writing need not be written. In fact, valuable planning may take place through thinking or oral discussion. These venues are no less important than written ones. Offering students space and time to discuss their writing ideas and plans, think through the story, and create connections in this time can help them develop stronger writing pieces down the line.

Revision Is Ongoing

Revision is not a destination; writers do not simply arrive at the revision step, complete the task, and move on to the final draft. Instead, revision—and writing for that matter—are recursive processes that are ongoing and certainly not linear. While I was drafting my mom's eulogy in my head, I was also revising and modifying the writing, whether it was in phrasing, word choice, or organizational structure. In addition, when I delivered her eulogy, I made some revision decisions right there in the pulpit. While I had included several stories about her, including humorous ones from when she was hospitalized, I looked out at my audience and realized that a couple of those stories might not go over well. (One, in particular, recounted my 60-year-old mother telling me after reading a chemo pamphlet that she could still take birth control, which I reminded her she did not need.) While the stories I had included in my draft were all relevant and on topic, my awareness of my audience reminded me that revision was still needed.

You see, revision is a sophisticated process and is not as simple as capitalizing letters and adding punctuation (That's editing.). Revision requires writers to revisit their pieces, consider their audience, think about the words they chose, and make decisions about the flow, purpose, and voice of their piece. And in all reality, revision never really is over.

Research Writing Needs to Be Relevant

While research writing often is a struggle for both teachers and students, it doesn't have to be. Most students, and individuals in general, research on a daily basis; they just don't call it that. Instead, it's called "looking something up," "looking up information," or "finding something out." Additionally, the research people do in their real lives has an important quality that much of the research in classrooms lack—authenticity and relevance. When my mother got sick, I began intensive research on brain cancer.

CHAPTER 1
Why Write Now?

CHAPTER 2
Parachute Writing

CHAPTER 3
Sum It All Up

CHAPTER 4
All the Right Words

CHAPTER 5
Digital Worlds

CHAPTER 6
Just the Facts

CHAPTER 7
Expecting the Unexpected

CHAPTER 1
Why Write Now?

CHAPTER 2
Parachute Writing

CHAPTER 3
Sum It All Up

CHAPTER 4
All the Right Words

CHAPTER 5
Digital Worlds

CHAPTER 6
Just the Facts

CHAPTER 7
Expecting the Unexpected

Prior to her illness, I knew nothing about anaplastic astrocytoma or glioblastoma. Today, I am much more knowledgeable due to the vast amount of research I conducted due to the necessity for information because it was relevant and authentic.

Students are no different. For example, they do research on their own time about their favorite singers, sports stars, and hobbies. Without having to explicitly instruct them, many are able to use the internet and other sources to locate appropriate information on these self-chosen topics. Classroom teachers can capitalize on this by including topics and content that students help select.

Making research writing relevant is another key component for successful integration of this sophisticated writing genre. When at all possible, students should be involved in generating research questions that relate to the worlds they live in. For example, recently a neighborhood near my university began an urban community garden. Several of the teachers I work with mentioned that some of their students were interested in how this project got started and how they could replicate it in their own neighborhoods. For those students, research on an urban community garden project is not only an authentic task, but it is relevant and directly related to the real worlds in which they reside.

Another possibility for research writing in the classroom is the integration of a Genius Hour. During this time, students are able to research topics and projects of interest to them. At my daughter's school, topics range from the design and creation of dog clothing, conservation of specific species, Emperor penguins, genres of dance, cupcake cooking techniques, and more. Dedicated space for this type of activity allows students the time and place to conduct research that is high interest and purposeful.

When designing and implementing writing engagements in the classroom, I implore teachers to consider the principles discussed above. Instead of focusing on a final product or the steps in the process, teachers can encourage and facilitate writers as they think through their writing while they plan, revisit, and revise. Acknowledging these simple principles offers opportunities to nurture and support writers as they wade through a variety of writing engagements in both the academic and personal realm.

Write Now . . . and Write On

Writing, in its truest form, serves as a vehicle for thought, reflection, and making sense of the world we live in. We use writing to help us construct narratives, tell our stories, give credence for an argument, and remind us of all the tasks we need to complete today. Yet writing is not static, but rather is constantly evolving, as new digital practices become integrated with traditional ones. Writing has a transformative power and offers opportunities for individuals to communicate ideas, challenge or support a position, and present a message for a specific purpose. Because of the vast potential of this often-neglected skill, writing in all classrooms is simply non-negotiable; it is an absolute necessity.

The following chapters include writing strategies and engagements that can be used in all classrooms in some form or fashion. My goal is to offer content teachers a number of "in-the-moment" writing strategies to increase the volume of writing students are doing daily—strategies that tap into their everyday literacies and interests. Plus, these strategies offer teachers another opportunity to gradually release the responsibility back to the students. Modeling the strategies, and then completing them together as a class before having students tackle them individually or with a partner, provides a safe and manageable space for writing instruction. This scaffolding allows students to engage with writing in a nonthreatening, low-stakes manner while working toward a larger writing goal as they complete smaller more manageable writing tasks.

Below are some highlights from each chapter that may help you determine just where you want to start reading first. Doing this can help ensure that the time spent is not wasted on strategies or engagements that don't fit your purpose. Don't worry if some lessons don't go exactly as planned or if you find that you gravitate toward certain types of strategies. The important component is simply to Write Now . . . and Write On!

Chapter 2—Parachute Writing: Strategies for Quick Writing

This chapter includes writing engagements that can be completed in quick bursts of time, called "parachute writings." These types of writings are dropped in during a day's lesson and can be completed in one quick sitting. Because of the versatile nature of these types of writings, they can be modified for a number of content areas and tasks.

Chapter 3—Sum It All Up: Strategies for Finding Key Details and Summarizing

Summarizing continues to be a skill that many students struggle with. Some aren't sure of what details to include in their summaries and end up including extraneous amounts of information, while others don't include enough material to adequately summarize a selection. In this chapter, strategies are provided to address this crucial skill.

Chapter 4—All the Right Words: Strategies for Learning Academic Vocabulary

Academic vocabulary often dominates the content classroom. Not only are students expected to be able to write and orally articulate a number of subject matter concepts, but they are also expected to utilize appropriate academic vocabulary and language to convey appropriate meaning and logical progression of ideas. In some cases, a student's unfamiliarity with discipline-specific words can result in underdeveloped written and oral responses. The strategies presented in this chapter focus on overcoming these challenges by scaffolding students toward appropriate academic vocabulary.

CHAPTER 1
Why Write Now?

CHAPTER 2
Parachute Writing

CHAPTER 3
Sum It All Up

CHAPTER 4
All the Right Words

CHAPTER 5
Digital Worlds

CHAPTER 6
Just the Facts

CHAPTER 7
Expecting the Unexpected

CHAPTER 1
Why Write Now?

CHAPTER 2
Parachute Writing

CHAPTER 3
Sum It All Up

CHAPTER 4
All the Right Words

CHAPTER 5
Digital Worlds

CHAPTER 6
Just the Facts

CHAPTER 7
Expecting the Unexpected

Chapter 5—Digital Worlds: Strategies for Meeting Students Where They're Already Hanging Out

Today's students are encountering changing literacy practices at an astounding rate. In fact, many of the literacy skills required in past generations for the real world and workplace are simply not enough for students today. Yet, in some instances, the vast amount of digital literacy capital is often unspent in the classroom. This chapter explores digital literacies and methods and strategies for maximizing them in the content classroom.

Chapter 6—Just the Facts: Strategies for Finding and Using Textual Evidence

In all content classrooms, students are required to cite textual evidence to answer document-based questions, articulate an argument, and justify their thinking. While this is not a new demand, students need additional practice with this skill, as it requires them to not only locate evidence from the text but use it effectively in their compositions as they pull together a well-constructed response. This section provides specific strategies to teach this skill.

Chapter 7—Expecting the Unexpected: Answers to Your Most Common Questions

Challenges will arise, we can count on that. So, how can you expect the unexpected? This chapter provides suggestions centered around questions that I often receive when working with teachers across the country.

Chapter
2

CHAPTER 1
Why Write Now?

CHAPTER 2
Parachute Writing

CHAPTER 3
Sum It All Up

CHAPTER 4
All the Right Words

CHAPTER 5
Digital Worlds

CHAPTER 6
Just the Facts

CHAPTER 7
Expecting the
Unexpected

PARACHUTE WRITING
Strategies for Quick Writing

As a literacy teacher, I write every day as part of my job. Manuscripts, responses to students, online class postings, and more. However, in all honesty, I probably write as much or more in my personal life, which, although heavily connected to my identity as a literacy professor, also exists on its own. The reality of writing is that most people use some form of it on a daily basis—and most of it is dropped into the day with purposeful intent. Think about the writing that drops in on you:

- Responses to emails—to colleagues, parents, students, and friends

- Text messages in response to an inquiry or issue

- Forms or surveys

- To-do lists (You saw mine in Chapter 1, and here is my son Vin's first-grade attempt at one.)

- Social media posts

- Workout/fitness logs

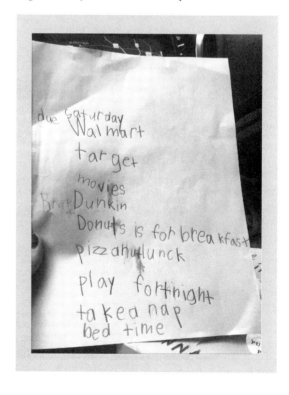

CHAPTER 1
Why Write Now?

CHAPTER 2
Parachute Writing

CHAPTER 3
Sum It All Up

CHAPTER 4
All the Right Words

CHAPTER 5
Digital Worlds

CHAPTER 6
Just the Facts

CHAPTER 7
Expecting the
Unexpected

- Notes/cards to friends

- Monthly/weekly budgets

- Notes taken while on the phone or while listening to podcasts

These are the types of writings that parachute in as part of the real world of literacy and the demands of daily life. Purposeful literacy instruction offers the same opportunities. Truthfully, I think that some type of writing can be dropped in just about anywhere. This chapter includes writing engagements that can be completed in quick bursts of time called "parachute writings." These types of writings are dropped in during a day's lesson and can be completed in one quick sitting. Because of the versatile nature of these types of writings, they can be modified for a number of content areas and tasks.

Parachute Writing Is Safe Writing

The name *parachute writing* might conjure up a number of possible mental images, but for the most part, when we think of parachutes, we think of safety. The most literal definition of parachute is the safety apparatus you need when you jump out of an aircraft, allowing you to float safely to the ground. I think of parachute writing as those types of writings that can be dropped safely into any lesson. A parachute offers safety, and for many teachers, writing instruction can be intimidating and scary. Parachute writing can provide students safe entry points to larger writing assignments, a safe place where they can connect or stretch their thinking, or a safe writing space where they can work through an argument. Plus, because many of these writings can be conducted in pairs or together as a class, they create a similar characteristic of safety that is present in an actual tandem jump. When learning to sky dive, or training in airborne school, individuals don't attempt their first jump alone. Instead, they jump in tandem with someone more experienced. This not only offers an added safety aspect but also the opportunity to learn from someone who has more experience and knowledge. Parachute writing offers some of those same aspects.

Pinpoint Placement

The main item for consideration is the placement of the strategy or engagement within the lesson. Parachute writing might seem like it's just drag and drop, but in reality, teachers still have to actively think about the lesson and what type of writing should be dropped in and when. For example, you can "drop in" the Neighborhood Map (page 45) after reading the picture book *My Brother Martin* or the young adult novel *Look Both Ways*, because the strategy capitalizes on the spatial relationship of landmarks woven together with a story. However, using the Neighborhood Map during a lesson on fractions or after a science lesson on genetics won't be effective. Why? Because the type of drop (Neighborhood Map) wasn't appropriate for the lesson. Knowing your coordinates for landing, or in teaching terms, your target objectives and standards, can aid in a successful implementation.

Timing Is Everything

The type of drop isn't the only item to consider. The time of the drop is also crucial. My friend who was a U.S. Army Airborne will concur; the timing of a drop and the moment when a parachute is deployed can mean success or failure. It's exactly why the First Impressions activity should be used at the beginning of a unit or lesson study. However, since the name implies the timing, that's probably an easy one to figure out. Others can be a little more difficult. For instance, although Drop Drafts can function at any given point in the lesson, they are most effective when used at a pivotal moment in instruction, like at a turning point, following a difficult problem, or after revisiting material that was previously learned. Similarly, Sketch to Stretch works best at a point in a lesson where visualization needs to be emphasized in order to improve comprehension or when you want students to take what they are learning and apply a visual element to it.

Regardless, it is imperative that teachers actively consider the type of material being addressed and then marry it appropriately with the best drop-in strategy. Doing so will yield better writing products as well as ensure that students are benefiting from the types of writing being used.

Each of the strategies listed in this section has one commonality: They can be dropped in at multiple points in a lesson and in multiple subject areas. Pay special attention to suggestions regarding when to use or modify and even how these parachute writings can carry over into more extended written responses.

CHAPTER 1
Why Write Now?

CHAPTER 2
Parachute Writing

CHAPTER 3
Sum It All Up

CHAPTER 4
All the Right Words

CHAPTER 5
Digital Worlds

CHAPTER 6
Just the Facts

CHAPTER 7
Expecting the
Unexpected

CHAPTER 1
Why Write Now?

CHAPTER 2
Parachute Writing

CHAPTER 3
Sum It All Up

CHAPTER 4
All the Right Words

CHAPTER 5
Digital Worlds

CHAPTER 6
Just the Facts

CHAPTER 7
Expecting the
Unexpected

DROP DRAFTS

Much of the writing that occurs in content writing classes never leaves the initial stages of development, due to the nature and purpose of this type of writing. In all honesty, it should be drafty and ugly, like me in middle school. (Remember the picture from the last chapter?) But don't let the looks of it fool you. Despite the fact that much of the writing that occurs in content classrooms doesn't ever make it to the final, polished stages, this kind of writing offers a vehicle for processing and understanding information and thinking through difficult material. It also gives students the opportunity to write and then move on. While much of this type of writing can be assessed or revisited, sometimes students just need time to write about something and then get rid of it. It doesn't always need to be graded or revisited, something that Schinske and Tanner (2014) outlined in their review of research regarding grading practices, motivation, and student impact. In many cases, grades impact student motivation in a negative manner and fail to stimulate interest or enjoyment in a learning task (Pulfrey et al., 2011). Sometimes students simply need to practice a skill and then move on. In fact, there is significant value in writing about something and then moving on. Writers need opportunities to write for multiple purposes, audiences, and within a variety of contexts. Plus, students learn to write by writing. In addition, writing is social: writers compose pieces meant for specific audiences (National Council of Teachers of English [NCTE], 2018). Even when students write pieces that are only intended for themselves, such as personal diaries and journals, they are their own audience (Bawarshi, 2003). The Drop Draft capitalizes on these factors.

Putting It to Work

1. After students have taken part in a lesson, content introduction, concept, or unit of study, have students take out a scratch sheet of paper.

2. Provide students with a prompt, question, or direction for the writing. For example, ask a question about the content, have students write about the basic tenets of a concept, or give them a statement to complete.

3. Allow students about five minutes to write.

4. At the end of class, have students drop their papers in the trash on the way out the door.

Quick Tip!

Write with them! While students are writing, you write, too. Lead by example.

CHAPTER 1
Why Write Now?

CHAPTER 2
Parachute Writing

CHAPTER 3
Sum It All Up

CHAPTER 4
All the Right Words

CHAPTER 5
Digital Worlds

CHAPTER 6
Just the Facts

CHAPTER 7
Expecting the
Unexpected

> I feel uncofortable when I wear the because the are hard to breath in and it does not feel normal. It makes me hot and frustrated when I wear them. When I go out in public I feel strange and unsual. I get kind of dizzy and light headed when I wear them for a long time. Also when I wear them at school I look hot + bothered. When we have mask breaks orange does not get as many mask breaks + yellow does I feel that its unfair. Orange always has to wear masks and yellow does not. When I feel my hot breath I feel uncofortable because it turnes my face red. We have to wear a mask when we are in groups which make me feel odd.

> I feel comforable about wearing a mask because it keeps me safe from others. I usually do not take my mask off during mask breaks. I like having my mask on I know that if I have my mask on I will be a safer year from the coronavirus. When I see others around me that do not have a mask on and I dont have one and I put up my mask so I will be safer.

When to Use It

- To quickly reflect on a concept or topic

- To write about something that doesn't need to be formally assessed

- To write about something, but not share it with the class or teacher

- As a brief opportunity to further process content taught in class

- As a no-pressure practice opportunity

CHAPTER 1
Why Write Now?

CHAPTER 2
Parachute Writing

CHAPTER 3
Sum It All Up

CHAPTER 4
All the Right Words

CHAPTER 5
Digital Worlds

CHAPTER 6
Just the Facts

CHAPTER 7
Expecting the
Unexpected

Why It Works

- Drop Drafts are low-stakes writing engagements with no formal assessment required.

- Because Drop Drafts are meant for the students' eyes only, there's no pressure to write with correct grammar, sentence structure, or spelling.

- Drop Drafts can be dropped into any lesson and at any point in the lesson with little planning and can be used in a variety of subject areas, even those that are nonacademic.

>>> *Writing to Process Feelings*

Sometimes students are distracted by emotions or issues that are not academic related. Recently I was in an upper elementary class for a scheduled demo writing lesson. When the students came back from music, it was apparent that something had happened in that class. Two students were crying, a third of the class was visibly angry, a few others looked confused, and the remainder of the kids were operating as "business as usual." I attempted to teach my lesson, but it became evident very quickly that the students were too distracted to proceed. Instead, I instructed everyone to take out a piece of paper and write down what was on their minds, including whatever it was that upset them in music. I instructed those who didn't have an issue with music to tell me all was well. For about five minutes the students wrote. After they wrote, I told them to ball it up and put it in the trash and I went back to my lesson. Once they had the opportunity to process their thoughts in writing, the class was ready to focus and we pressed on.

Modifications

- Use this strategy for nonacademic-related issues, such as the example shared in the sidebar or for topics that aren't standards based.

- Use this strategy to discuss difficult or controversial topics. For example, sometimes students are not comfortable writing their true feelings about a polarizing topic for fear of how their classmates, or even their teacher, may respond. Drop Drafts can reduce or eliminate that obstacle.

- Have students draft a picture or image instead of using words.

- Have students write in a word document on their laptops and then click "no" when asked to save or drag it to the trashcan icon.

Extensions

- Have students craft questions that they developed after writing their Drop Drafts.

- This strategy could be extended with other strategies such as Quick Writes (page 24), Written Conversations (page 54), or Sketch to Stretch (page 19) as these offer more opportunity for extension.

Content Area Connections

- Incorporate student responses to current events in social studies.

- Support studying novels that have debatable pivotal points in the story.

- Practice low-stakes mathematical explanations or drafting constructed responses.

- Practice playing with the language and new words without worry of accuracy in language classes.

- Draft a new play formation or write about their best or worst play in the game in PE.

- Safely write about politics and polarizing figures.

- Use to address socially charged topics that might make students uncomfortable such as racism, police brutality, and drug abuse.

CHAPTER 1
Why Write Now?

CHAPTER 2
Parachute Writing

CHAPTER 3
Sum It All Up

CHAPTER 4
All the Right Words

CHAPTER 5
Digital Worlds

CHAPTER 6
Just the Facts

CHAPTER 7
Expecting the Unexpected

CHAPTER 1
Why Write Now?

CHAPTER 2
Parachute Writing

CHAPTER 3
Sum It All Up

CHAPTER 4
All the Right Words

CHAPTER 5
Digital Worlds

CHAPTER 6
Just the Facts

CHAPTER 7
Expecting the
Unexpected

QUICK WRITES

When I was teaching middle school, Quick Writes were my absolute favorite way to incorporate writing into my teaching on a daily basis. Why? They required limited planning and were nonscripted. How else can a teacher use a poem about owl pellets one day, an 80s hair band song another day, and an excerpt from "Letters From a Birmingham Jail" the next during the same class? Quick Writes offer teachers the flexibility of student-specific prompts, nudge questions, and tasks, and also provide much-needed exposure to multigenre materials. They also allow students the opportunity to practice writing in a variety of genres for quick, short bursts. Plus, they create a coffer full of potential writing ideas for a later date.

Often students don't get enough exposure to different genres of writing because of the sheer volume of standards and material that must be covered. For example, as a social studies teacher, I never felt like I included enough primary sources in my regular instructional block of time. Quick Writes became a fantastic venue for the incorporation of a variety of historical photos, video clips, and primary sources that otherwise might not have been implemented. Plus, in my writing class, I could experiment with all kinds of genres from argument to narrative to poetry. Because the engagements were quick and fast paced, I could introduce a variety of writing types in class *and* emphasize different components of the writing. It also gave me reason to integrate selections from larger literary works and novels to entice students to read the entire book.

 Quick Tip!

Some primary sources I used as Quick Writes in my social studies classes included historical diary entries, legislation, political cartoons, historical photos, and letters.

Putting It to Work

1. First, decide whether you want your Quick Write to stand alone or function as a springboard into the day's lesson objectives. If it is connected to your day's lesson, the prompts, questions, or actions the students complete should be calculated and deliberate. For a stand-alone Quick Write, the prompts can be more random.

2. Display the selected text for the Quick Write displayed for the entire class to see. If it is a portion of written text, make sure that students also have individual copies in front of them. If it is an image, video clip, or sound, ensure that all students are able to view it from their seats.

-⚡- Quick Tip!

If your school allows students to bring their own devices, consider having a QR code for students to scan so they can listen and view on their own devices.

CHAPTER 1
Why Write Now?

CHAPTER 2
Parachute Writing

CHAPTER 3
Sum It All Up

CHAPTER 4
All the Right Words

CHAPTER 5
Digital Worlds

CHAPTER 6
Just the Facts

CHAPTER 7
Expecting the
Unexpected

3. Allow students time to view the image, video clip, or read the text excerpt provided. It's a good idea to read aloud any excerpts of texts if they are used.

4. If you are teaching virtually, provide a link to the text or share your screen. You might also consider utilizing a recording of the text as well. This is especially important if you are using a children's picture book, as I have found that it is sometimes difficult to read and show the pictures adequately in a virtual environment.

5. Provide students with sample prompts or nudge questions to get them writing. Some examples include the following:

   • *This piece made me think of* _____.

   • *I wondered* _____.

   • Borrow a line from the text and put your own spin on it.

   • Take the same event, but write from a different point of view. For example, if using an excerpt from the novel *Three Times Lucky*, write about the event in the excerpt from the point of view of a different character.

   • Draw a picture that best captures the mood of this piece.

   • Write a list of words that describe the image (if using an image).

6. Take students through two or three prompts or exercises with the Quick Write text.

7. Allow them anywhere from one to three minutes per prompt. Don't spend too much time on one particular prompt or nudge question. You want students to write quickly, so it is perfectly acceptable if they don't finish a sentence or if they don't write much for a prompt that didn't resonate with them.

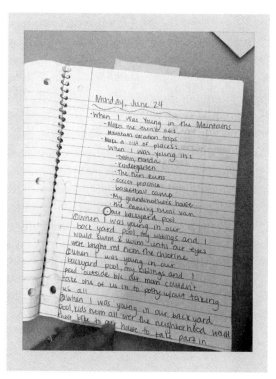

8. Allow students the opportunity to share their thoughts with the class or in small groups.

When to Use It

• As a bell ringer or stand-alone opening activity

• As a springboard into the day's lesson that is directly linked to the content you are

CHAPTER 1
Why Write Now?

CHAPTER 2
Parachute Writing

CHAPTER 3
Sum It All Up

CHAPTER 4
All the Right Words

CHAPTER 5
Digital Worlds

CHAPTER 6
Just the Facts

CHAPTER 7
Expecting the
Unexpected

teaching that day (For instance, during a unit on the Civil War, you might choose to use an excerpt from "What to a Slave is the Fourth of July" as a lead-in to the lesson.)

- To practice a certain skill using a brief, informal mode of delivery

- To review a previous skill to ensure proficiency

- To incorporate writing even when there's not a lot of time

- To incorporate material that otherwise you might not have the occasion to implement (e.g., primary sources and current events)

Why It Works

- Quick Writes require little planning. Unless you are specifically linking the Quick Write to your daily content, there is little up-front planning needed.

- It is a low-stakes writing engagement. Little attention is paid to neatness, sentence structure, or other formal rules of writing.

- The purpose of the Quick Write can easily be changed based on the questions asked during the engagement.

- Quick Writes can be extended into more developed and polished pieces of writing, if there is need.

- Quick Writes can incorporate a variety of modalities (e.g., alphanumeric texts, movie clips, images, concrete objects, sounds, music, primary sources, and more).

Modifications

- Instead of making the prompts teacher led, assign a student to be responsible for giving classmates the nudge questions for the Quick Write.

- For some students, it may be best to have the prompts written on the board or on individual notecards at the students' desks. This would be helpful for students who might forget the prompts or instructions.

- Differentiate the activity by giving each student unique notecards that include a mixture of different prompts or engagements to try with the Quick Write. This way, the entire class isn't doing the same activities with the text.

- Use a Quick Write choice board instead. This allows students to pick the prompts or engagements they want when working with the text.

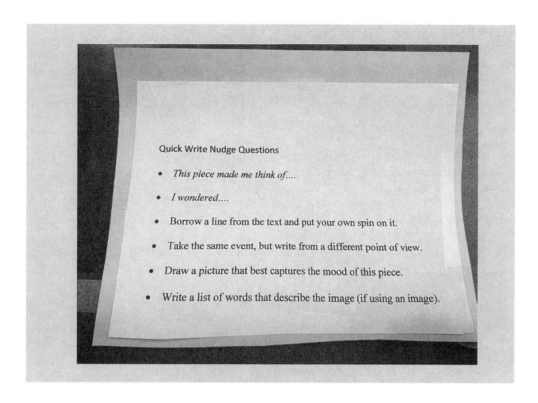

Quick Write Nudge Questions

- *This piece made me think of....*
- *I wondered....*
- Borrow a line from the text and put your own spin on it.
- Take the same event, but write from a different point of view.
- Draw a picture that best captures the mood of this piece.
- Write a list of words that describe the image (if using an image).

Extensions

- Quick Writes are great places for seed ideas to start. Have students use their Quick Writes folder as a place to keep their ideas for pieces of writing they want to continue.

- Use portions of Quick Writes as springboards for fully involved writings down the road.

- Have students create an illustrated accompaniment to their Quick Writes.

- Use Quick Writes for integrated grammar lessons on a variety of skills including sentence combining, descriptive language, effective hooks, and dialogue incorporation.

- Have students partner up and swap Quick Writes. Give them two to three minutes to read through their partner's piece and then another one or two minutes to add to their classmate's writing.

>>> *Write Alongside Students*

When I taught middle school, I wrote alongside my students during Quick Writes. That allowed them to see that I was also a writer, and it helped them see how writers think, revise, and even struggle with topics. While I did not write with every class every day, I did make sure that each class saw me writing with them two or three times a week. I also made sure to share my writing too.

CHAPTER 1
Why Write Now?

CHAPTER 2
Parachute Writing

CHAPTER 3
Sum It All Up

CHAPTER 4
All the Right Words

CHAPTER 5
Digital Worlds

CHAPTER 6
Just the Facts

CHAPTER 7
Expecting the Unexpected

CHAPTER 1
Why Write Now?

CHAPTER 2
Parachute Writing

CHAPTER 3
Sum It All Up

CHAPTER 4
All the Right Words

CHAPTER 5
Digital Worlds

CHAPTER 6
Just the Facts

CHAPTER 7
Expecting the Unexpected

Content Area Connections

- Use images for students to describe using only math vocabulary.

- Have students look at a completed math problem and draft what they believe the student was thinking as they solved the problem.

- Use historical photos in social studies to jumpstart conversations about historical topics.

- Use different play formations for students to brainstorm and comment on the configurations in physical education.

- Use music videos in ELA to draw attention to voice, symbolism, and mood.

1) This song is about people who spend their time sending homobopic and transphobic messages online. This song addresses those people and tells them to just shut up and calm down. This makes me think about the times in my life where people have been homophobic towards me whether it be online or in person. This song makes me happy because it reminds me that they are wasting their time hating and being angry.

2) I think people are critical of Swifts video, because they are bigoted and don't want to come to terms with the fact that their view on gay and trans people is wrong and outdated.

3) One of my favorite lines in this song is "shade never made anybody less gay", I like this cause its true. Yelling at someone to try and make them straight never works. If I were to add something to this line I would probably say something along the lines of "so stop wasting your time cause you aint changing our minds."

- Have students listen to musical scores and draw pictures that best illustrate the mood and tone of the music

- Have students pick out the words or phrases they know in the text and translate them into the language they are studying during foreign language

HEAR THIS!

Visualization is a major key to comprehension and understanding. For elementary students, much of what they read or come in contact with is heavily laden with images and pictures. Yet, when students get older, pictures go away and are replaced by longer paragraphs. For that student who used the images in the book to assist with their understanding of the story or text, a chapter book offers none of that security. Instead, that visual image now becomes the duty of the reader to construct. However, many students do not actively acknowledge that while they are reading they should be conjuring up an image or a moving picture in their heads of what is happening in the story. Plus, many elementary standard sets include listening and speaking components. For the listening component, strategies that allow students to focus on what they hear and create products using this information are important, yet many times, these lessons are a little more difficult to develop. Hear This is a great strategy to emphasize not only the important skill of visualization but also listening. This strategy is useful for a wide range of readiness levels and subject areas.

>>> Books and poems that work well with this strategy:

- *Mojave, Mississippi, Heartland,* and *Sierra* by Dianne Siebert
- *Momma, Where Are You From?* by Marie Bradby
- *Eleanor and Park* by Rainbow Rowell
- *The Gruffalo* by Julia Donaldson
- *The Land of Stories* series by Chris Colfer
- *Night in the Country* by Cynthia Rylant
- *See the Ocean* by Estelle Condra
- *Crown: An Ode to the Fresh Cut* by Derrick Barnes
- *The Last Stop on Market Street* by Matt de la Peña
- *Finger Paints* by Brod Bagert
- *Filling Station* by Elizabeth Bishop
- *My Papa's Waltz* by Theodore Rothke

Putting It to Work

1. Select a text that is highly descriptive. There need to be lots of descriptive details that students can include in their drawings. Use the list above as a starter.

CHAPTER 1
Why Write Now?

CHAPTER 2
Parachute Writing

CHAPTER 3
Sum It All Up

CHAPTER 4
All the Right Words

CHAPTER 5
Digital Worlds

CHAPTER 6
Just the Facts

CHAPTER 7
Expecting the Unexpected

CHAPTER 1
Why Write Now?

CHAPTER 2
Parachute Writing

CHAPTER 3
Sum It All Up

CHAPTER 4
All the Right Words

CHAPTER 5
Digital Worlds

CHAPTER 6
Just the Facts

CHAPTER 7
Expecting the
Unexpected

2. Have students take out a scratch sheet of paper or provide them with a blank sheet of paper.

3. Tell students that as you read, they are to draw what they hear or what is happening in the text.

4. Read aloud from the chosen text. Do not show the students any of the pictures from the text if there are any.

5. Have students share their pictures with the class.

When to Use It

1. To pay close attention to the importance of visualization and its link to comprehension

2. As support for texts that have few or no accompanying images

3. As an arts extension for a unit or concept

4. To support students who are writing or reading below grade level or who are learning English as a new language

Why It Works

- Hear This is a low-stakes strategy that incorporates artistic components as an extension.

- Students who struggle or feel uncomfortable with writing can complete this task because no writing of words is required.

- Hear This emphasizes the need for students to visualize, which aids in improved comprehension.

Modifications

- Divide the class into groups and have some students draw pictures and others write accompanying sentences for the images.

- Instead of reading a text to the students, play music and have them draw a picture that captures the mood and tone of the music.

- Prepare images ahead of time and have students choose the images that best fit the written text being read.

Extensions

- Use the Hear This images that were created to compile a picture-only version of the written text being studied.

- Use Hear This as an opening strategy for a comic strip or graphic novel construction.

- Use Hear This as a kickoff to the Post-it Poems strategy (page 29).

- Have students incorporate textual evidence by going back to their pictures and, using address labels, include textual evidence from the story on their pictures.

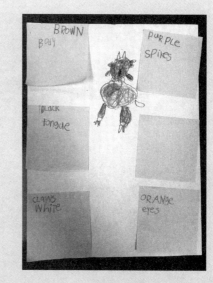

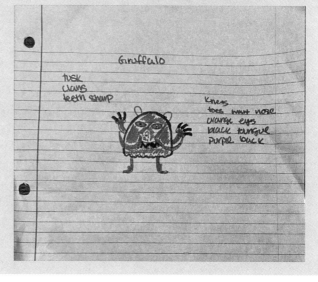

CHAPTER 1
Why Write Now?

CHAPTER 2
Parachute Writing

CHAPTER 3
Sum It All Up

CHAPTER 4
All the Right Words

CHAPTER 5
Digital Worlds

CHAPTER 6
Just the Facts

CHAPTER 7
Expecting the Unexpected

CHAPTER 1
Why Write Now?

CHAPTER 2
Parachute Writing

CHAPTER 3
Sum It All Up

CHAPTER 4
All the Right Words

CHAPTER 5
Digital Worlds

CHAPTER 6
Just the Facts

CHAPTER 7
Expecting the Unexpected

Content Area Connections

- Use Hear This when studying historical battles, tracing the movement of people across time, or when studying geographic features in history.

- Have students draw supplemental images that accompany a math problem or real-world math scenario.

- In science, have students draw an animal's habitat or home based on readings.

- Use Hear This with old radio show clips for students to draw the characters, setting, and problem.

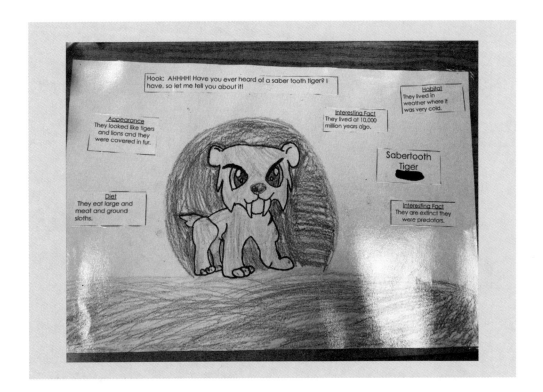

CHAPTER 1
Why Write Now?

CHAPTER 2
Parachute Writing

CHAPTER 3
Sum It All Up

CHAPTER 4
All the Right Words

CHAPTER 5
Digital Worlds

CHAPTER 6
Just the Facts

CHAPTER 7
Expecting the
Unexpected

ATTACK OR DEFEND WRITING

Argument writing is a genre common to a number of subject areas and grade levels. This is a sophisticated genre, one that requires a solid understanding of a claim, but also a clear direction regarding the organization and positioning of evidence to support a claim. It's more than persuasive and more than just research. (And if your students don't know persuasive writing cold, then writing an argument may be difficult for them.) Instead, argument is the juxtaposition of components of both of those genres, yet with nuances exclusive to argument.

For many students, argument writing is one of the hardest genres to master. However, arguments are fully cemented in our daily lives whether we actively notice this or not. Here's where I have recently seen argument show up in my professional world:

- Budget justifications at work

- ESPN's *Pardon the Interruption*

- Editorials

- Proposals for board meetings

- Grant applications

- Responses to accusations

- Appeals

- Policy rebuttals

Now, granted, not all of these examples have all the components of a fully involved argument, but all of them have characteristics of an argument: claims, evidence, responses, rebuttals, research, and the like. All are necessary characteristics of well-developed arguments.

Despite the fact that these and many other real-world examples don't include all the required academic components of argumentative writing, they are excellent examples of this genre in the real world. Plus, this gives students another example of how writing is relevant and real.

 Stop & Think:

Attack or Defend can bring in content that otherwise might not be included in instruction. For example, recently while taking my daughter to school, we saw a sign that said "Men Working." My daughter read it out loud and then said, "Men Working? Not Women Working or People Working. Hmmm." Showing students signs, commercials, or ads from their contemporary lives makes for great material to "argue" about.

CHAPTER 1
Why Write Now?

CHAPTER 2
Parachute Writing

CHAPTER 3
Sum It All Up

CHAPTER 4
All the Right Words

CHAPTER 5
Digital Worlds

CHAPTER 6
Just the Facts

CHAPTER 7
Expecting the
Unexpected

A favorite way to introduce students to the idea of argument is through Attack or Defend writing. This strategy allows students to practice taking a side while compiling evidence that supports their choice. I love this strategy because it has great benefits for all subject areas, can be completed in a short amount of time, and can serve as a springboard for fully involved writing. Plus, due to its nature, it's fantastic for incorporating unique information, sources, and quotes that otherwise might not be used in instruction. When I was a history teacher, I often found unique historical facts, interesting primary sources, and supplemental material that either didn't really fit in with a big unit or wasn't meaty enough to warrant an entire lesson or unit. Attack or Defend is a great way to incorporate these types of materials that otherwise might fall into the periphery.

Putting It to Work

1. Identify several specific quotes that are content related (e.g., historical quotes) or quotes that are credited to popular contemporary figures. Make sure your students have some background information about the people who said the words you want them to examine. Otherwise, you will end up with just random guesses.

2. Create two notecard sets. One notecard set includes a quote and the name of the person who said it. The other notecard set should include the quote but not the name of who said it.

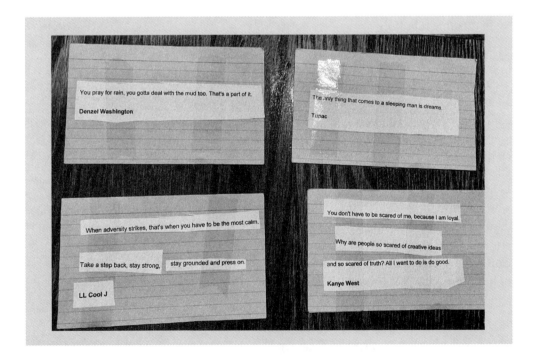

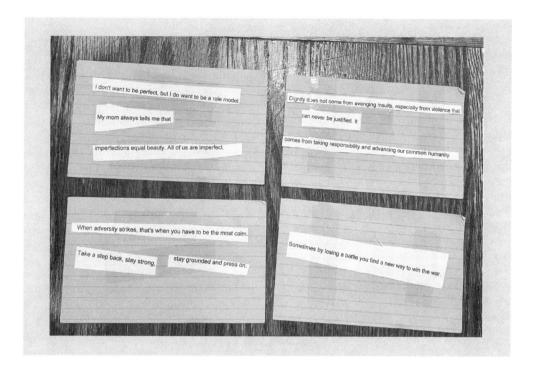

Quick Tip!

Try using two different color notecards for the two sets. This makes it easy to see that you have distributed the appropriate number of matching sets. Plus, you can quickly look at the room and see which students have the information with the speaker listed as well as those who only have a quote in front of them.

CHAPTER 1
Why Write Now?

CHAPTER 2
Parachute Writing

CHAPTER 3
Sum It All Up

CHAPTER 4
All the Right Words

CHAPTER 5
Digital Worlds

CHAPTER 6
Just the Facts

CHAPTER 7
Expecting the
Unexpected

CHAPTER 1
Why Write Now?

CHAPTER 2
Parachute Writing

CHAPTER 3
Sum It All Up

CHAPTER 4
All the Right Words

CHAPTER 5
Digital Worlds

CHAPTER 6
Just the Facts

CHAPTER 7
Expecting the Unexpected

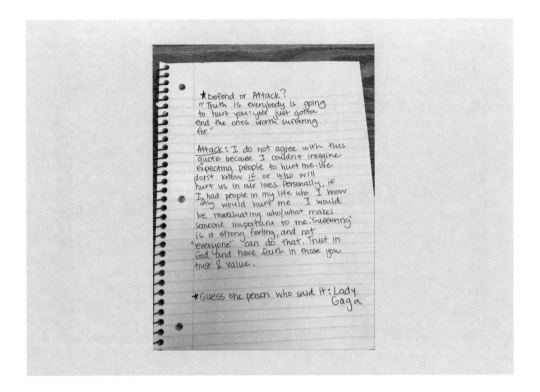

3. Distribute the notecards so that half of the students receive ones that include the quote and name and half receive cards that include only the quote.

4. Tell the students that they are not to use any technology to search for information about the quotes.

5. Give students the following instructions: Read the quote on your notecard. Talk with your partner or group about the quote. Decide whether you want to attack or defend the quote. "Attack" means you do not agree with the message of the quote while "defend" means you do support the message of the quote.

6. Model an appropriate response to the entire class if they are new to this strategy so that they understand your expectation.

7. Once students have determined whether they are going to attack or defend the quote, have them provide one to three sentences or evidence or justification as to why they took that position.

CHAPTER 1
Why Write Now?

CHAPTER 2
Parachute Writing

CHAPTER 3
Sum It All Up

CHAPTER 4
All the Right Words

CHAPTER 5
Digital Worlds

CHAPTER 6
Just the Facts

CHAPTER 7
Expecting the
Unexpected

8. For students who do not know who said their quote, also have them brainstorm two or three people who they think might have said those words. (This is where the prior knowledge and background information come in handy.)

9. After students have had time to discuss and write, provide time for each group to share.

10. Begin with a group that had an anonymous quote. Once that group has shared their response, invite the group that knew the speaker to give their position without revealing the speaker to the class.

11. Following the discussion, return to the original group and ask them to share who they thought might have said the quote. Then, invite the other group to reveal the true owner of the quote.

12. Repeat this sharing process for the other groups and quotes.

When to Use It

- To explore both sides of an issue

- As a lead-in to crafting a succinct argument

- To practice using one source of information

- As practice for argument throughout the year

- As a way to explore bias

Why It Works

- Attack or Defend is a brief, confined writing task.

- Contemporary topics and current events can be integrated into the strategy.

- Students are given specific instructions: either attack the statement or defend it. They then have to give a reason to justify their answer.

- The debated topic can be extended or dropped after the Attack or Defend strategy is completed; the teacher and students decide which route to take.

CHAPTER 1
Why Write Now?

CHAPTER 2
Parachute Writing

CHAPTER 3
Sum It All Up

CHAPTER 4
All the Right Words

CHAPTER 5
Digital Worlds

CHAPTER 6
Just the Facts

CHAPTER 7
Expecting the
Unexpected

Modifications

- Use one quote without a speaker as a Quick Write or bell ringer for the whole class.

- After students have practiced this strategy, allow them to complete this individually, and then locate their partner for a think-pair-share.

- Use quotes with similar thematic messages and have students find their partners in theme instead of determining who said the quote.

- Use signs or other images (propaganda, ads, commercials, etc.) to build students' critical literacy skills.

Extensions

- Have students conduct a mini-inquiry on their speaker.

- Extend this into an ESPN-inspired argument using the show *Around the Horn* as a model.

- Use this as a springboard for the Say What? strategy (page 40).

- Have students develop this assignment into a fully involved argument.

Content Area Connections

- Debate the best methods for solving a particular math problem.

- Use nutrition, exercise regimens, or healthy lifestyle habits as content for this strategy during physical education.

- Use this strategy to compare viewpoints on environmental issues in science.

- Examine historical figures, war battles, or court decisions in history.

- Use quotes from characters in novels and have students determine who said it and why.

Equation- Way #1

$$2r - (5-r) = 13 + 2r$$
$$2r - 5 + r = 13 + 2r$$
$$\underline{\quad -r \qquad\qquad -r \quad}$$
$$2r - 5 = 13 + r$$
$$\underline{\quad +5 \qquad +5 \quad}$$
$$2r = 18 + r$$
$$\underline{\quad -r \qquad\qquad -r \quad}$$
$$r = 18$$

Attack or Defend:

I am going to attack this way to solve the equation.

Write 1-3 sentences explaining your position.

You can solve this problem in many ways, but I do not like this way to solve it. On the second line, it automatically subtracted the "r" on the left side whereas I would have combined all of my like terms before I solved the equation. In my opinion, it is easier to single out the variable if you combine your like terms first.

Equation- Way #2

$$2r - (5-r) = 13 + 2r$$
$$2r - 5 + r = 13 + 2r$$
$$3r - 5 = 13 + 2r$$
$$\underline{\quad -2r \qquad\qquad -2r \quad}$$
$$r - 5 = 13$$
$$\underline{\quad +5 \quad +5 \quad}$$
$$r = 18$$

Attack or Defend: Defend

Write 1-3 sentences explaining your position.

I would like to defend the way she solved this equation for a few reasons. First off, she combined like terms, making it easier to solve. She also used the distributive property first, also making it easier to solve.

CHAPTER 1
Why Write Now?

CHAPTER 2
Parachute Writing

CHAPTER 3
Sum It All Up

CHAPTER 4
All the Right Words

CHAPTER 5
Digital Worlds

CHAPTER 6
Just the Facts

CHAPTER 7
Expecting the Unexpected

CHAPTER 1
Why Write Now?

CHAPTER 2
Parachute Writing

CHAPTER 3
Sum It All Up

CHAPTER 4
All the Right Words

CHAPTER 5
Digital Worlds

CHAPTER 6
Just the Facts

CHAPTER 7
Expecting the Unexpected

SAY WHAT?

One of the important components of drafting an argument is the ability to not only state your position but also include information about what the opposing side believes. In some instances, it is difficult for students to identify what the opposing side might say about their topics and even more difficult for them to weave the counterclaim into their compositions. True, the art of weaving information and evidence into a paper in an effective and fluid manner is a sophisticated skill, but it becomes easier when students can accurately outline what the opposing side might counter. The Say What? strategy does just this by allowing students to consider not only their side but also anticipate the argument that may arise from the opposing side. Plus, it can help them as they begin to rank their evidence or rebuttals, something that comes when writing a more sophisticated argument.

A favorite component of this strategy is the fact that this engagement helps students build up to a more fully involved writing piece. Sometimes, drafting an argument can be daunting due to the multiple components. Yet by incorporating an activity such as this, students begin by listing possible supporting statements and their counterparts. Later, when students are tasked with completing the entire writing piece, the material they collected using Say What? can be easily integrated into their fully involved piece.

Putting It to Work

1. Start with a concept or topic that can be debatable or can be viewed through different or opposing lenses (e.g., animal testing, genetically modified foods, opposing sides of current laws or policies, battle tactics from historical conflicts, or historical figures with opposing views).

2. Now would be a great time to have a mini-lesson review on claims. Once students have determined what their claim will be, they will begin to stockpile their evidence on their paint strips.

3. Discuss as a class what the opposing viewpoints or lenses might be.

4. Provide each student with a paint strip that has four or more large color gradient blocks. This color will serve as the visual cue for the side of the argument students are attempting to prove and will become their I Say card. For example, students may include all their information for their I Say card on the paint strip that includes a blue gradient strip while they compile all their opposing side They Say information on a yellow gradient strip.

-⚡- Quick Tip!

Need a great resource for argument writing text sets, or other lesson ideas? The National Writing Project's Community, College, and Careers Writing Program (C3WP) website is a great resource.

https://sites.google.com/nwp.org/c3wp/home

CHAPTER 2
Why Write Now?

CHAPTER 2
Parachute Writing

CHAPTER 3
Sum It All Up

CHAPTER 4
All the Right Words

CHAPTER 5
Digital Worlds

CHAPTER 6
Just the Facts

CHAPTER 7
Expecting the
Unexpected

5. Have students list reasons or evidence that support their claim on their I Say paint strips, filling in one point per color block. This should include one reason or detail per block so students end up with about four or five reasons depending on the length of the paint strip.

6. Once students have filled up their supporting evidence for their claim, have each student share with a partner or with the class.

7. Provide students with a second paint strip that shows a different color gradient. This will become their They Say card.

8. Information on the They Say card at first should be details that the opposing might present. As students move through the engagement, they will begin to match up reasons that correspond with the same topic. For example, if students are researching athletes' use of performance-enhancing drugs, initially, they will list details that each side would present. However, after digging into the topic more, they will begin to link details. As a result, one side's comments about the dangers of performance-enhancing drugs would be matched up with the benefits.

9. Have them collect evidence on the paint strip for the opposing side, filling in one point per color block. It may be necessary to provide students with supplemental material or sources to use to research the evidence from the opposing side of their topic.

10. Allow students to share their evidence with a partner or the class.

When to Use It

- To practice debating on paper

- To discuss a topic or concept that has definite opposing sides

- To examine multiple viewpoints of an issue

- As a review or reminder of persuasive and argumentative writing throughout the year

- As a working list that can be used for an argument writing task later

Why It Works

- Say What? serves as a springboard into argument writing.

- Say What? allows for examination of an issue using opposing viewpoints.

CHAPTER 1
Why Write Now?

CHAPTER 2
Parachute Writing

CHAPTER 3
Sum it All Up

CHAPTER 4
All the Right Words

CHAPTER 5
Digital Worlds

CHAPTER 6
Just the Facts

CHAPTER 7
Expecting the Unexpected

- Students can practice outlining what different groups might say about the same topic (e.g., conservatives, liberals, independents).

- Say What? feels low stakes for students because it can be completed using sticky notes or paint strips.

Modifications

- Instead of using paint strips, use different colored sticky notes and have students collaboratively work to develop the evidence. You can also use individual blocked paint strips (shown below) or notecards.

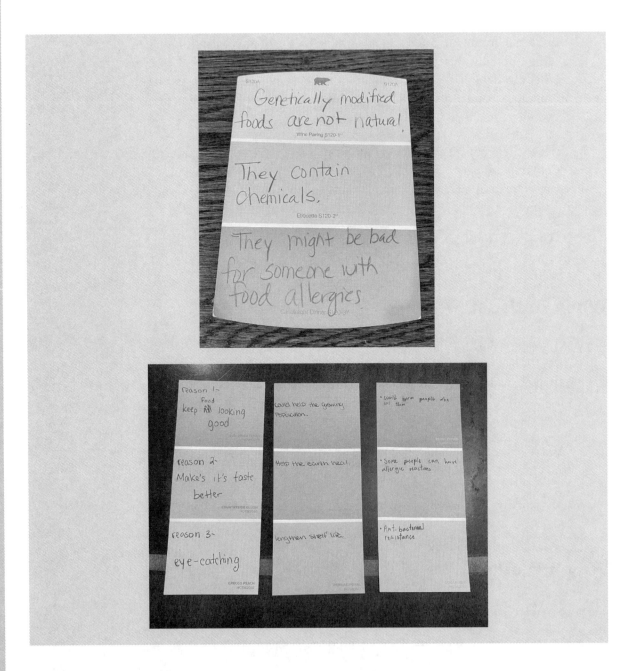

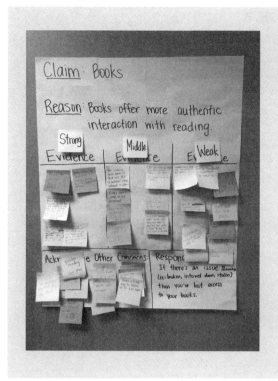

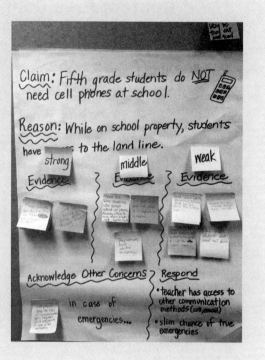

- Use the I Say card only when working with the persuasive genre.

- To add detail and cite more evidence, insert a Back It Up card in between. In this modification, after students use the I Say card, they then begin conducting research to find evidence that supports the material they included initially. This is a great way to incorporate citation of evidence, APA/MLA formatting, direct quotes, and paraphrasing.

Extensions

- Add a third paint strip called I Respond where students take the information from the They Say card and respond to each of the items.

- Have students use the direct quotes they have lifted from their sources and paraphrase them in their own words.

- Use Say What? as a springboard for students to develop a fully involved argument piece.

CHAPTER 1
Why Write Now?

CHAPTER 2
Parachute Writing

CHAPTER 3
Sum It All Up

CHAPTER 4
All the Right Words

CHAPTER 5
Digital Worlds

CHAPTER 6
Just the Facts

CHAPTER 7
Expecting the
Unexpected

CHAPTER 1
Why Write Now?

CHAPTER 2
Parachute Writing

CHAPTER 3
Sum It All Up

CHAPTER 4
All the Right Words

CHAPTER 5
Digital Worlds

CHAPTER 6
Just the Facts

CHAPTER 7
Expecting the
Unexpected

Content Area Connections

- Have students debate the best way to solve a particular multistep math problem.

- Have students debate issues that have two distinctive sides in history (e.g., Vietnam War, immigration, or taxes).

- Have students discuss the pros and cons of contemporary science topics (e.g., genetic engineering, animal testing, or climate change).

- Compare contemporary health claims or recommendations (e.g., what experts say about training regimens or diet and lifestyle plans).

- After reading material that addresses a debatable topic, have students use the Say What? writing activity as a comprehension check.

- Use Say What? in social studies classes as a way to respond to historical speech clips.

NEIGHBORHOOD MAP

Most teachers employ some type of "getting to know you" activity to build community and develop relationships at the beginning of the year or semester. Unfortunately, sometimes the methods in which this is directed result in material and information about students that is somewhat canned or artificial. You end up with vanilla information about everyone. (Think bio poems: friend of _____, lover of _____, who fears _____.)

Neighborhood Maps offers a brand new way of getting to know students through the use of pictures, words, and stories. While Ralph Fletcher (2007) utilizes this writing engagement as a sort of prewriting activator for students when they are writing their life stories, I love using it as a getting-to-know students activity or as a way to incorporate a different kind of writing into class. When using this strategy, students develop an oral narrative along with an illustration and active drawing of the narrative they are constructing. In other words, they tell the story orally and draw it at the same time. The drawing helps the student explain, elaborate, and clarify details in the narrative. This strategy is also extremely flexible and can be utilized for all levels of students, content areas, and grades. In addition, the ability to draw and talk can allow students to not only tell stories about their worlds using words but also in pictures. Plus, in today's virtual world, Neighborhood Maps can serve as another community builder in an online platform.

Putting It to Work

1. Set up a sheet of chart paper or use a document camera to display a blank sheet of paper.

2. Model a Neighborhood Map by telling students what the map will consist of (your current neighborhood, childhood home, church, school hallway, etc.).

3. Tell your story orally and use the paper to help draw images, words, and other items that help you tell your story, remember details, or explain the material. Take about five minutes for this think-aloud.

4. Divide students into pairs and give them each a sheet of paper.

Quick Tip!

Teaching virtually? Have students partner up online and present to their partner virtually. This summer, my Writing Project class did just that. We utilized the breakout room feature in Zoom, and each took turns in a small group completing the activity.

CHAPTER 1
Why Write Now?

CHAPTER 2
Parachute Writing

CHAPTER 3
Sum It All Up

CHAPTER 4
All the Right Words

CHAPTER 5
Digital Worlds

CHAPTER 6
Just the Facts

CHAPTER 7
Expecting the
Unexpected

CHAPTER 1
Why Write Now?

CHAPTER 2
Parachute Writing

CHAPTER 3
Sum It All Up

CHAPTER 4
All the Right Words

CHAPTER 5
Digital Worlds

CHAPTER 6
Just the Facts

CHAPTER 7
Expecting the Unexpected

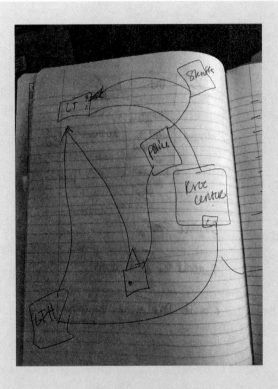

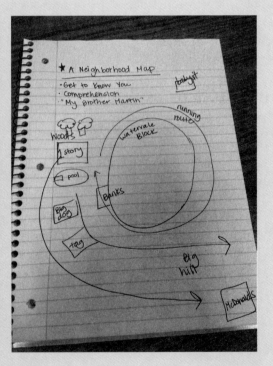

5. Have students take turns telling their story to their partner while drawing on the paper provided. During this time, one person draws and tells and the other listens.

6. After five minutes, have students switch roles.

Quick Tip!

Still not sure how this works? Go to https://www.augusta.edu/education/community-outreach/writing_project/videos.php and watch my Neighborhood Map video to see this strategy in action.

When to Use It

- As a means to practice oral narrative construction

- To create a multimodal story

- As a strategy to scaffold instruction for English learners

- To construct a diagram or visual example that corresponds with oral or written language

- As a way to draw attention to the various forms and types of writing

Why It Works

- Neighborhood Maps combines multiple aspects of literacy (words, pictures, storytelling).

- Neighborhood Maps has students focus on their own lives—the one thing they probably know the most about!

- There's no script so the story can flex based on the author.

Modifications

- Instead of leaving the task open ended with few parameters on what to draw or include, provide students with a specific time period they should write about or a certain number of details or images to include on their maps. (These might include items like who was there, where the story occurred, and what was the main event.)

CHAPTER 1
Why Write Now?

CHAPTER 2
Parachute Writing

CHAPTER 3
Sum It All Up

CHAPTER 4
All the Right Words

CHAPTER 5
Digital Worlds

CHAPTER 6
Just the Facts

CHAPTER 7
Expecting the Unexpected

CHAPTER 1
Why Write Now?

CHAPTER 2
Parachute Writing

CHAPTER 3
Sum It All Up

CHAPTER 4
All the Right Words

CHAPTER 5
Digital Worlds

CHAPTER 6
Just the Facts

CHAPTER 7
Expecting the
Unexpected

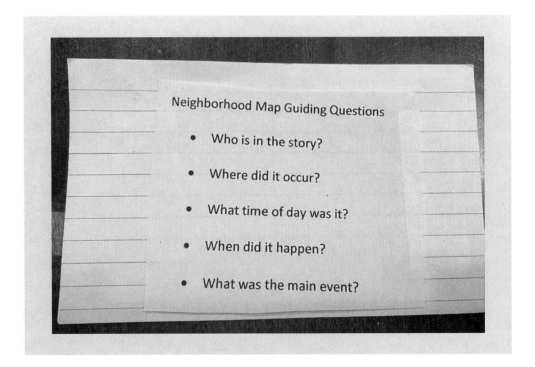

- Have students draw their pictures first and then share their story with a partner, using the picture to aid with the construction of the story.

- Have a partner write down details from the oral retelling of the story for inclusion in a more formal written assignment.

- Use a ready-made map of a place you know they have been (school, cafeteria, library, etc.) and have them use the prefab map as a starter for them to annotate as they tell their story.

Extensions

- Have students create final pieces of artwork based on their maps and video or audio record their stories.

- Have students construct a story based on historical images or artwork.

- Use Neighborhood Maps as a springboard or pre-writing for a unit on small moments, exploding the moment, or memoirs.

- Have students use multiple photographs, artwork, or other images to construct a story using traditional collage methods or a web program such as PicCollage.

- Use Neighborhood Maps in conjunction with Georgia Heard's (1999) *Heart Maps* where students draw and write about items in their lives that are important to them and that they love.

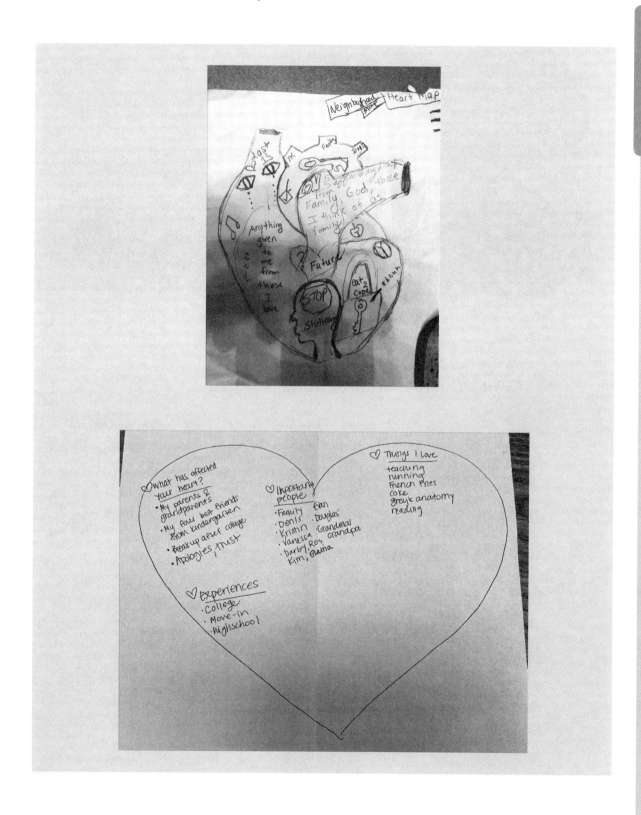

CHAPTER 1
Why Write Now?

CHAPTER 2
Parachute Writing

CHAPTER 3
Sum It All Up

CHAPTER 4
All the Right Words

CHAPTER 5
Digital Worlds

CHAPTER 6
Just the Facts

CHAPTER 7
Expecting the
Unexpected

CHAPTER 1
Why Write Now?

CHAPTER 2
Parachute Writing

CHAPTER 3
Sum It All Up

CHAPTER 4
All the Right Words

CHAPTER 5
Digital Worlds

CHAPTER 6
Just the Facts

CHAPTER 7
Expecting the
Unexpected

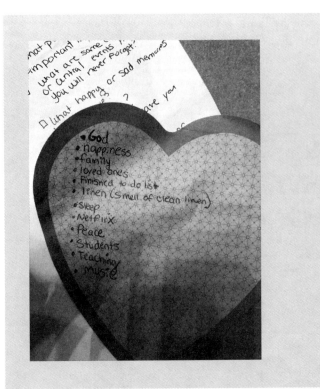

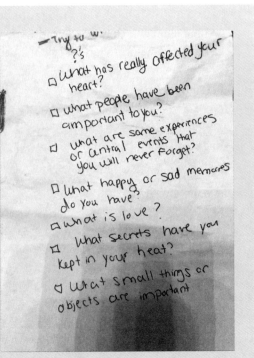

Content Area Connections

- Improve comprehension in history when discussing geographic regions, battle plans, and movement of groups of people across locations.

- Assess comprehension for literature that includes characters who move around a lot, are highly descriptive about place, or involve multiple settings. Some books that work great with this strategy are *Look Both Ways* by Jason Reynolds, *My Brother Martin* by Coretta Scott King, and *The Last Stop on Market Street* by Matt de la Peña.

- Explain the movement of players in a particular formation in physical education.

- Explain diagrams of scientific concepts using the basic idea of a Neighborhood Map.

- Construct and deconstruct complex mathematical word problems.

✏️▷ FIGURE THIS

As teachers, we can gain a lot of insight into students' background knowledge, comprehension or understanding about a topic or concept when they write in a genre that is not the same as the content being studied. Using figurative language to describe how content area ideas, concepts, or topics are related allows students to be creative in their response and dig deeper into what they know. Additionally, looking at what the students compare the material to and how they use figurative language to describe it can potentially offer teachers insight into their attitudes or underlying feelings about a particular subject or topic. When students are required to compare something in a content area to an unrelated photo or image, they must truly examine both the content and the image with a critical eye. They must look beyond the surface layer of what is in the image and dig deeper, considering the image, the content, and their own attitudes when making the comparison.

This type of strategy can fit well anywhere in a lesson and does not involve much preparation in order to do so. It works great as a way to start off a unit of study to give you insight into what students already know. It can also be used as an entrance or exit ticket to check in on student learning, or it can be used at the end of the unit as a way to sum up what was studied. Plus, because students are able to use multiple types of figurative language (similes, metaphors, alliteration, personification, idioms, or onomatopoeia), they can choose the one that they have the most knowledge of. This allows them to capitalize on background knowledge so they can create a better quality product.

Putting It to Work

1. Review the main types of figurative language and provide students with the Figure This Reference Guide (page 232).

2. Provide students with examples of content-connected figurative language (e.g., cumulus clouds are like the whales of the sky).

3. Give students a concept or idea and have them draft an example that corresponds with the topic. If needed, you could provide students with a sentence frame, like this: _____ is like _____ because _____.

4. Allow students to share their work and discuss as the class.

When to Use It

- At the beginning, middle, or end of a unit of study

- To compare the content to another concept

- To uncover students' perceptions and attitude toward a concept, topic, or subject

CHAPTER 3
Sum It All Up

CHAPTER 4
All the Right Words

CHAPTER 5
Digital Worlds

CHAPTER 6
Just the Facts

CHAPTER 7
Expecting the Unexpected

CHAPTER 1
Why Write Now?

CHAPTER 2
Parachute Writing

CHAPTER 3
Sum It All Up

CHAPTER 4
All the Right Words

CHAPTER 5
Digital Worlds

CHAPTER 6
Just the Facts

CHAPTER 7
Expecting the
Unexpected

Why It Works

- Figure This is informal, low stakes, and quick.

- It can be implemented anywhere in the lesson or unit of study.

- It allows students to draw on personal experiences and opinions.

- It offers students opportunities to creatively think about a content area concept.

Modifications

- Instead of figurative language, have students write a "_____ reminds me of" statement.

- Put possible comparison items on notecards and because statements on other notecards. Have students build a simile from the word or phrase bank.

Extensions

- Have students add to their writings by providing informative facts about the concept.

- Have students include an illustration to go with the figurative language they created.

- Start the semester with this strategy and have students write about their feelings toward your entire content area (e.g., chemistry is like _____ because _____.).

Content Area Connections

- Address the specific steps of solving a problem or obtaining a solution.

- Have students compare historical figures, policies, or historical events.

- Have students compare characters or events from different literary works.

- Use lyrics from songs that already utilize figurative language. Have students write the lyrics using a different type of figurative language.

- Use this as a response to video clips of historic speeches (John F. Kennedy's inauguration speech is like _____.).

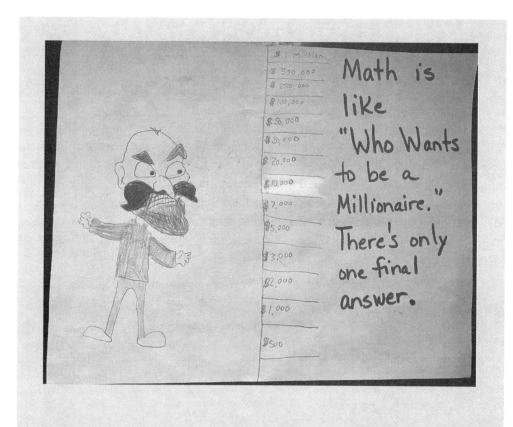

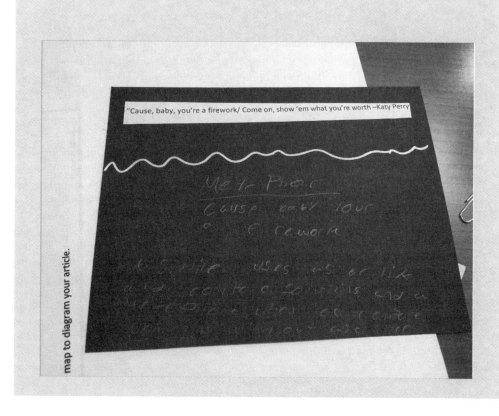

map to diagram your article.

CHAPTER 1
Why Write Now?

CHAPTER 2
Parachute Writing

CHAPTER 3
Sum It All Up

CHAPTER 4
All the Right Words

CHAPTER 5
Digital Worlds

CHAPTER 6
Just the Facts

CHAPTER 7
Expecting the
Unexpected

CHAPTER 1
Why Write Now?

CHAPTER 2
Parachute Writing

CHAPTER 3
Sum It All Up

CHAPTER 4
All the Right Words

CHAPTER 5
Digital Worlds

CHAPTER 6
Just the Facts

CHAPTER 7
Expecting the Unexpected

WRITTEN CONVERSATIONS

As a former middle grades teacher, I can't tell you how many notes I intercepted or simply found left around my classroom. It seems that students have no problem writing to each other, and do so on a frequent basis. In fact, on one occasion I caught a student writing what looked to be a bunch of random letters but turned out to be a note in code. I proceeded to decode it during my planning period. When he came into class the next day, he found a note from me on his desk written in the same code that said, "David, Your code is too easy to crack. Don't write notes in my class. Love, Mrs. Harper." Over ten years later, whenever I see that student, we still have a good laugh over that incident. Apparently, code writing is still popular, as my daughter Macy Belle's friend recently sent her a letter written in code along with a key, too.

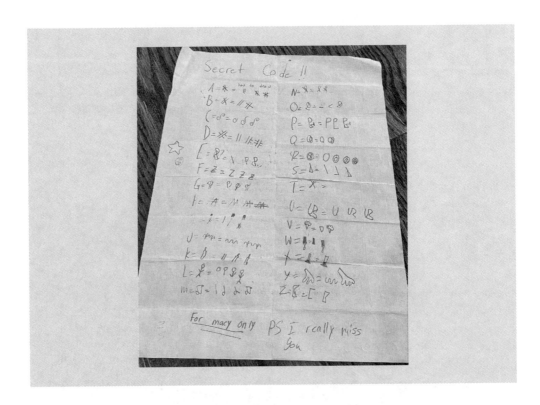

Although I told David not to write notes in class, student note writing can serve as an effective instructional tool. Because we know that students write notes back and forth to each other, and more often text and message back and forth, Written Conversations can be a great strategy to utilize in the classroom.

Here are some tips for success:

- Set specific time limits and keep the written conversations brief.

- Set parameters for responding and discussing: Exactly what should the students be talking about and what are appropriate means to respond?

- If desired, strategically pair students with partners who work well together.

- Alternate with partnering students based on writing proficiency level. In some cases, pair similar proficiency levels, while in other cases, partner up those with differing proficiency levels.

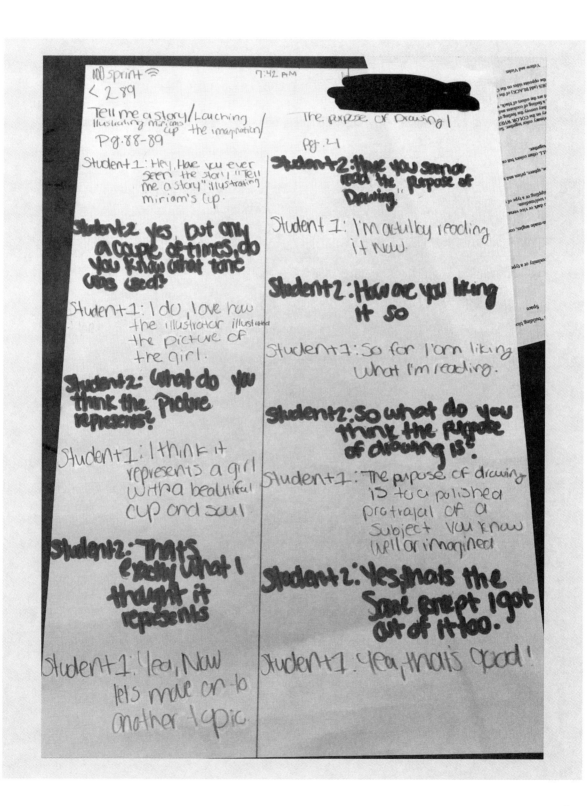

CHAPTER 1
Why Write Now?

CHAPTER 2
Parachute Writing

CHAPTER 3
Sum It All Up

CHAPTER 4
All the Right Words

CHAPTER 5
Digital Worlds

CHAPTER 6
Just the Facts

CHAPTER 7
Expecting the Unexpected

CHAPTER 1
Why Write Now?

CHAPTER 2
Parachute Writing

CHAPTER 3
Sum It All Up

CHAPTER 4
All the Right Words

CHAPTER 5
Digital Worlds

CHAPTER 6
Just the Facts

CHAPTER 7
Expecting the
Unexpected

Putting It to Work

1. Prior to implementing the strategy, provide students with an overview of what is expected and the parameters for their responses.

2. Give students a prompt, question, or nudge statement.

3. Set a timer for a short amount of time (1–2 minutes) for students to write their initial responses.

4. Divide students into pairs and have them respond to each other's work by writing the next part of the conversation. Remind students that they are not evaluating their peer's writing but rather are responding to the content.

5. Repeat for a few rounds or until students have written and responded to their classmate multiple times to conclude the written conversation.

6. Allow students to share their conversations and discuss them as a class.

Quick Tip!

Teaching virtually? Use the chat feature found on many lesson delivery platforms.

When to Use It

- To review after studying a concept or reading a selection of text

- To quickly integrate writing into a lesson

- To "discuss" material in a silent setting

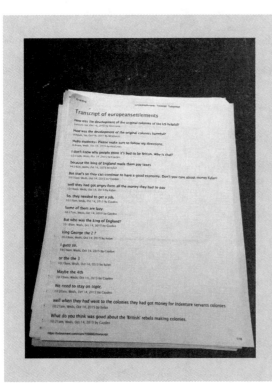

Why It Works

- Written Conversations are informal and don't follow a rigid structure.

- Students do not have to worry if they follow all the appropriate grammar or spelling rules.

- Students are free to use slang, draw pictures or emojis, and use abbreviations and humor in their responses.

- It is quick, can be implemented with little planning, and has the potential to spark quality classroom conversations during follow up.

Modifications

- Have students complete a virtual written conversation using an online platform such as Google Classroom or Microsoft Teams.

- Instead of a written conversation, have students complete a tweet or a text conversation.

- Turn the written conversation into a snowball fight by having students ball up their papers and toss them across the room. Students pick up one of the crumpled papers and write the next response in the conversation before balling it up and tossing it again for another student to contribute.

Extensions

- Use Written Conversations as an extension to the Hashtag strategy (page 163), Write Around the Text (page 195), or Text Mapping strategies (page 190).

- Have students translate their written conversations into formal language.

- Have students incorporate illustrations that correlate with the conversations.

- Have students develop a supplemental key that "decodes" any abbreviations or slang used in the conversation.

Content Area Connections

- Use this strategy as a springboard for introducing new types of literary texts.

- In math, have students discuss what type of figure or model should accompany a specific problem.

CHAPTER 1
Why Write Now?

CHAPTER 2
Parachute Writing

CHAPTER 3
Sum It All Up

CHAPTER 4
All the Right Words

CHAPTER 5
Digital Worlds

CHAPTER 6
Just the Facts

CHAPTER 7
Expecting the Unexpected

CHAPTER 1
Why Write Now?

CHAPTER 2
Parachute Writing

CHAPTER 3
Sum It All Up

CHAPTER 4
All the Right Words

CHAPTER 5
Digital Worlds

CHAPTER 6
Just the Facts

CHAPTER 7
Expecting the
Unexpected

- In art, insert an image of a piece of artwork on the paper that is being used for the conversation. Have students respond to the artwork with a partner.

- Use written conversations for nonacademic tasks, much like the Drop Draft before. Written conversations are good tools when students need to talk about something that might be bothering them or something that is somewhat controversial.

- Have students assume the roles of different historical figures and create conversations based on those points of view.

- Use Written Conversations as a springboard to teach dialogue.

- Have students discuss different ways to solve a complex problem.

Quick Tip!

The OMG Shakespeare and OMG Classics collections translate classic works of literature into text messages and emojis. They are great companion pieces to this strategy.

CHAPTER 1
Why Write Now?

CHAPTER 2
Parachute Writing

CHAPTER 3
Sum It All Up

CHAPTER 4
All the Right Words

CHAPTER 5
Digital Worlds

CHAPTER 6
Just the Facts

CHAPTER 7
Expecting the
Unexpected

Chapter 3

SUM IT ALL UP

Strategies for Finding Key Details and Summarizing

Many students feel that summarization is only used in the classroom. They often don't realize how frequently we use the skill in our daily lives. Being able to summarize key events and important details helps us in a number of ways, as it assists us in providing both written and oral recaps of events and ideas. From general conversational summaries that answer questions like "Tell me about your day," "What did you do over the weekend?" and "What was that movie about?" to written summaries such as emails, résumés, and meeting minutes, summaries are a key component of daily life. Even a subject line on an email is a summary or a main idea since it is meant to function as the overarching topic or gist of the actual written email that follows.

Recently a colleague asked me why students don't engage with reading and writing like we want them to. My response was one that I have repeated often: "Because we don't do a good job of making connections between the real and academic worlds and we don't use authentic examples of literacy." Instead of incorporating what students are already seeing and using, we continue to fall back on traditional methods of teaching like book reports, grammar exercises, and traditional knowledge-based assessments. That is especially true of many of the approaches and strategies that are used when teaching students to summarize. Instead of finding examples and means to teach this skill through traditional methods, I advocate that we look for ways to incorporate real-world writing.

CHAPTER 1
Why Write Now?

CHAPTER 2
Parachute Writing

CHAPTER 3
Sum It All Up

CHAPTER 4
All the Right Words

CHAPTER 5
Digital Worlds

CHAPTER 6
Just the Facts

CHAPTER 7
Expecting the Unexpected

Clarity Is Key

Many students struggle with developing the skill of summarization. Finding the right amount of details and evidence to craft a concise and relevant summary can be difficult. Teachers comment that students either include extraneous information or not enough when they craft written summaries. This may happen because the purpose has not been made clear. Think about it. What happens when teachers ask students to recall important details? Often, students may recall numerous details from the material, but the word "important" is a high-stakes word. It's like the word *favorite*; a student may like a lot of movies, but asking them to tell you their favorite means that one is elevated above all the other examples.

When we ask students to identify important details, the word *important* becomes the qualifying word that posits specific parameters on the detail. It means that when compared to *all* the other details in the text, the important ones are those that carry the most weight. For a student who recalls numerous details about a text, that *one* qualifying word can cause hesitancy from the student. What if the detail they provide isn't important? What if there are other answers that are more important? A better way to approach summary may be to ask students first to recall as many details as they can from the material and then categorize these details or rank them in order of importance. (The Summary Sweep strategy in this chapter employs these methods.) This creates a safer way to summarize.

Get Real With Real-World Examples of Summarization

Another important tactic when addressing summary is making clear connections between real-world examples and academic demands. Without even realizing it, students take part in real-world summaries all the time—recaps of television shows, sports replays, movie trailers. And just this week, I saw T-shirts for sale with one-line movie summaries of popular holiday films. Plus, many jobs in the real world require individuals to be competent at the skill of summarization. Think about attorneys who write summary briefs, realtors who have to summarize a home's key features and selling points, and physicians who have to summarize a diagnosis in a medical chart. However, I am not sure we (including myself) do the best job of drawing attention to these types of real-world summaries in the classroom. These are prime opportunities to clap back at students who ask *why* they need to learn something. Students want to know how it affects them in the real world. By paying deliberate attention to real-world examples, students can begin to see that they may possess the skills needed to complete an academic summary simply by employing their everyday skills.

Regardless of the difficulties some students may have or *think* they have with the crafting of summaries, this is a crucial skill that all disciplines and grade levels require. Like every other written task, students need multiple opportunities to practice this skill using several strategies and text types. Plus, they need opportunities to see this skill reflected in the real world. Think about it: When do you see summaries used? If you are thinking that people don't actively summarize on a daily basis, ponder these possibilities:

- Meeting minutes

- Eyewitness accounts

- Emails (especially ones whose purpose is to follow up on a conversation or meeting)

- Hashtags

- Text messages

- Tweets

- Commercials

- Television and sports recaps

- "Tell me about your day" requests

- Annual performance reviews

- Résumés/vitas

Are you convinced now? There may be some items on this list that you never considered as a summary. A résumé? Yes, that is a type of summary. It's a summary of your work history and skill set. Meeting minutes? Yes. It's a short summary of that hour-long meeting you just sat through. And it doesn't stop there. Attorneys draft title opinions (summaries) and briefs, news anchors give abbreviated reports of events, student progress reports summarize achievement, discipline referrals summarize an infraction, and pastors summarize sections of scripture in sermons. In summary, there's no denying that summarizing is a skill needed across the board.

Quick Tip!

Have students make a list of any task they would consider as a summary. They'll likely come up with things you haven't yet considered!

Regardless of the content or grade level you teach, students need to develop the skill of summarizing. This chapter contains strategies to use in a variety of subjects and grade levels for several purposes. When considering the use of these strategies in the classroom, keep in mind these questions:

- How much background knowledge does the student have about the topic? Lack of appropriate prior knowledge can dramatically affect the final summary product.

CHAPTER 1
Why Write Now?

CHAPTER 2
Parachute Writing

CHAPTER 3
Sum It All Up

CHAPTER 4
All the Right Words

CHAPTER 5
Digital Worlds

CHAPTER 6
Just the Facts

CHAPTER 7
Expecting the Unexpected

CHAPTER 1
Why Write Now?

CHAPTER 2
Parachute Writing

CHAPTER 3
Sum It All Up

CHAPTER 4
All the Right Words

CHAPTER 5
Digital Worlds

CHAPTER 6
Just the Facts

CHAPTER 7
Expecting the
Unexpected

- Does the student need to complete a full-length summary or a shortened summary version? (For full-length summaries, consider the Pizza Slice (page 63), Summary Sweep Sentence (page 67), or Three-Panel Summary (page 76). For abbreviated summaries, consider using the Summary Meme (page 83), or Hashtag (page 163) strategies.)

- Do I want my student to revise and revisit their summary or is a "one-shot" try OK?

- Would peer collaboration offer benefits for the content you are addressing? Is there value in having the students collaborate with a peer or revisit a summary with a peer?

- How could I extend the summary task or is there a need to do so?

Considering these questions can help you choose the most appropriate strategy for the goals and purposes of the lesson. Clearly articulating the lesson purpose and choosing strategies that are well-suited for the lesson purpose can help you capitalize on precious time and resources.

CHAPTER 1 Why Write Now?

CHAPTER 2 Parachute Writing

CHAPTER 3 Sum It All Up

CHAPTER 4 All the Right Words

CHAPTER 5 Digital Worlds

CHAPTER 6 Just the Facts

CHAPTER 7 Expecting the Unexpected

PIZZA SLICE SUMMARY

The Pizza Slice Summary capitalizes on knowledge of social media to summarize in chunks, all the way down to the main idea. Students sometimes get bogged down in too much text when summarizing, so this strategy asks them to provide less text each time. They provide a summary first as an email format at the top of the wedge/pizza crust, then as a text message summary, then as a hashtag—showing how to whittle down to the main kernel of an idea. Plus, since the image mirrors the whittling down process of summarization, this helps students to visually see how a summary differs from the main text.

Quick Tip!

The material that students are summarizing does not have to be text they read. As with other strategies in this chapter, you can have students summarize a lecture, video clip, or other material.

Putting It to Work

1. Place the main selection of the material being summarized at the top of the flipped triangle.

2. Have students read the material and then discuss it as a class, in a group, or with a peer. It is important to provide adequate time for dialogue and conversation about the material to make certain that the students comprehend what was read or addressed.

3. Ask students questions to support their comprehension. Examples include

   - How does the length of the summary text change as you move down the pizza slice?

   - What type of language is used? Is it informal or formal?

   - How does the audience impact the language used?

4. Show students authentic examples of emails and discuss the key qualities of an email.

5. Instruct students to take the main selection they have just read and discussed and summarize it in an email format. (This is the second component of the triangle.)

Quick Tip!

Students MUST see examples of all mediums that they are expected to craft. Keep in mind that many students do not email as much as adults, so this form may be a little more difficult for them to complete. An example is an absolute necessity.

6. Show students examples of real text messages and discuss the key qualities of a text, highlighting how it is different than an email.

CHAPTER 1
Why Write Now?

CHAPTER 2
Parachute Writing

CHAPTER 3
Sum It All Up

CHAPTER 4
All the Right Words

CHAPTER 5
Digital Worlds

CHAPTER 6
Just the Facts

CHAPTER 7
Expecting the
Unexpected

7. Ask students to summarize the selection again, but this time, in the form of a text message. (This is the third component of the triangle.) Remind students that instead of focusing on the entire topic, text, or concept studied, they should focus their attention to summarize the email portion only. They are looking at less text this time.

8. Now have students create the hashtag. (This is the last component of the triangle.) Remind them that they should only focus on the previous summary they constructed (the text message), and that the hashtag should capture the kernel of the main idea of the original text read.

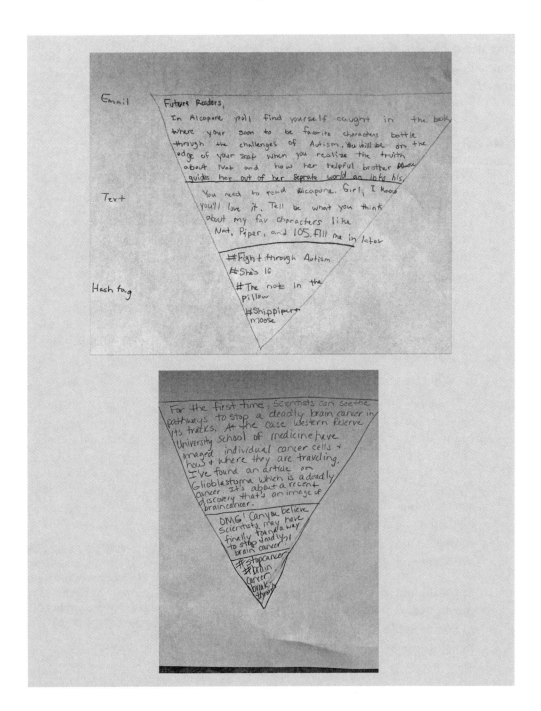

When to Use It

- As an assessment at the end of a short assigned reading

- As an overall summary of an important concept or unit

- As a means to summarize nontraditional texts (movies, conversations, photographic evidence, dramas, etc.)

- To work collaboratively to develop a group summary

 Quick Tip!

Each reduction in text can aid students in constructing an effective summary because they are able to focus their attention on less material.

Why It Works

- Students use modes and materials that are familiar so summarizing the material is easier and more achievable.

- Students eliminate extra fluff each time they move from one format to another, so they can focus on smaller sections of the text each time.

- Because the shape of the triangle narrows as the student continues to summarize, students recognize visually that their summaries should become condensed. (I often use a funnel as a visual metaphor.)

- Sections can be modified and adjusted based on the needs of the students.

Modifications

- Allow English learners to complete a section of the flipped triangle in their native language. Then partner English learners with native English speakers. Have each student share their written summary. This allows each student to have an oral example of the summary in their native language and a written one.

- Omit the email section and replace it with an image instead. (Think Instagram here!) Have students add a picture, drawing, or other visual representation of the concept they are summarizing.

- Flip the triangle to start with the hashtag or main idea first, and complete the activity in reverse. Have students write extensions of the main idea by elaborating and adding details, which is a great way to get them to write an extended response.

CHAPTER 1
Why Write Now?

CHAPTER 2
Parachute Writing

CHAPTER 3
Sum It All Up

CHAPTER 4
All the Right Words

CHAPTER 5
Digital Worlds

CHAPTER 6
Just the Facts

CHAPTER 7
Expecting the Unexpected

CHAPTER 1
Why Write Now?

CHAPTER 2
Parachute Writing

CHAPTER 3
Sum It All Up

CHAPTER 4
All the Right Words

CHAPTER 5
Digital Worlds

CHAPTER 6
Just the Facts

CHAPTER 7
Expecting the
Unexpected

Extensions

The purpose of the extensions is for students to see how these formats can be modified and extended to encapsulate the main idea and the overarching ideas of larger pieces of information.

- Students can use the text message section to craft Instagram captions by adding an image that corresponds with their written text.

- Students can create news headlines instead of hashtags for their summaries. Journalists everywhere use these examples of summary statements.

- Have students determine the best summary email subject line for their selection. These subject lines are nothing more than main ideas and topic sentences.

- Have students work in cooperative groups to take the text message component that they each wrote and modify them into a single tweet to represent their group. Students can use a sheet of chart paper to record their tweets and then share them with the rest of the class.

Content Area Connection

- Use this strategy to summarize key historical events, create concise summaries of primary sources, or summarize a historical figure's most important accomplishments.

- Have students summarize their thinking and mathematical computations for a problem by moving from showing all their work and explaining their thinking (top of triangle), all the way down to the final answer without any supplemental explanation (bottom point of the triangle).

- Have students summarize a science lab report or lab safety instructions.

- Have students describe and summarize a particular art movement or period of art, then craft a list of summarizing, descriptive words that capture the period, and conclude with the best overall image representation of this period.

SUMMARY SENTENCE SWEEPS

Determining exactly which details are necessary to include in a strong summary can often be challenging for students. We can help them build this skill using the Summary Sentence Sweeps. When creating a summary, sometimes students have difficulty determining which details are important and which ones aren't. This often creates summaries that are either overly verbose or extremely short, or worse, summaries that never get off the runway because students can't decide what should be included. With this strategy, students first eliminate details that are not important in order to narrow the field. Sometimes coming into it from a different angle makes the importance of details clearer.

When students start this activity, they begin by recalling any details from the selection. Teachers should be careful NOT to ask for important details, but rather for any detail from the lesson. Removing the qualifier "important" can help students when recalling details since they are not bound to the word *important*.

Once they have provided a variety of details, students categorize details into three main subheadings: Important, Not Important, and Don't Know. Because they are only looking at one detail each time, grouping details into one of those categories is easier. The category "Don't Know" is important because it allows students to get assistance from their classmates. "Don't Know" functions much like a life raft or the "phone a friend" lifeline on popular game shows. It allows students to admit they are unsure of where the detail goes without penalty.

After a discussion about the piles, the teacher *uses a broom to sweep* away the "not important" pile in order to focus on the other two piles. Yes, I said to use a broom and sweep them away. Students love this part! Sweeping those details out into the hallway really cements the fact that they are not needed for their summaries. (Just make sure you remember to pick up the swept-out pile! In fact, more than once I have had a custodian knock on the door and ask if those notecards in the hall are important or can they trash them!)

Keep in mind, too, there is not a set order to how you address the remaining two piles. In many instances, conversations require you to bounce between the two. The major point is to determine which of the details in the Don't Know pile are needed and which can be swept away.

CHAPTER 1
Why Write Now?

CHAPTER 2
Parachute Writing

CHAPTER 3
Sum It All Up

CHAPTER 4
All the Right Words

CHAPTER 5
Digital Worlds

CHAPTER 6
Just the Facts

CHAPTER 7
Expecting the Unexpected

CHAPTER 1
Why Write Now?

CHAPTER 2
Parachute Writing

CHAPTER 3
Sum It All Up

CHAPTER 4
All the Right Words

CHAPTER 5
Digital Worlds

CHAPTER 6
Just the Facts

CHAPTER 7
Expecting the Unexpected

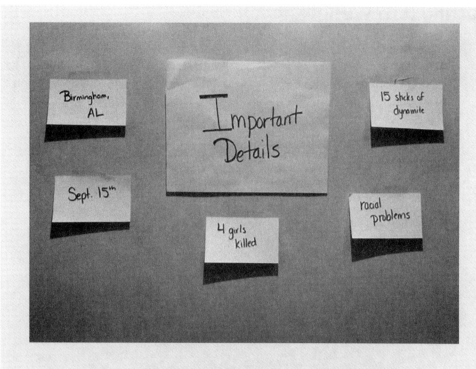

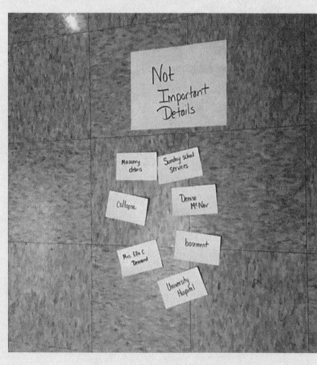

CHAPTER 1
Why Write Now?

CHAPTER 2
Parachute Writing

CHAPTER 3
Sum It All Up

CHAPTER 4
All the Right Words

CHAPTER 5
Digital Worlds

CHAPTER 6
Just the Facts

CHAPTER 7
Expecting the
Unexpected

CHAPTER 1
Why Write Now?

CHAPTER 2
Parachute Writing

CHAPTER 3
Sum It All Up

CHAPTER 4
All the Right Words

CHAPTER 5
Digital Worlds

CHAPTER 6
Just the Facts

CHAPTER 7
Expecting the
Unexpected

Putting It to Work

1. After students have read the text or completed a unit of study, provide them with notecards or sentence strips. Remember, this text just doesn't have to be one that they read. It can be a movie, a collection of images, an overall unit of study, works of art, or a concept.

 Quick Tip!

Don't use sticky notes because you don't want the papers to stick to the floor, but you can use solid block paint strips shown below.

2. Have students recall a detail from the text and write it on the sentence strip or notecard. (This can be any detail at all.)

3. Have students bring their detail up to the front of the room and throw it in a pile on the floor. Read a few of the details to the class to share.

4. Display sentence strips with the headings Important, Not Important, and Don't Know on the floor.

5. Instruct students to come back to the piles and pick up any sentence. It does not have to be their own. Have them read it to themselves and place it in the appropriate pile.

   • Important = important details

   • Not Important = not important details

   • Don't Know = don't know or uncertain of correct importance

6. After students have grouped the details into piles, have a quick class discussion about each pile. Ask students the following kinds of questions:

- How do we know this detail is important?

- Is this detail necessary for us to understand the overall text?

- Do you agree that this detail is important or not important?

- Are there any details that we left out that need to be included?

7. Use a *broom to sweep* away the Not Important pile and begin to focus on the other two piles.

8. Once the Don't Know pile is eliminated and all extraneous details are swept away, only the Important pile remains. Have students examine all of the details in that pile to determine which of the important details are the most important.

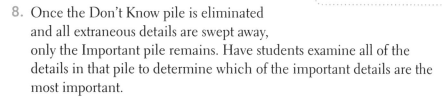

I typically start with the Not Important pile and then move to the Important pile. This allows time to clarify any confusion or correct any misconceptions about the text. If there are any details in the wrong piles, simply rearrange them.

When to Use It

- To summarize after reading a section of text—content area reading, novel, digital text, etc.

- To create an overall summary of an important concept or unit

- As a way to summarize nontraditional texts—movies, conversations, photographic evidence, dramas, etc.

- To work collaboratively to develop a group summary

- To process and summarize a particularly dense selection of text

- To check for reading comprehension and understanding

Why It Works

- There's less pressure on having the correct or best answer because students aren't asked to recall important details, but are prompted to recall any detail.

- Students can easily get bogged down in too much text. This strategy can help them focus on smaller amounts of text.

- As students eliminate details that are not important, it allows them to look at smaller amounts of text to write a more concise summary without getting

CHAPTER 1
Why Write Now?

CHAPTER 2
Parachute Writing

CHAPTER 3
Sum It All Up

CHAPTER 4
All the Right Words

CHAPTER 5
Digital Worlds

CHAPTER 6
Just the Facts

CHAPTER 7
Expecting the Unexpected

CHAPTER 1
Why Write Now?

CHAPTER 2
Parachute Writing

CHAPTER 3
Sum It All Up

CHAPTER 4
All the Right Words

CHAPTER 5
Digital Worlds

CHAPTER 6
Just the Facts

CHAPTER 7
Expecting the
Unexpected

bogged down by the entire text. (This same characteristic is evident in the Pizza Slice Summary.)

- Students get practice in categorizing specific details based on level of importance. This helps them differentiate information and label and categorize it appropriately.

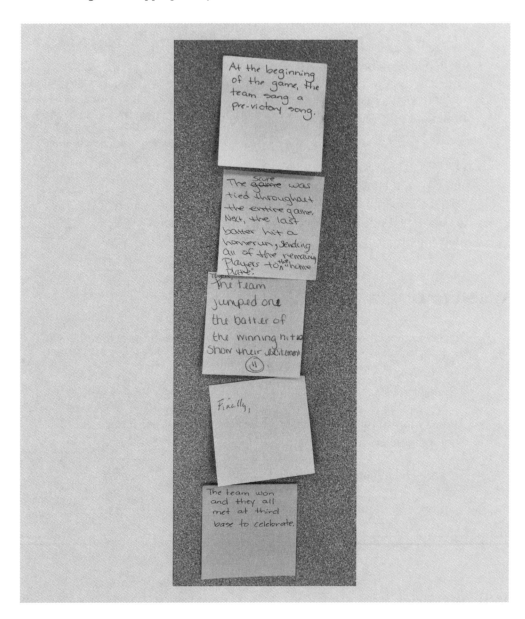

Modifications

- Provide students with premade detail cards (one detail per card) to use for the activity instead of having them recall and write the details on their own.

- Have students create their own summaries using a certain number of the important details in the pile instead of condensing the important details down to a specific number.

- Allow students to draw pictorial representations of details instead of utilizing words.

- Have students recall the details from the story on notecards as a method for checking understanding rather than going through all of the steps of classification.

Extensions

- Have students use the words from the important details pile to craft their own summaries of the concept.

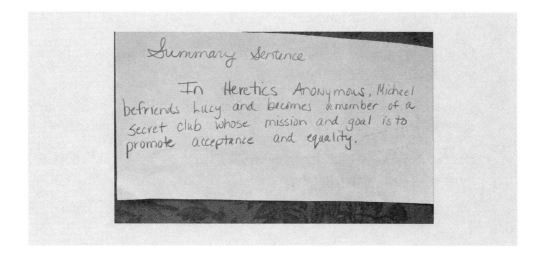

CHAPTER 1
Why Write Now?

CHAPTER 2
Parachute Writing

CHAPTER 3
Sum It All Up

CHAPTER 4
All the Right Words

CHAPTER 5
Digital Worlds

CHAPTER 6
Just the Facts

CHAPTER 7
Expecting the Unexpected

CHAPTER 1
Why Write Now?

CHAPTER 2
Parachute Writing

CHAPTER 3
Sum It All Up

CHAPTER 4
All the Right Words

CHAPTER 5
Digital Worlds

CHAPTER 6
Just the Facts

CHAPTER 7
Expecting the Unexpected

- Put a variety of qualifiers on the summaries that students write using the details. For example, require students to use all the details in some form or require them to use only five of the important details in their summaries.

- Ask students to collaborate with a partner and add illustrations that complement the individual details, or practice a grammar skill such as sentence combination.

- Have students choose an important detail and create a visual accompaniment that compliments the sentence.

- Using the details from the pile, have students create collaborative summaries in partners or groups.

- Have students rank the details in order of importance and write a justification sentence supporting why they assigned that ranking to the sentence.

- Have students convert the details to tweets or hashtags as a means to further summarize and engage with the text.

Content Area Connections

- Break mathematical word problems up onto notecards (one sentence of the word problem per notecard) and have students categorize the cards based on which information is needed to solve the problem and which cards have extraneous information.

- Analyze key battles in wars, overarching themes or issues based on historical perspectives, and historical figures and their key accomplishments.

- Illustrate key information needed in an effective lab report or key ideas of a particular science concept such as photosynthesis.

- Sort different pieces of artwork into piles to rank their level of influence on other artists.

CHAPTER 1
Why Write Now?

CHAPTER 2
Parachute Writing

CHAPTER 3
Sum It All Up

CHAPTER 4
All the Right Words

CHAPTER 5
Digital Worlds

CHAPTER 6
Just the Facts

CHAPTER 7
Expecting the Unexpected

CHAPTER 1
Why Write Now?

CHAPTER 2
Parachute Writing

CHAPTER 3
Sum It All Up

CHAPTER 4
All the Right Words

CHAPTER 5
Digital Worlds

CHAPTER 6
Just the Facts

CHAPTER 7
Expecting the
Unexpected

THREE-PANEL SUMMARIES

This summarization strategy was inspired by Lisa Brown's book *Depressed, Repressed, Obsessed* (2014), which offers a series of three-panel book reviews of classic literature. This text provides readers with a succinct book review using three panels of details along with images. While this serves as an excellent resource for introducing classic literature, it also offers inspiration for summary writing.

To create a Three-Panel Summary, students first need to determine the three most important details, then depict each with an illustration and one or two sentences in order to summarize the text. Three-Panel Summaries work well as a bridge from similar elementary activities that focus on details that occur at the beginning, middle, and end; this strategy positions the student to continue with the three most important details, scenes, or events of a story or concept. One way to bridge a beginning, middle, and end writing to a Three-Panel Summary is by having students start with details from different parts in the story and then rank them based on importance for each section of the story. For example, from a pile of four or five details from the beginning of a story, students would pick the most important one from that part of the story. They would continue this for the middle and end. Later, students could move from this to the Three-Panel Summary where the task requires them to automatically choose the most important detail out of the gate. Merging these strategies in this manner is an effective way to scaffold students to more sophisticated tasks that require more independence.

Quick Tip!

If students struggle with identifying the most important details of the text, before moving on with this strategy have them practice the Summary Sentence Sweep strategy (page 67) or the modification in which students rank their evidence on paint strips. You can also show them examples from Brown's book or other student-created samples.

Putting It to Work

1. Following the completion of a unit, novel, short story, or concept, have students brainstorm details they recall. Students can brainstorm important details from the beginning, middle, and end. This gives them a reference point for where to find their details and what to include.

2. Instruct students to determine which of the brainstormed details are most important for their summaries and have students write them on notecards. Alternatively, you could have ready-made images and statements on index cards for the students to sort.

3. Explain to students that they should put one detail in each panel.

4. Have students write the sentence form of their details on each corresponding panel.

5. Invite students to draft pictures that complement their important details and include them within each of the three panels.

6. Allow students to share with a partner for feedback.

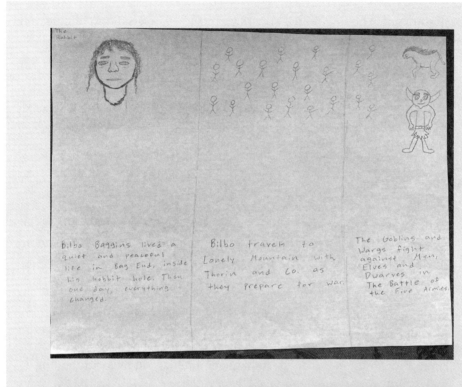

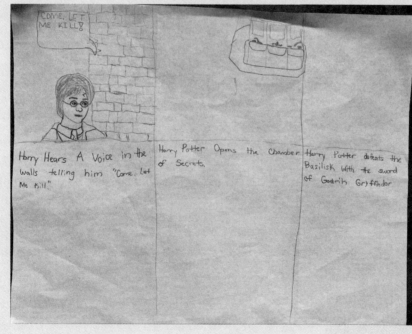

CHAPTER 1
Why Write Now?

CHAPTER 2
Parachute Writing

CHAPTER 3
Sum It All Up

CHAPTER 4
All the Right Words

CHAPTER 5
Digital Worlds

CHAPTER 6
Just the Facts

CHAPTER 7
Expecting the Unexpected

CHAPTER 1
Why Write Now?

CHAPTER 2
Parachute Writing

CHAPTER 3
Sum It All Up

CHAPTER 4
All the Right Words

CHAPTER 5
Digital Worlds

CHAPTER 6
Just the Facts

CHAPTER 7
Expecting the
Unexpected

When to Use It

- To create a summary after reading a section in the text (e.g., content area texts, novels, digital texts, or other forms of text)

- As an overall summary of an important concept or unit

- To summarize nontraditional texts (e.g., movies, conversations, photographic evidence, or dramas)

- To work collaboratively to develop a group summary

- As a springboard into writing an extended graphic novel excerpt or comic strip

Why It Works

- Students already have some background knowledge about summarizing in a series of three. (Think about all the primary grades' emphasis on beginning, middle, and end.)

- Three-Panel Summaries incorporate an artistic element, which allows students to capitalize on another strength and a different style of thinking.

- Three-Panel Summaries aid in student comprehension by incorporating a written and visual depiction in each panel.

- The short length of the assignment—only three panels—makes it seem easier for students to complete and achieve.

- It mimics a real-life medium: the comic strip.

Modifications

- Have students brainstorm the important details as well as their corresponding images. Then, have students use these to determine which sentences and images to incorporate in their Three-Panel Summaries.

- For struggling students, begin this strategy using details from the beginning, middle, and end before transitioning to summary details.

- Use paint strips and address labels instead of having students complete the summary on a comic strip template.

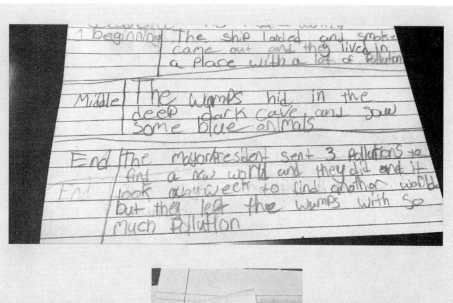

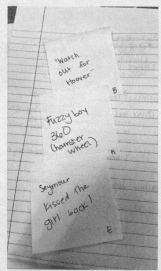

CHAPTER 1
Why Write Now?

CHAPTER 2
Parachute Writing

CHAPTER 3
Sum It All Up

CHAPTER 4
All the Right Words

CHAPTER 5
Digital Worlds

CHAPTER 6
Just the Facts

CHAPTER 7
Expecting the
Unexpected

CHAPTER 1
Why Write Now?

CHAPTER 2
Parachute Writing

CHAPTER 3
Sum It All Up

CHAPTER 4
All the Right Words

CHAPTER 5
Digital Worlds

CHAPTER 6
Just the Facts

CHAPTER 7
Expecting the
Unexpected

- Have English learners complete a dual language Three-Panel Summary with their native language on the bottom of the image and English on the top (or vice versa).

- Allow students to use photographs instead of drawing pictures in the summary panels.

Extensions

- Use this activity as a bridge or storyboard to a more comprehensive written assignment like a graphic novel or comic strip.

- Have students complete Three-Panel Summaries multiple times throughout reading a novel so the end product resembles a graphic novel.

- Use this as a tool for revision by having students peer edit and suggest alternate images or details that would better convey meaning.

Content Area Connections

- Use Three-Panel Summary in lab science for a three- (or more) panel lab report.

- Use Three-Panel Summary to provide a synopsis of a period of art or a movement.

- Have students complete a Three-Panel Proof for math problems that benefit from a visual element, such as geometric proofs.

CHAPTER 1
Why Write Now?

CHAPTER 2
Parachute Writing

CHAPTER 3
Sum It All Up

CHAPTER 4
All the Right Words

CHAPTER 5
Digital Worlds

CHAPTER 6
Just the Facts

CHAPTER 7
Expecting the Unexpected

CHAPTER 1
Why Write Now?

CHAPTER 2
Parachute Writing

CHAPTER 3
Sum It All Up

CHAPTER 4
All the Right Words

CHAPTER 5
Digital Worlds

CHAPTER 6
Just the Facts

CHAPTER 7
Expecting the
Unexpected

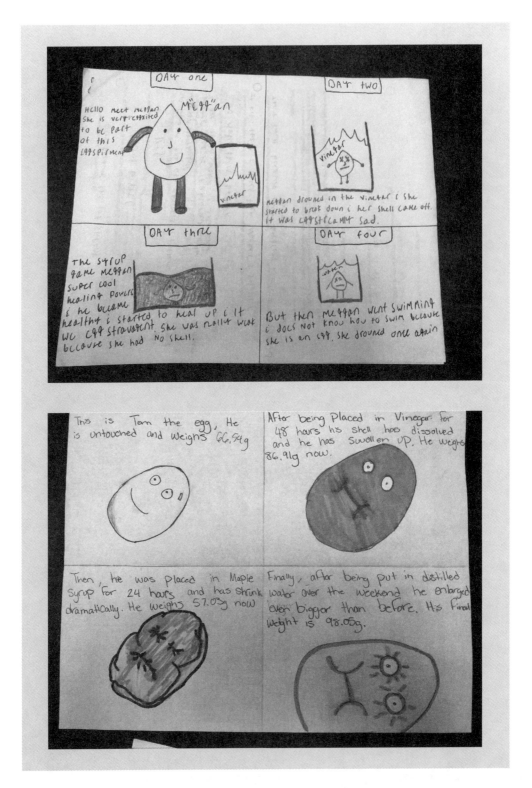

- Use Three-Panel Summary to summarize the process when solving a mathematical problem.

- Have students use this strategy to create a Three-Panel Character Analysis.

SUMMARY MEMES

Who doesn't love a good meme? You know, the ones that show a picture of a screaming baby with a great caption about the extended faculty meeting? Memes are great tools for teaching concepts such as main idea, summarization, theme, voice, audience, topic, purpose, and humor. In order to create an effective meme, you must have a clear sense of purpose, audience, and the message you intend to convey. In fact, meme generation can require pretty sophisticated thought processes because there really is a lot to consider when creating an effective meme.

In addition to the numerous items to consider when creating a meme, there's a significant amount of revision that occurs because you have to be conservative with the word count. An overly verbose meme just isn't effective. Part of the meme's appeal is the fact that the image and short caption work in tandem to create an effective overall message and there is a significant level of skill needed when selecting the right picture and accompanying words. Knowing this, memes become great tools for summarizing material.

Putting It to Work

1. Following the completion of a lesson, unit, or concept, introduce the meme genre.

2. Provide students with examples of appropriate memes and have them critique each one looking specifically for details such as sentence structure, image and sentence congruence, purpose, audience, font size, and word count.

3. Draft a list of these observations on the board for students to reference as they complete their own.

Quick Tip!

There are a variety of meme generators available online, including websites (makeameme.org and kapwing.com) and apps (Mematic and Memeto).

4. Using the list, complete a class meme together using applicable course content.

5. Once students have completed a class meme, pair them with a partner and have each pair create their own meme. Allow about fifteen minutes for this activity.

6. Have students share with the class, critique, and make revisions if needed.

CHAPTER 1
Why Write Now?

CHAPTER 2
Parachute Writing

CHAPTER 3
Sum It All Up

CHAPTER 4
All the Right Words

CHAPTER 5
Digital Worlds

CHAPTER 6
Just the Facts

CHAPTER 7
Expecting the Unexpected

CHAPTER 1
Why Write Now?

CHAPTER 2
Parachute Writing

CHAPTER 3
Sum It All Up

CHAPTER 4
All the Right Words

CHAPTER 5
Digital Worlds

CHAPTER 6
Just the Facts

CHAPTER 7
Expecting the
Unexpected

When your teacher asks you to give an example of simplifying an expression

$$2(537+473)=2020$$
$$\div 2$$
$$537+437=1010$$

Then, all the class cheers because you simplified an expression and a whole year! Happy New Year!

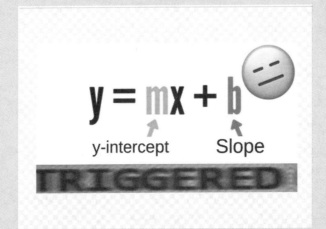

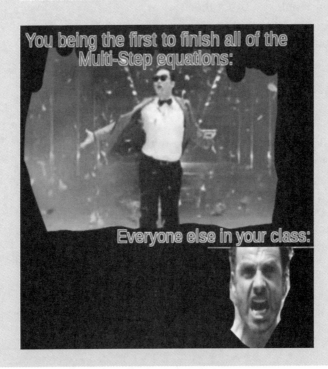

When to Use It

- To create a summary after reading a section in the text (e.g., content area texts, novels, digital texts, or other forms of text)

- To focus on the main idea or theme of a concept

- As a ticket out the door or exit slip

- As a bell ringer or class opener

- To include both a sentence component and a visual component

- To incorporate technology (meme generator apps make this strategy super easy)

Why It Works

- Memes offer students the ability to work in a medium they are familiar with.

- Memes require limited word counts and can be completed in a short class period.

- Memes aid in student comprehension: By incorporating a written sentence along with a visual depiction of what is written in sentence form, creating memes adds another layer of understanding.

- Memes offer the opportunity to incorporate additional elements such as humor, figurative language, and voice.

CHAPTER 1
Why Write Now?

CHAPTER 2
Parachute Writing

CHAPTER 3
Sum It All Up

CHAPTER 4
All the Right Words

CHAPTER 5
Digital Worlds

CHAPTER 6
Just the Facts

CHAPTER 7
Expecting the Unexpected

CHAPTER 1
Why Write Now?

CHAPTER 2
Parachute Writing

CHAPTER 3
Sum It All Up

CHAPTER 4
All the Right Words

CHAPTER 5
Digital Worlds

CHAPTER 6
Just the Facts

CHAPTER 7
Expecting the
Unexpected

Modifications

- Have students play "Meme Matchup" where they match the most appropriate image to the best caption.

- Allow students to work with partners, where one partner submits the image and the other is responsible for writing the meme. Then swap roles.

- Instead of using the digital meme generator, allow students to do it "old school" and cut images from magazines or draw pictures.

- Have students critique memes that are found online and revise them if needed, instead of creating a summary meme.

Extensions

- Use memes as a starter for the Three-Panel Summary (page 76).

- For an end of quarter, semester, or year review, show students a meme and have them guess the concept.

- Create memes for a certain character in a novel, scientist, or famous figure and create a collection of "Best Rated Memes."

- Have students create an end of chapter, section, or lesson meme that they compile over the course of the unit of study.

Content Area Connections

- Have students create memes that best represent that figure's beliefs or accomplishments when studying different historical figures.

- Have students translate popular memes into a different language in world language classes.

- Use memes in math to determine a student's attitude toward a math concept or to share their understanding about a certain concept such as fractions, functions, or geometric proofs.

- Create memes to show proper form when weight training or rules of a sport in physical education.

- Have students choose a character and draft memes based on the events in the character's life when studying novels.

CHAPTER 1
Why Write Now?

CHAPTER 2
Parachute Writing

CHAPTER 3
Sum It All Up

CHAPTER 4
All the Right Words

CHAPTER 5
Digital Worlds

CHAPTER 6
Just the Facts

CHAPTER 7
Expecting the Unexpected

BROCHURE SUMMARIES

While visiting Bryson City recently, my children and I picked up a plethora of brochures from the lobby on a variety of restaurants, activities, and excursions. Typically a brochure consists of one folded piece of paper that includes a mixture of images and information. Brochures can be about any number of topics, but because of their limited space, items such as word count and image size are extremely important, and brochure designers have to rely on summarization to create the most effective advertisement. For example, when you open a brochure on the popular attractions of a particular city, you expect that the material in this text would address a number of services. You might expect to see some information about the restaurants, activities, and locations of several relevant places that are in that area. Readers need to see succinct information on a variety of topics that can provide an effective overview of that geographic area.

The same concepts are prevalent even in brochures that advertise different products and services. While the audience and purpose may differ, most brochures include similar components. Take this example from a design company. Look at the section under the Copying & Bindery/Finishing heading. In a short amount of text, the business owners are able to give the reader/audience a brief summary of the types of copying services they offer.

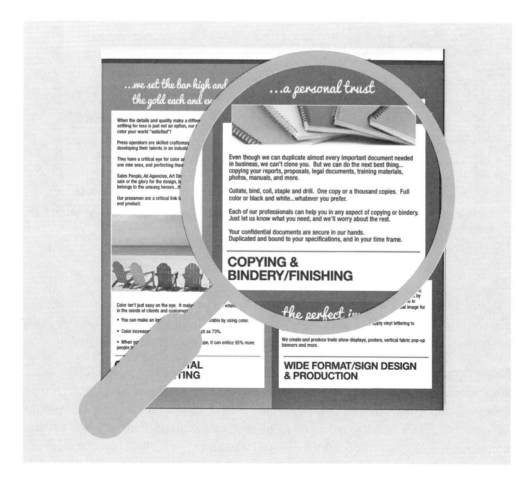

CHAPTER 1
Why Write Now?

CHAPTER 2
Parachute Writing

CHAPTER 3
Sum It All Up

CHAPTER 4
All the Right Words

CHAPTER 5
Digital Worlds

CHAPTER 6
Just the Facts

CHAPTER 7
Expecting the
Unexpected

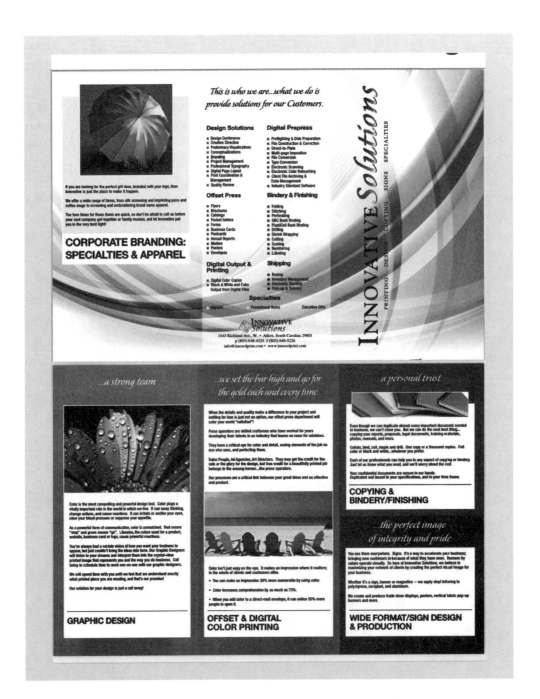

Creating brochures is a great way for students to practice the skill of summary using a real-world application. Plus, utilizing brochures in a writing lesson also allows students the opportunity to critique brochures for quality, relevance, and key information.

Before beginning the activity, it is a good idea to collect brochures for similar attractions, services, or purposes. For example, collect a variety of brochures that address attractions found in different cities' downtown areas. Students may not be familiar with brochures (because they can find most information on the internet), so building a bit of background may be helpful here. And it's helpful for students to all look at the same *type* of brochure so they are able to see similarities that run across all examples.

Putting It to Work

1. Show students several brochures to make sure they understand the general components and overall purpose.

2. Divide students into pairs or small groups. Provide each pair or group with a set of brochures all around a similar topic, theme, or service (e.g., white water rafting, day spas, or restaurants).

3. Have students examine their brochures and make a list on chart paper of all the main items or focuses of the brochures. For example, if students are looking at brochures that all address white water rafting adventures, they may expect to see the following in all of the brochures, regardless of the company or location:

   - Photos of the excursion
   - Pricing
   - Location
   - Preparation for the excursion
   - Maps
   - Overview of the excursion or experience

4. Once they have completed their list, provide pairs or groups with additional brochures on that same topic, service, or theme. Have students critique the additional brochures. This is important to support conversations about what is and is not included.

5. Ask the class to come together and use what they have learned from their brochure analysis and critique to draft a list of nonnegotiables that should be included for creating their own brochures on their content topics.

6. Using the list of class-created nonnegotiables, students will now develop and create their own brochures on their assigned topics. Students can do this "old school" with paper and pencil or use a digital tool such as Microsoft Publisher, Adobe Spark, or Canva.

7. Provide students with a checklist of items that you want to be included in their brochures that might not make the class-created nonnegotiables. These should be included regardless of the topics (e.g., a specific number of images, specific number of categories, contact information).

When to Use It

- As an overall summary of an important concept or unit
- To work collaboratively to develop a group summary

CHAPTER 1
Why Write Now?

CHAPTER 2
Parachute Writing

CHAPTER 3
Sum It All Up

CHAPTER 4
All the Right Words

CHAPTER 5
Digital Worlds

CHAPTER 6
Just the Facts

CHAPTER 7
Expecting the Unexpected

CHAPTER 1
Why Write Now?

CHAPTER 2
Parachute Writing

CHAPTER 3
Sum It All Up

CHAPTER 4
All the Right Words

CHAPTER 5
Digital Worlds

CHAPTER 6
Just the Facts

CHAPTER 7
Expecting the Unexpected

- To have a final piece of work that is "publishable"

- As a culminating assessment or a presentation for a storyboard or Three-Panel Summary (page 76)

Why It Works

- Brochures are visually appealing and utilize a unique blend of images, fonts, color schemes, and words.

- Brochure Summaries blend the skill of summarization with the persuasive genre.

- Students are able to work collaboratively to create a final product.

- Brochure Summaries allow students to practice both their written and presentation skills.

Modifications

- Have students create a public service announcement (PSA) instead of utilizing the brochure format.

- Have students draft an infographic instead of a brochure. Use a digital tool such as Canva, Venngage, or Piktochart to create crisp infographics for this activity.

- Have students create a condensed version of the brochure that would be appropriate for sharing on social media. (Think pop-up ads that appear in your web searches or social media.)

- Have students create a billboard advertisement instead of a brochure.

Extensions

- Use brochures as an additional component for assessment when teaching persuasive essay construction.

- Have students develop companion commercials, radio ads, or other forms of advertising in conjunction with their brochures.

- Allow students to develop a marketing strategy or ad campaign for the product or service included in their brochure.

Content Area Connections

- Have students create a reversible brochure with one side in one language and the flip side in another they are studying in foreign language class.

- Have art students create brochures advertising specific movements in art, or create hand-illustrated brochures using an art technique(s) they are studying.

- Have students use address labels or sticky notes to draw attention to math concepts included in their brochures, such as price discounts, angles, or statistics.

- When students are researching a controversial topic such as animal rights or gun control, have them create a flip side brochure where they address the opposing side.

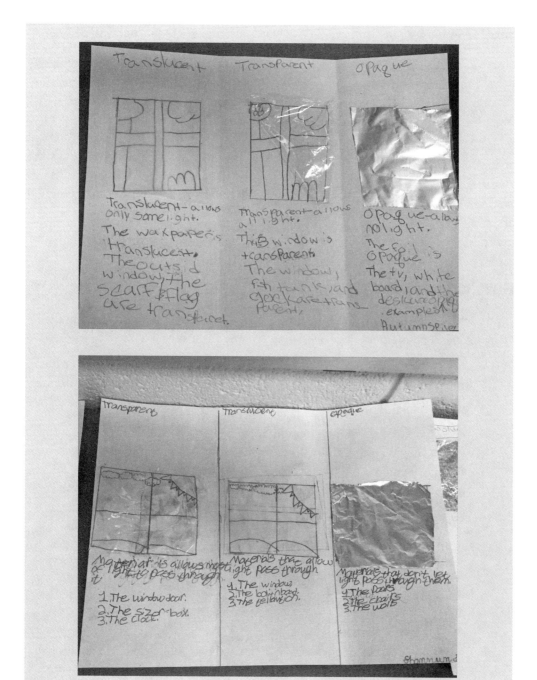

CHAPTER 1
Why Write Now?

CHAPTER 2
Parachute Writing

CHAPTER 3
Sum It All Up

CHAPTER 4
All the Right Words

CHAPTER 5
Digital Worlds

CHAPTER 6
Just the Facts

CHAPTER 7
Expecting the
Unexpected

CHAPTER 1
Why Write Now?

CHAPTER 2
Parachute Writing

CHAPTER 3
Sum It All Up

CHAPTER 4
All the Right Words

CHAPTER 5
Digital Worlds

CHAPTER 6
Just the Facts

CHAPTER 7
Expecting the
Unexpected

COMMERCIALS

Most students see and hear advertisements on YouTube or other streaming services, on social media channels, and on television, billboards, and the radio. The writer of a commercial only has a short amount of time to convey their message. The main purpose is to persuade the viewer or purchase an item or service, but in order to do this, the writer must summarize what the service or product does AND persuade in order to be effective. Think about campaign advertisements, radio ads, and pop-up ads that you have to watch to move on to the video you actually wanted to see. These are short bursts of persuasion that utilize effective words and images to persuade an audience.

Commercials are great opportunities for students to explore not only the persuasive genre but also the skill of summarization. I am a huge fan of teaching multiple standards in a layered approach and commercials are a fantastic way to do this. Plus, really effective commercials have staying power. Think about the Geico commercials, Wendy's "Where's the Beef?" and the new Alexa commercials. They combine effective persuasive writing, coupled with engaging visual elements. What great venues for teaching!

 Quick Tip!

Don't box yourself in by only using video commercials. Make sure to utilize radio ads as well because these rely more on words than on visuals.

Putting It to Work

1. Share with students several commercials to make sure they understand the general components and overall persuasive purpose.

2. Divide students into pairs or small groups. Provide each pair or group with a link or QR code to a set of commercials all around a similar product, theme, or service (e.g., cereal, cleaning products, or travel destinations).

3. Have students examine their commercials and make a list on chart paper or in a Google Doc of all the main items or focuses of the brochures. For example, if students are looking at commercials that all are promoting a type of cereal, they are to make note of the components, which might include

- Setting
- Dialogue
- Cost of product
- Features of product
- Cast of characters

4. Once they have completed their list, provide pairs or groups with additional commercials on that same topic, service, or theme. Have students critique

the additional commercials. This is important to support conversations about what is and is not included.

5. Have the class come together and use what they have learned from their commercial analysis and critique to draft a list of nonnegotiables for creating their own commercials on their content topics.

6. Have students use the list of nonnegotiables to develop and create their own commercials on their assigned topics. Provide specific parameters regarding the commercial construction including length of an ad, written script, presentation of the final product, for example. Depending on the technology at your disposal and your time parameters, the commercials can be presented live or recorded and edited.

When to Use It

- As an overall summary of an important concept or unit

- To work collaboratively to develop a group summary

- To practice public speaking skills

- As a culminating assessment or a presentation for a storyboard or Three-Panel Summary

- As a way to engage students in a virtual environment

CHAPTER 1
Why Write Now?

CHAPTER 2
Parachute Writing

CHAPTER 3
Sum It All Up

CHAPTER 4
All the Right Words

CHAPTER 5
Digital Worlds

CHAPTER 6
Just the Facts

CHAPTER 7
Expecting the
Unexpected

CHAPTER 1
Why Write Now?

CHAPTER 2
Parachute Writing

CHAPTER 3
Sum It All Up

CHAPTER 4
All the Right Words

CHAPTER 5
Digital Worlds

CHAPTER 6
Just the Facts

CHAPTER 7
Expecting the
Unexpected

Why It Works

- Commercials are modes that students are familiar with and see across a variety of platforms on a regular basis.

- Commercials blend the skill of summarization with the persuasive genre.

- Students are able to work collaboratively to create a final product.

- Commercials allow students to practice both their written and presentation skills.

Modifications

- Have students create a public service announcement (PSA). Follow similar steps as the lesson, giving plenty of examples of PSAs.

- Have students draft a storyboard of their commercial without actually filming it.

- Instead of creating a full commercial, have students develop a one-sentence product slogan.

Extensions

- Have students write multiple versions of a script for their commercial as practice with formal and informal tone.

- Allow students to incorporate ad spots into their commercials.

- Use the Commercial activity in conjunction with the Brochure Summaries (page 87) for another layer of instruction.

- Have students who speak a second language provide a translated version of the commercial for a foreign television network.

Content Area Connections

- Students can draft subtitles of the commercial in foreign language class.

- Ask students to create commercials for novels in English classes.

- Have students create commercials for different eating plans or fitness regimes in physical education.

- Allow students to create a commercial for a specific composer or artist or style of music while using that artist's musical works.

CHAPTER 1
Why Write Now?

CHAPTER 2
Parachute Writing

CHAPTER 3
Sum It All Up

CHAPTER 4
All the Right Words

CHAPTER 5
Digital Worlds

CHAPTER 6
Just the Facts

CHAPTER 7
Expecting the Unexpected

CHAPTER 1
Why Write Now?

CHAPTER 2
Parachute Writing

CHAPTER 3
Sum It All Up

CHAPTER 4
All the Right Words

CHAPTER 5
Digital Worlds

CHAPTER 6
Just the Facts

CHAPTER 7
Expecting the Unexpected

OBITUARIES

Although I no longer subscribe to the print or online version of any newspapers, about three times a week I do check the local paper online just to read the obituaries section. In fact, according to Legacy.com, obituaries are the most engaging section of a newspaper site. Now that certainly sounds a little morbid, but Legacy's studies have determined that, when reading newspapers online, individuals spend a significant amount of time reading the obituary section.

Morbid or not, obituaries are another real-world example of a summary. In several paragraphs, one can learn about a person's life—from their birth and death dates to their family members, accomplishments, hobbies, and other important details. Granted, some obituaries are more detailed than others and the voice and tone certainly vary. Some are extremely formal and stick to the expected categories of information, while others offer humorous anecdotes using a more playful tone. Regardless, they serve as an effective representation of summary and are certainly utilized in the real world.

When utilizing this assignment, I try to find examples of humorous and unique obituaries, as well as ones for historical figures. Obituaries or different historical figures offer excellent opportunities for students to revise and rewrite with new information. In addition, fictional characters can become useful models for this engagement as well.

Stop & Think

It is important when using this strategy that you be mindful of students who have experienced death in their families. If writing an obituary is sensitive for a student, please offer them an alternate assignment to complete.

Putting It to Work

1. Ask students what they know about obituaries and show them several examples.

2. Have students work with a partner to analyze an example obituary. Have them create a list of the information that is included in their example.

3. Have students share the information from their examples to create a class master list of components for an obituary.

Quick Tip!

Tip: Use obituaries from newspapers that are not local. This reduces the likelihood that a student might encounter a relative or friend.

4. Using the master list, have a class discussion to narrow the list to only the essential components of an obituary. Your class list may vary, but some suggested components are as follows:

- Birth and death dates
- Family members
- Residence
- Occupation and hobbies
- Interesting facts
- Memorial requests

5. Using the condensed list, have students develop their own obituary for an assigned topic, word, concept, figure, or idea.

When to Use It

- As an overall summary of an important concept or unit

- To use summarization in a genre that is unique and typically has a different, specific purpose

- To summarize all the important pieces of a large unit or important concept from start to finish

- As a culminating assessment

Why It Works

- Obituaries are examples of real-world relevant summaries.

- Obituaries can blend the skill of summarization with other elements such as tone, figurative language voice, and humor.

- Students can work collaboratively to create a final product.

- Obituaries allow students to practice both their written and presentation skills.

Modifications

- Have students create a social media–post tribute to a concept, idea, or figure.

- Have students create a comic strip obituary to incorporate a pictorial element to the assignment.

CHAPTER 1
Why Write Now?

CHAPTER 2
Parachute Writing

CHAPTER 3
Sum It All Up

CHAPTER 4
All the Right Words

CHAPTER 5
Digital Worlds

CHAPTER 6
Just the Facts

CHAPTER 7
Expecting the Unexpected

CHAPTER 1
Why Write Now?

CHAPTER 2
Parachute Writing

CHAPTER 3
Sum It All Up

CHAPTER 4
All the Right Words

CHAPTER 5
Digital Worlds

CHAPTER 6
Just the Facts

CHAPTER 7
Expecting the
Unexpected

IN LOVING MEMORY..... NOT

On December 3 2020, after fighting a rather grievous battle with modern day slang, Grammar suffered a rather painful death. Born from the early Greeks. When Grammar was first introduced into the school systems, it began its long life of repetion and confusing students for years to come. Being implemented into the school system was Grammar's greatest achievement in its long life. Grammar is survived by the people who still use its techniques in everyday life. The funeral services will be privately held, and memorial donations can be made to any school or school system. The family asks for privacy and respect for their wishes during this time.

CHAPTER 1
Why Write Now?

CHAPTER 2
Parachute Writing

CHAPTER 3
Sum It All Up

CHAPTER 4
All the Right Words

CHAPTER 5
Digital Worlds

CHAPTER 6
Just the Facts

CHAPTER 7
Expecting the
Unexpected

Proctor's Eulogy

We are gathered here today to mourn the loss of John Proctor. Mr. Proctor was a very complex man. Imagine being convicted of witchcraft. Although there is no way you could possibly be a witch, you have to make a choice. Do you plead guilty and live with guilt of lying to everyone, or do you proclaim your innocence and be hanged for your lies? This is the very choice that our beloved John had to make. Add one last lie to his list, or wipe his slate clean and be a hero of Salem.

When Proctor pleaded innocent, he not only showed his wife that he was a better man and was making up for all his sins, he also showed the town how to stand up for themselves. John made the decision that dying an innocent man was worth much more than living as a sinner.

Did John Proctor die with goodness? Yes, he did. His death shows us that lying just to get your way is wrong and can NEVER be justified. However, the most important thing about his death is that it MEANT something. His death was IMPORTANT. John's death reminds us that even those of us with flaws can become heroes.

- Allow students to write the obituary in list or bulleted format instead of a traditional paragraph.

- Have students create a tombstone epitaph instead of an entire obituary.

Extensions

- Have students write their obituaries in both a formal and informal tone.

- Have students create a last will and testament in conjunction with their obituary.

- Have students create a pictorial storyboard that can be used as a visual addition to the obituary.

- Have students use their obituary to craft a eulogy that could be used as an oral presentation assessment.

- Use my bio poem template from my first book, *Content Area Writing That Rocks (and Works!)* (2017), as a springboard into this activity or an idea generator.

Content Area Connections

- Use Obituaries for words that you do not want students to use in their writing anymore.

CHAPTER 1
Why Write Now?

CHAPTER 2
Parachute Writing

CHAPTER 3
Sum It All Up

CHAPTER 4
All the Right Words

CHAPTER 5
Digital Worlds

CHAPTER 6
Just the Facts

CHAPTER 7
Expecting the
Unexpected

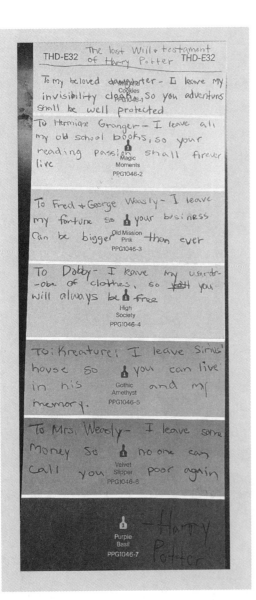

- Have students create an obituary for an art movement, style, or artist.

- Use obituaries at the end of a math or science unit to summarize learning.

- Have students rewrite the obituaries of historical figures using obscure or little-known facts. Three great books that include this kind of little-known information are *How They Croaked: The Awful Ends of the Awfully Famous; Caught: Nabbing History's Most Wanted;* and *How They Choked: Failures, Flops, and Flaws of the Awfully Famous* by Georgia Bragg.

CHAPTER 1
Why Write Now?

CHAPTER 2
Parachute Writing

CHAPTER 3
Sum It All Up

CHAPTER 4
All the Right Words

CHAPTER 5
Digital Worlds

CHAPTER 6
Just the Facts

CHAPTER 7
Expecting the
Unexpected

ALL THE RIGHT WORDS

Strategies for Learning Academic Vocabulary

Words dominate our lives, both in written and spoken form. Though studies vary, they say we speak on average anywhere from 7,000 to 16,000 words per day (Ahearn, 2017; Swaminanathan, 2007). And if you are the parent of a teenager like myself, sometimes that count fluctuates, from one day at about 100 words to the next at 50,000!

When writing this, I was reminded of the opening chapter of Sharon Draper's *Out of My Mind*:

> *Words. I'm surrounded by thousands of words. Maybe millions.*
> *Cathedral. Mayonnaise. Pomegranate. Mississippi. Neapolitan.*
> *Hippopotamus. Silky. Terrifying. Iridescent . . . Deep within me,*
> *words pile up in huge drifts. Mountains of phrases and sentences and*
> *connected ideas.*

And while Draper's main character is providing us with a thoughtful account of the words in her world, readers are shocked or at least surprised by the last sentence of that chapter that simply states

> *I have never spoken one single word. I am eleven years old.*

This piece reminds me that, even for those who do not speak yet or ever and even for those who do not hear, words are a significant part of how we humans make sense of the world. They are part of almost all our daily lives. Recently at the post office,

CHAPTER 1
Why Write Now?

CHAPTER 2
Parachute Writing

CHAPTER 3
Sum It All Up

CHAPTER 4
All the Right Words

CHAPTER 5
Digital Worlds

CHAPTER 6
Just the Facts

CHAPTER 7
Expecting the
Unexpected

I overheard the postal worker ask the woman ahead of me in line if the items in her package were liquid, perishable, or potentially hazardous or harmful, to which she replied, "No, they're just words on the paper." Yet words are never "just words." They are so much more. Words name items, give us a means of expression and response, and help us understand the world around us. They hurt; they heal; they comfort; they love. They matter. And they are all around us.

Background Knowledge Matters

Think about this. When you consider the word *bird*, what do you think of? A red bird? A blue bird? Is it small? Is it large? Perhaps it's flightless? If I were to ask you to draw a picture of that bird, would it look like this?

Or this?

Or even this?

My guess is that everyone's bird is going to look somewhat different because the meaning lies not in the letters B-I-R-D. Rather meaning lies in our knowledge, association, and construction. When those four letters are put together in that order, they spell *bird*, which truly means nothing until we have experience and background that match with that combination of letters. That's why your bird may have been red while mine was blue. We use our past experience and our conceptualization of what a bird is to link that experience and knowledge to those four letters placed together in that particular order. Letters and words are simply symbols or signs for something else that conjure up meaning. One of my favorite people and professors in this great wide world, Dr. Diane Stephens, addressed this in my very first doctoral class, Semiotics and Literacy. This helped cement my understanding that reading and writing are about understanding and not simply word calling and copying.

Comprehension vs. Word Calling

Many of our students might be able to decode and pronounce a word, meaning they are able to apply their knowledge of letter–sound relationships and phonics when reading a new word, but they have no clue what that word means. Does this sound familiar? This often occurs in content area classrooms simply because many of the words that are regularly used in specific disciplines aren't frequently used in everyday language. Consider the word *amoeba* for example. How often do you hear that word outside of a science classroom? Probably not too often unless you teach or work in this field. Yet for a biology or life science student, it is an important word to know.

A few years ago I was reminded of this after I picked up the *Journal of American Physics* from the magazine swap table at our local library. I remember standing at the table considering *Southern Living* instead, then thought, "Hey, I have a PhD; I can read this journal." So I took the physics journal to my car because for a brief moment I thought I was smart enough to read and understand it. I came off that cloud quickly when I opened it up, "word called" two paragraphs, and had no idea what I had just read. Then I did what any self-respecting person would do; I took that physics journal back up to the magazine swap table and got myself a *Southern Living*.

Now, why is this story important? First, it is a reminder to me that just because someone doesn't understand what he or she has read does not mean they are not intelligent. When students pick up an algebra textbook and don't understand functions or linear equations, that doesn't mean that they can't or won't understand the concept. Yet many times students who struggle with vocabulary don't realize this is not indicative of how smart they are or their ability to do well in that subject. Not knowing a word does not indicate inability. Instead, it means we have not had enough

Stop & Think

Think about students' acquisition of new slang or expressions. Those words are picked up rather easily and seem to make a fluid entrance into their conversations. However, acquisition of those new terms rarely occurs in the manner that we typically teach academic vocabulary. There is no defining of the term, sentence construction, or test on Friday. However, students can learn these new words readily and often employ them in both their oral conversations and written construction. How are they able to master these types of words? Because these new words are active parts of their world and don't exist just in fifth period.

CHAPTER 1 Why Write Now?

CHAPTER 2 Parachute Writing

CHAPTER 3 Sum It All Up

CHAPTER 4 All the Right Words

CHAPTER 5 Digital Worlds

CHAPTER 6 Just the Facts

CHAPTER 7 Expecting the Unexpected

CHAPTER 1
Why Write Now?

CHAPTER 2
Parachute Writing

CHAPTER 3
Sum It All Up

CHAPTER 4
All the Right Words

CHAPTER 5
Digital Worlds

CHAPTER 6
Just the Facts

CHAPTER 7
Expecting the Unexpected

exposure to and experience with certain content-specific vocabulary that is essential for comprehension and proficiency for that discipline.

Context Is Key

Sometimes students do in fact know the word, but their working definition or conceptualization of that word doesn't match the new context they encounter. For example, I have a colleague who is a long-distance runner. After an ultra-marathon, he mentioned the number of *rabbits* on the trail. I was disappointed to learn that he wasn't referring to actual rabbits, but instead was talking about other humans who served as the pace runners for the race. Another example is the word *subway*. Where I live in South Carolina we don't have underground public transit, but we do have Subway restaurants. The "subway" that refers to transportation isn't part of the world of many students and may not be what they think of first when they encounter that word in text or in conversation. Imagine how much confusion that might cause a student who only knows *subway* as a restaurant and imagines a person getting on a sandwich to ride to work!

Think on that for a minute: How often are we using words that aren't part of our students' worlds, or how often are we using a word meaning that is different than students typically understand? Here are some everyday multiple-meaning words that can be confusing to students:

- *Suburban*: Are you talking about the car or a populated area?

- *Drape*: The curtains or a verb?

- *Draw*: The artistic rendition or a stalemate?

- *Compact*: The container for your makeup or small in size?

- *Fair*: An okay grade or a carnival?

- *Project*: An assignment for class, to display on a board, or to speak loudly?

- *Fine*: A penalty or a measure of someone's mood? Or how about the texture of someone's hair?

- *Illustrate*: To show or to draw?

- *Party*: A group or celebration?

Now, think about the academic vocabulary in your content area. What are the words that can cause a breakdown in students' understanding because of multiple meanings? Now consider the rigor of expectation that we hold for our students' vocabulary understanding. Not only are they expected to be able to write and orally articulate a number of subject matter concepts, but they are also expected to utilize appropriate academic vocabulary and language to convey appropriate meaning and a logical progression of ideas. In some cases, a student's unfamiliarity with discipline-specific words can result

CHAPTER 1
Why Write Now?

CHAPTER 2
Parachute Writing

CHAPTER 3
Sum It All Up

CHAPTER 4
All the Right Words

CHAPTER 5
Digital Worlds

CHAPTER 6
Just the Facts

CHAPTER 7
Expecting the
Unexpected

in underdeveloped written and oral responses and even a lack of comprehension of key concepts due to gaps in their vocabulary.

One strategy I detailed in my first book, *Content Writing That Rocks! (and Works!)* (2017), was an AKA Chart, or an Also Known as Chart. This functioned as an anchor chart that was buildable and flexible over the course of a semester. Teachers and students used this chart to display academic vocabulary or other words seen in the content classroom that had multiple meanings, such as *passage* and *excerpt*. This strategy assists with calling student attention to words with multiple meanings and aids in comprehension improvement.

Sometimes, a student's unfamiliarity with a set of words might be because English is not his/her first language. Research indicates that the development of vocabulary plays a pivotal role in English learners' language acquisition and academic achievement (August et al., 2005; Chung, 2012). Because gaps in vocabulary instruction can negatively affect comprehension, research suggests that explicit and purposeful vocabulary instruction can combat this issue (Beck et al., 1982; Graves, 2007; McKeown et al., 1983; National Reading Panel, 2000).

Stop & Think

Sometimes students simply need a reminder of what to do when they come across a specific type of academic word when it shows up in texts such as word problems, lab activities, or procedures. In many instances, these key words give clues or signals about what the student needs to do. Try creating an anchor chart to help students remember what each of those key words means and what it signals them to do.

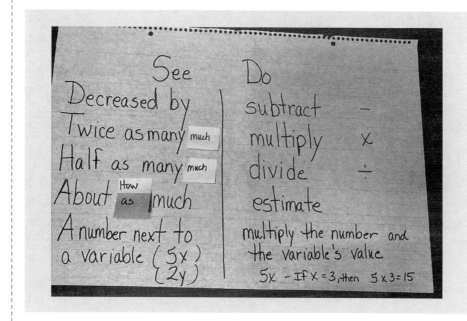

CHAPTER 1
Why Write Now?

CHAPTER 2
Parachute Writing

CHAPTER 3
Sum It All Up

CHAPTER 4
All the Right Words

CHAPTER 5
Digital Worlds

CHAPTER 6
Just the Facts

CHAPTER 7
Expecting the Unexpected

Additionally, students may show they understand a concept, but they don't remember the academic vocabulary that is part of the concept. For example, a student may refer to the denominator in a fraction as the "bottom number." In this case, they might not know the academic term, and let's face it, "bottom number" *is* easier to spell, which also may be why some students still refer to it as such when they write constructed responses. It is helpful for students to have a word bank of appropriate academic vocabulary that should be used in constructed responses. Having a list of words available can assist students who have spelling difficulties or those who don't recall all the needed academic vocabulary.

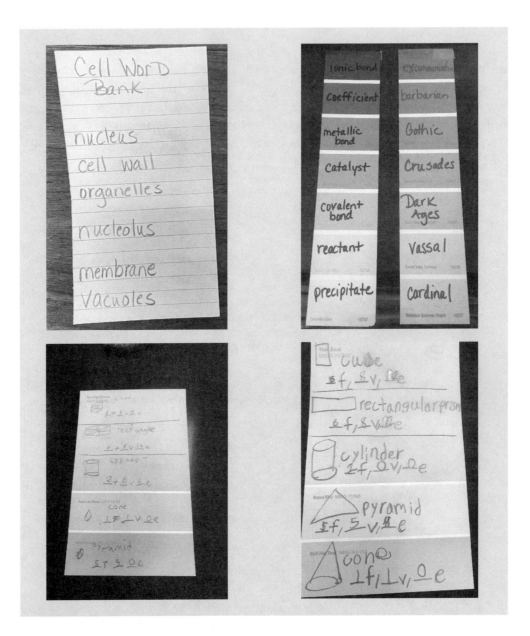

Yet content classrooms are filled with academic jargon that can result in a student not understanding a concept. There are three widely accepted tiers of words (Beck et al., 2013). Tier 1 words are the most informal, Tier 2 words are those that are kind of in the middle, and Tier 3 words are those that are the most formal. Often, students are proficient in Tier 1, but making the jump to Tier 3 is daunting. It's always a good idea to have anchor charts in your classroom with examples of words from different tiers. While you can use three tiers, you may find that simply having two tiers works well in your content area. The point is to have examples that are relevant in your content area so that students can see what each looks like. It also helps students to better understand what you are talking about when they are reminded of the differences that are sometimes subtle but other times blatant.

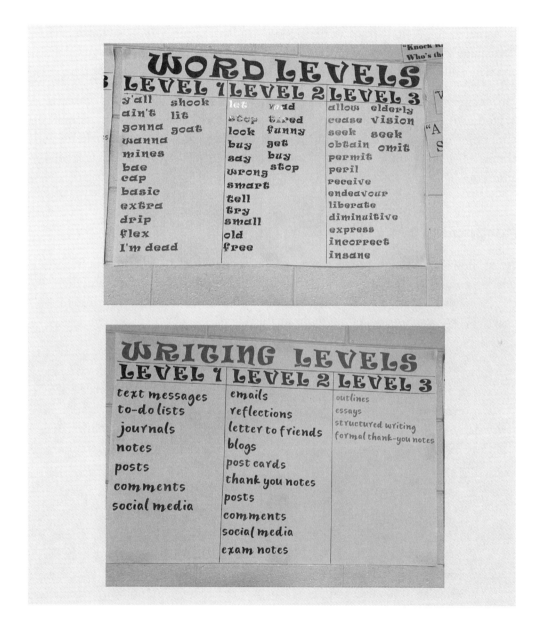

The goal now is to find ways and means to help students acquire and understand a variety of academic vocabulary in a manner that doesn't feel like traditional vocabulary instruction. This chapter offers a variety of strategies for teaching vocabulary in multiple content areas using a variety of tools and methods.

CHAPTER 1 Why Write Now?

CHAPTER 2 Parachute Writing

CHAPTER 3 Sum It All Up

CHAPTER 4 All the Right Words

CHAPTER 5 Digital Worlds

CHAPTER 6 Just the Facts

CHAPTER 7 Expecting the Unexpected

CHAPTER 1
Why Write Now?

CHAPTER 2
Parachute Writing

CHAPTER 3
Sum It All Up

CHAPTER 4
All the Right Words

CHAPTER 5
Digital Worlds

CHAPTER 6
Just the Facts

CHAPTER 7
Expecting the
Unexpected

SURVIVAL WORDS

Would you agree that in some instances, when students are reading content area passages or material, there are certain words that are essential for comprehension? Are there specific words that a student must know to understand the material? Enter Survival Words. No, these aren't words you need to know to survive. Instead, they are words that students need to know ahead of time before they read a selection or begin a unit in order to comprehend it. Survival Word charts are a great prereading or pre-unit assessment activity that allows students to use a Likert rating scale to self-assess while the teacher is able to determine whether the students are ready to tackle a piece of text or a new unit of study based on their responses.

This strategy is one of the few times when I will advocate using a list of words in isolation. In most instances, words without context are not effective in supporting student learning, but in the case of Survival Words, the missing contextual clues are exactly what you want. The point of this strategy is to see IF your students have any prior knowledge or conceptualization of a specific list of words.

Putting It to Work

1. Prior to beginning a new unit or reading a new text, determine which content-specific words are essential for students to fully comprehend the material. Make a list of these words and create a chart that is like this one below (see Appendix for a reproducible chart).

Survival Words for Section on Cells	Self-Assessment of Word Knowledge	Key
Spindle		**A:** I know the word and meaning, and I use it.
Chromatids		**B:** I know the word and meaning, but I really don't use it.
Nuclear envelope		
Cleavage furrow		**C:** I've heard of it, but I am not sure what it means.
		D: I have no idea what this word means.

2. Before reading, have students complete the chart based on their knowledge of the listed words. (I typically create these on notecard size pieces of paper.)

3. Informally assess students' charts. If there are a majority As and Bs, then proceed with the unit or text. If you notice that most students recorded Cs or Ds, don't proceed. Instead, spend some time preteaching the words before moving forward.

When to Use It

- To informally assess the students' knowledge of content-specific vocabulary

- As a measure of prior knowledge

- To build engagement for an upcoming unit or text

- To support students when the material has a significant amount of content-specific vocabulary

Quick Tip!

Don't forget about students who responded with Cs and Ds! If you choose to move forward because the majority of your class responded with As and Bs, consider conducting a small-group lesson with the other students to preteach the necessary vocabulary or fill in the gaps in their understanding. Or, team up the students with others who responded with Aa and Bs for a peer learning experience.

Why It Works

- It requires students to look at words in isolation and determine whether they have any prior knowledge regarding the material.

- Survival Words provide a quick and informal assessment of student knowledge.

- Survival Words give students a chance to self-assess their knowledge and learning.

- It is a quick and easy assessment.

Modifications

- Include the word *apply* to the Category A description in math (I know the word and meaning **and** can apply it in math.).

- For English Learners, use emojis in addition to the statements describing their knowledge.

Quick Tip!

In my experience using Survival Words in math, some students would choose A because they knew the word and could use it in a sentence, but they could not apply it to a problem. Therefore, I recommend making the language adjustment to Description A.

- Add a column for peer collaboration or explanation so that students have to explain their understanding of the word to a peer.

- Add a column for questions that students can pose about the word.

Extensions

- At the end of a unit, have students make additions to the Survival Words chart and add those that they feel were challenging.

CHAPTER 1
Why Write Now?

CHAPTER 2
Parachute Writing

CHAPTER 3
Sum It All Up

CHAPTER 4
All the Right Words

CHAPTER 5
Digital Worlds

CHAPTER 6
Just the Facts

CHAPTER 7
Expecting the Unexpected

CHAPTER 1
Why Write Now?

CHAPTER 2
Parachute Writing

CHAPTER 3
Sum It All Up

CHAPTER 4
All the Right Words

CHAPTER 5
Digital Worlds

CHAPTER 6
Just the Facts

CHAPTER 7
Expecting the
Unexpected

- Use the Survival Word lists to develop pictorial definitions, paint strip lists, or alphabet books.

- Add a fourth column to the chart and have students create their own definition of each word or create a fourth column that includes where you might see the word in context.

Content Area Connections

- Have students include a column that shows a problem, graph, or operation that illustrates the word in math. If a formula is associated with the term, have students include this as well.

- Use Survival Words when learning about an art movement or period, and add a column where students can add the names of specific artists or examples of art pieces.

- Have students include the appropriate formulas that might accompany a word in physics (e.g., force, acceleration, or velocity).

- Include a fourth column on the chart for students to enter examples of when this phenomenon might occur during history.

- Instead of Survival Words, create a chart of Survival Formulas for math or science, Survival Figures for Social Studies, or Survival Genres for ELA.

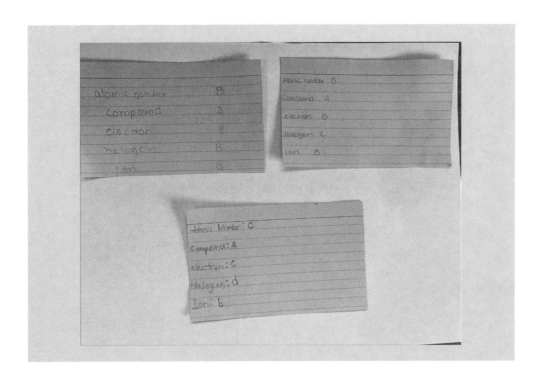

CHAPTER 1
Why Write Now?

CHAPTER 2
Parachute Writing

CHAPTER 3
Sum It All Up

CHAPTER 4
All the Right Words

CHAPTER 5
Digital Worlds

CHAPTER 6
Just the Facts

CHAPTER 7
Expecting the
Unexpected

PICTORIAL DEFINITIONS

Sometimes, a picture really is worth a thousand words. In many cases, images help students associate the meaning with a particular word. The image might be of something that the word does or an action of sort or it might be an example of some component of a word. In short form, it serves as a visual definition of a content-specific word that students need to know. Pictorial Definitions offer students one more layer of meaning when it comes to a vocabulary word. These layers of meaning are especially important for comprehension. Remember that many students are visual learners or may still be learning English; they need more than a simple definition to cement the understanding of a word. These visual vocabulary definitions can be bound together or hole-punched and secured with a ring so students can have their own personal pictorial dictionaries at their desks to reference when needed.

Think about what happens to many readers and writers when they graduate from books with lots of images to ones with only words. For some, the task of reading AND writing becomes that much more difficult. With books that utilize numerous images, students can use those images to help them figure out what some of the words are. This is one of the reasons that graphic novels are so popular with students.

CHAPTER 1
Why Write Now?

CHAPTER 2
Parachute Writing

CHAPTER 3
Sum It All Up

CHAPTER 4
All the Right Words

CHAPTER 5
Digital Worlds

CHAPTER 6
Just the Facts

CHAPTER 7
Expecting the
Unexpected

Putting It to Work

1. Select a list of words that support the text or unit of study and can be easily illustrated in some way.

2. Choose a word from the list for the class to work on together as an example.

3. Have students work with a partner to develop a picture or locate a digital image that best represents the meaning of the example word.

4. Allow students to share their images and discuss as a class the strengths and weaknesses of the chosen images.

5. Assign a word or list of words for students to work with either collaboratively or individually.

6. Have students share their finished products and post them on class charts for students to reference.

 Quick Tip!

These words need to be ones that students are familiar with so that they can create pictorial definitions. If students do not have experience with the words, they will not be successful with the strategy.

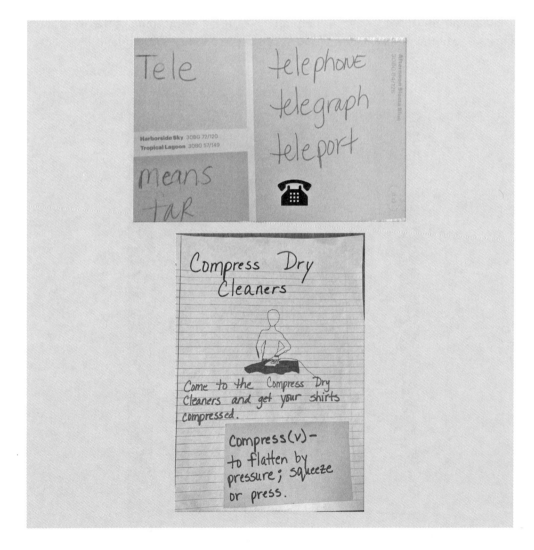

When to Use It

- To help study prefixes, suffixes, roots, and stems

- As a break from traditional vocabulary assessments

- To help visualize a word that employs an action or specific type of example

- To aid in reading comprehension

Why It Works

- It provides students with a visual reminder or a word and its meaning.

- It offers another layer of meaning for words that might be foreign or unknown to students.

- Pictorial Definitions allow students to think deeply about a concept and the meaning behind a word to determine the best visual representation for it.

- For words that are a little more abstract, Pictorial Definitions provide students with concrete examples.

Modifications

- Ask students to perform a dramatic interpretation of the word instead of a pictorial definition.

- Encourage students to create a sound that represents a word.

- Allow students to work in pairs or groups of three to create a group pictorial definition. To do this, divide the page into two or three parts, depending on the number of kids in the group. Have each partner locate an image or diagram that they believe best represents the word and place it on their side of the paper.

- Have students add a definition to their image.

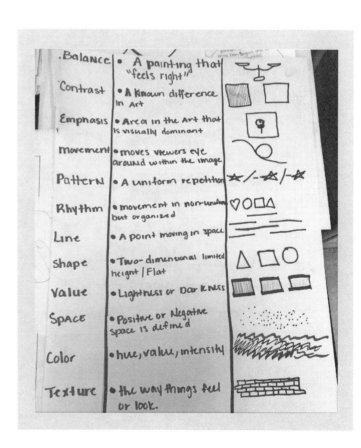

CHAPTER 1
Why Write Now?

CHAPTER 2
Parachute Writing

CHAPTER 3
Sum It All Up

CHAPTER 4
All the Right Words

CHAPTER 5
Digital Worlds

CHAPTER 6
Just the Facts

CHAPTER 7
Expecting the Unexpected

CHAPTER 1
Why Write Now?

CHAPTER 2
Parachute Writing

CHAPTER 3
Sum It All Up

CHAPTER 4
All the Right Words

CHAPTER 5
Digital Worlds

CHAPTER 6
Just the Facts

CHAPTER 7
Expecting the
Unexpected

Extensions

- Have students create a digital collage (e.g., using a program like PicCollage) of multiple images that best define or exemplify their word.

- Give students a concept or topic and have them find images that best represent the overall topic.

- Have students create visual nonexamples to add to their visual examples of the word.

Content Area Connections

- Have students include multiple visual models for the same mathematical word problem, vocabulary word, concept, or mathematical operation.

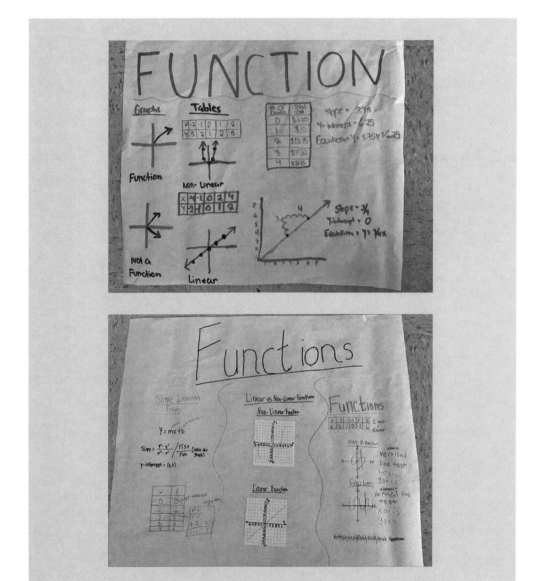

- Have students find multiple images of foods associated with a specific diet or food group in physical education.

- Have students find multiple images for a specific art movement, such as surrealism.

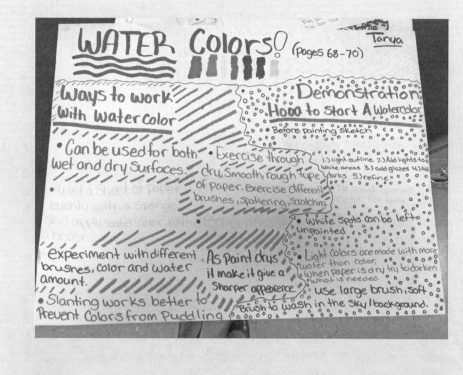

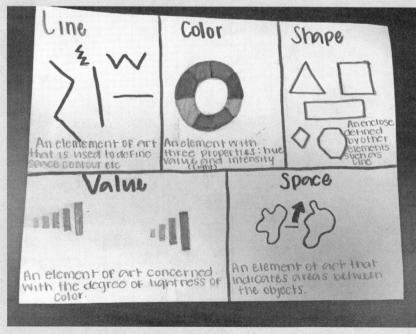

CHAPTER 1
Why Write Now?

CHAPTER 2
Parachute Writing

CHAPTER 3
Sum It All Up

CHAPTER 4
All the Right Words

CHAPTER 5
Digital Worlds

CHAPTER 6
Just the Facts

CHAPTER 7
Expecting the Unexpected

CHAPTER 1
Why Write Now?

CHAPTER 2
Parachute Writing

CHAPTER 3
Sum It All Up

CHAPTER 4
All the Right Words

CHAPTER 5
Digital Worlds

CHAPTER 6
Just the Facts

CHAPTER 7
Expecting the
Unexpected

- Use pictorial definitions in English to describe specific roots, stems, or prefixes where the finished product can assist students in defining multiple words.

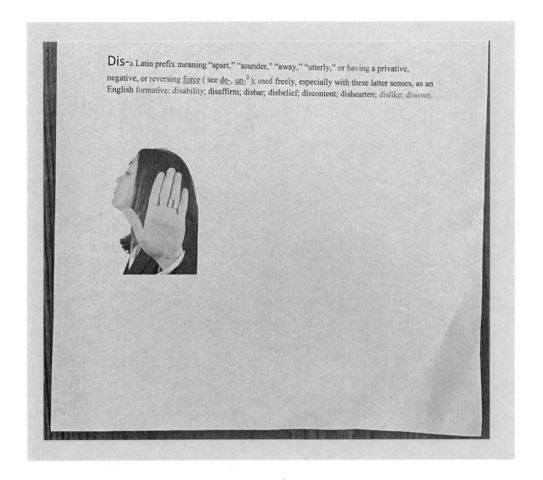

CHAPTER 1
Why Write Now?

CHAPTER 2
Parachute Writing

CHAPTER 3
Sum It All Up

CHAPTER 4
All the Right Words

CHAPTER 5
Digital Worlds

CHAPTER 6
Just the Facts

CHAPTER 7
Expecting the
Unexpected

WHAT'S THE WORD?

While there are many activities I enjoy, I am far from a sports enthusiast. However, while watching ESPN with my husband, I saw a great opportunity for teaching with the show *Pardon the Interruption*. For several years, I have been using this show to teach argumentative writing, the persuasive genre, and the creation of thesis statements. However, one of my favorite segments of this show is "What's the Word?" During this segment, one of the hosts or special guests takes an example from sports and develops a sentence with a missing word that the hosts fill in. Think of it as a shortened cloze passage for cool sports people.

During this segment, the commentators take a specific sports event and a fill-in-the-blank statement where they have to pick a word that best fits the context and content of the statement and defend their choice of the word. Each host defends his choice of word in a short succinct argument. In this particular segment, there are often two or three sentences with one word omitted for the hosts to complete. Each host chooses a word to complete the sentence and then explains their choice.

For example, in one episode, one of the commentators stated, "Deron Williams's decision to pass up the game-winning shot to Jordan Farmar was _____." Each host was then asked to fill in the blank with an appropriate word. During this time, the hosts provided the word they believed filled in the blank appropriately and defended it. In this specific segment, the first host responded with, "It was LeBronian." The second host responded with "What Deron Williams did was Magical, as in Earvin Magic Johnson." This method of argument and the utilization of evidence to support a claim is one that is echoed in the classroom. Students have to

Quick Tip!

Check out ESPN's video archives for clips of *Pardon the Interruption* that would be appropriate to show to your students as a real-life example of this strategy.

1. Choose a topic

2. Find evidence that supports it

3. Orally articulate their stance

4. Compose a rebuttal

Putting It to Work

1. Introduce the strategy by showing students examples of the segment from *Pardon the Interruption*.

CHAPTER 1
Why Write Now?

CHAPTER 2
Parachute Writing

CHAPTER 3
Sum It All Up

CHAPTER 4
All the Right Words

CHAPTER 5
Digital Worlds

CHAPTER 6
Just the Facts

CHAPTER 7
Expecting the
Unexpected

2. Discuss the examples with the class using questions such as the following:

- What types of words are used?
- Are phrases employed as well?
- How does the host defend their choice?
- What kinds of explanations or justifications are utilized?

3. Provide students with a sample prompt to complete as a class. Examples might include:

- Katniss's decision to volunteer as Tribute in her sister's place was _____.
- Purchasing locally grown foods from the neighborhood farmer's market is _____.
- Using valuable land for wind farms to create energy is _____.
- JFK's pledge to put a man on the moon was _____.

4. Allow ample time to discuss the choices and justifications behind the words they chose.

5. Provide students with a notecard that has a new "What's the Word?" statement on it. Make sure these cards are centered on the same topic, period in history, or novel, for example.

6. Instruct students to write information on the back of the notecard that explains and justifies their word choice.

7. Divide students into pairs to complete the activity.

8. After about ten minutes, have students share their work with the class, including their justifications for their words.

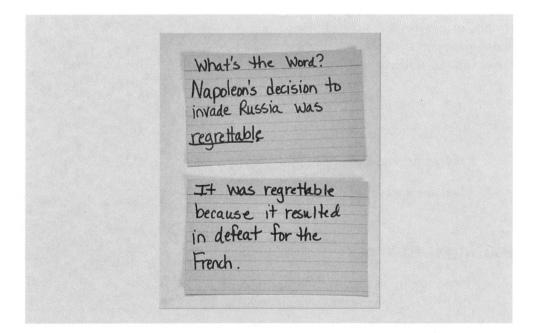

When to Use It

- To incorporate academic vocabulary in classroom discussions and writing

- As a real-world reading and writing connection

- As an opportunity to draft and defend an argument

- As a ticket out the door or a quick review

Why It Works

- "What's the Word?" allows students to practice the skill of argument in a short time frame.

- "What's the Word?" has a limited word count, so students aren't required to create an extended response.

- It offers a real-world connection for students.

- It provides teachers with a variety of ready-made examples from the archives of television shows that can be utilized in the classroom.

Modifications

- Provide students with a list of choices to use to fill in the blank and have them explain their choices.

- Use images or emojis instead of words as choices.

- Provide each student or pair of students their own "What's the Word?" statement. Have them solicit responses to the statement from their classmates and record those responses in a chart.

- Have ready-made created sentences with explanations. Have students orally read the sentences with the explanations but mute themselves when it comes to the actual word choice. Then have the class guess the word based on the explanation and descriptions.

Extensions

- Have students use their completed statements as a framework for a fully involved writing engagement.

 Quick Tip!

This extension requires students to construct adequate justification for their word choice. The ability to justify an answer or response is important across the disciplines and allows students to practice many skills in addition to the focus on vocabulary.

CHAPTER 1 Why Write Now?

CHAPTER 2 Parachute Writing

CHAPTER 3 Sum It All Up

CHAPTER 4 All the Right Words

CHAPTER 5 Digital Worlds

CHAPTER 6 Just the Facts

CHAPTER 7 Expecting the Unexpected

CHAPTER 1
Why Write Now?

CHAPTER 2
Parachute Writing

CHAPTER 3
Sum It All Up

CHAPTER 4
All the Right Words

CHAPTER 5
Digital Worlds

CHAPTER 6
Just the Facts

CHAPTER 7
Expecting the
Unexpected

- Allow students to critique a peer's completed statement. Have them draft questions for their partner on notecards, and then have the original student respond to the questions on another notecard.

Content Area Connections

- Change the name of the strategy in math to "What's the Work?" or "What's the Formula?" to help students justify their problem-solving steps (e.g., "Nicole's decision to use the multiplicative inverse when dividing fractions was _____.").

- Use this strategy in English for attacking or defending a character's motives or decisions (e.g., From the novel *The Giver*, "Jonas's decision to take baby Gabriel away was _____.").

- Have students complete a "What's the Word?" activity for historical figures. This can be used to critique their war strategies, decisions, and so on.

- Use this strategy in art and change the name to "What's the Work?" when discussing works of art.

RANSOM NOTE WRITING

Years ago, when I was in elementary school, one of my teachers had us complete a Ransom Note poem. While I certainly don't remember what I wrote about, I do remember that I loved the final product. It just looked cool and it was a different way for me to write. Plus, I could use someone else's words as a shortcut and was able to discover new words and sentences to make my own.

Ransom Note Writing has some of the same appeal that writing on sticky notes and paint strips does, as it lowers the affective filter for students, especially for struggling writers. Ransom Note Writing looks different and doesn't feel like traditional writing because it's a collection of cut-out words that are pasted together focused on a specific topic. The completed project resembles a ransom note because of all the cut-up words and mismatched fonts. Plus, it is a great opportunity for students to locate and use premade words and mold them into a brand new product.

To prep for this strategy, make sure you have plenty of old magazines and newspapers for students to use. Students will also need scissors, tape, glue, and paper. In order for students to be successful, make sure they have experience and strong background knowledge of the concepts or topics selected for this strategy.

CHAPTER 1
Why Write Now?

CHAPTER 2
Parachute Writing

CHAPTER 3
Sum It All Up

CHAPTER 4
All the Right Words

CHAPTER 5
Digital Worlds

CHAPTER 6
Just the Facts

CHAPTER 7
Expecting the Unexpected

CHAPTER 1
Why Write Now?

CHAPTER 2
Parachute Writing

CHAPTER 3
Sum It All Up

CHAPTER 4
All the Right Words

CHAPTER 5
Digital Worlds

CHAPTER 6
Just the Facts

CHAPTER 7
Expecting the
Unexpected

Putting It to Work

1. Determine the concept, idea, or topic that students will be focusing their work around. For example, in biology, you might choose topics like genetics, cells, or respiration, while in a math class, you might choose a topic such as fractions or linear equations.

2. Select a related concept or topic to use as a class example. (For example, if you were planning to use a topic such as fractions in a math class, your class example might be on something that is related, like decimals.)

3. Divide students into pairs. Explain to students that they have five minutes to work with their partners to skim the provided newspapers and magazines and find as many words and images related to the class example.

4. Have students cut out and glue the words they find with their partners on a class poster and discuss the selections as a class.

5. During this discussion, have students share ideas for other words and phrases that could have been included on the poster.

6. Provide students with the selected topic or concept to explore with their partner.

7. Allow them to use magazines and newspapers to find words and phrases as well as images that are related to their topics. Then have students glue their selections onto chart paper or construction paper for display.

When to Use It

- To focus on a cluster of words or phrases around a content topic or unit

- As a way to incorporate vocabulary instruction into an informal writing piece

- To indirectly teach the reading strategy of skimming and scanning

- As a real-world reading and writing connection

- As a collaborative group or partner activity

Why It Works

- Ransom Note Writing is informal and approachable, not an extended written response.

- It allows students the opportunity to incorporate a unique aesthetic element into a written engagement.

- Ransom Note Writing offers students the opportunity to peruse reading materials and texts that they might ordinarily skip through, while utilizing the skills of scanning and skimming during the selection and search process.

Modifications

- Have precut words in a basket for students to choose from instead of having students find the words in magazines or newspapers.

- Use an internet program or application such as PicCollage or Glogster for students to create a virtual version of their Ransom Note.

- Have groups complete this activity in two parts: Part 1 involves finding the images that go with the topic while Part 2 involves finding the corresponding words.

Extensions

- Have students swap their work with another group and locate additional words, phrases, and images that could also go with that concept.

- Use the selected words and phrases to draft complete sentences or even a Ransom Note poem, like the one in the image below.

CHAPTER 1 Why Write Now?

CHAPTER 2 Parachute Writing

CHAPTER 3 Sum It All Up

CHAPTER 4 All the Right Words

CHAPTER 5 Digital Worlds

CHAPTER 6 Just the Facts

CHAPTER 7 Expecting the Unexpected

CHAPTER 1
Why Write Now?

CHAPTER 2
Parachute Writing

CHAPTER 3
Sum It All Up

CHAPTER 4
All the Right Words

CHAPTER 5
Digital Worlds

CHAPTER 6
Just the Facts

CHAPTER 7
Expecting the
Unexpected

- Use the selected words and phrases to write a constructed response to a focused question on their topic.

Content Area Connections

- Use Ransom Note Writing as a reminder for clue words in written problems that designate a particular operation or real-world applications in data analysis, statistics, or fractions.

- Use this strategy to support grammar instruction (e.g., parts of speech) or when teaching dialogue or figurative language.

- When researching a historical figure, use Ransom Note Writing as a means to capture information about their significant contributions, famous words, quotes, or speeches.

CHAPTER 1
Why Write Now?

CHAPTER 2
Parachute Writing

CHAPTER 3
Sum It All Up

CHAPTER 4
All the Right Words

CHAPTER 5
Digital Worlds

CHAPTER 6
Just the Facts

CHAPTER 7
Expecting the
Unexpected

WORD SORT

Sometimes, students know how to use a word in the correct context, but they have a hard time explaining the definition in their own words. I find this to be true as an adult as well when my children ask me what a particular word means. Often, I can use it in a sentence or provide an example but can't seem to articulate it into a succinct definition. In many instances, I end up giving them a list of words that are similar to the word they asked about when I just can't quite come up with a definition that makes sense.

This same sort of categorizing or list of synonyms is played out in a Word Sort. This is a great strategy for when students might know something about a word or are able to make connections with the word but may have trouble defining it traditionally. It also works to expose students to words they may not have seen before. Even without knowing the explicit definitions for each word, students are able to determine certain characteristics or aspects of a word based on what category it gets sorted into. It is not always necessary for individuals to know the full working definition of a word; sometimes it is enough to know related words and concepts, which can help a student determine the meaning when reading and when to use it in their own writing.

⚡ Quick Tip!

Word Sorts work great as an alternative style of question on an assessment. Try swapping out a traditional test question for a Word Sort instead!

CHAPTER 1
Why Write Now?

CHAPTER 2
Parachute Writing

CHAPTER 3
Sum It All Up

CHAPTER 4
All the Right Words

CHAPTER 5
Digital Worlds

CHAPTER 6
Just the Facts

CHAPTER 7
Expecting the Unexpected

Putting It to Work

1. Display a list of ten to twenty related words based on a selected topic or unit of study. The words can be displayed on the board, a sheet of chart paper, or a document projector.

2. Explain to students that they need to use all of the words in the displayed list and sort them into new categories. Once they have sorted them, they name the categories based on the types of words that are included in the group. Have students work in pairs or in small groups to complete the Word Sort.

3. Have students share their groupings and reasoning with the class.

 Quick Tip!

This strategy works great as a bell ringer to get students ready for the day's lesson. It also works well as a rotating workstation activity.

4. Provide students with an additional Word Sort on a similar topic or concept to be completed individually or in pairs.

5. Allow students ten to fifteen minutes to complete the sort and then discuss as a class.

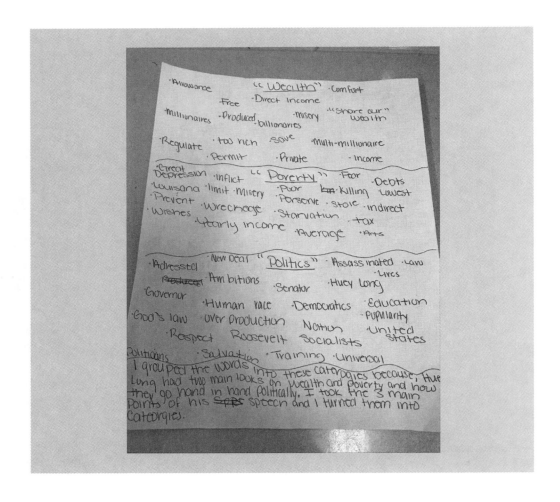

When to Use It

- To focus on a cluster of words or phrases around a content topic or unit

- As a way for students to make connections between words

- To sort and classify a ready-made list of words

- When there isn't time to fully complete the List, Group, Label, Share strategy (page 168)

- As a collaborative group or partner activity

Why It Works

- Because the words are provided, students do not have to spend time developing a list of words for the topic.

- Word Sort is an informal and approachable strategy, not an extended written response.

- It allows students to make connections between types of words and locate similarities between different words.

- Students can create their own categories for each group of words and can label them based on their similarities and attributes.

Modifications

- Instead of having students complete an entire Word Sort, write each word on a separate notecard. Post four or five chart papers around the classroom and include at least two related words on each chart. Have students complete a gallery walk and place their word on the chart paper they feel their word best fits.

- Have students develop their own Word Sorts by using the bolded vocabulary words from a chapter(s) in their textbooks or a set of informational text passages. Then, complete the sort as written in the lesson plan.

- Use images for the sorting activity instead of words.

- Have students work in small groups to use ready-made notecards (one word per card) for the sort.

- Use paint strips for the Word Sort. Give students different color paint strips and have them list all the related words on the same color paint strip. With this modification, students are able to color-code the related words.

CHAPTER 1
Why Write Now?

CHAPTER 2
Parachute Writing

CHAPTER 3
Sum It All Up

CHAPTER 4
All the Right Words

CHAPTER 5
Digital Worlds

CHAPTER 6
Just the Facts

CHAPTER 7
Expecting the Unexpected

CHAPTER 1
Why Write Now?

CHAPTER 2
Parachute Writing

CHAPTER 3
Sum It All Up

CHAPTER 4
All the Right Words

CHAPTER 5
Digital Worlds

CHAPTER 6
Just the Facts

CHAPTER 7
Expecting the
Unexpected

Extensions

- Have students swap their work with another group and locate additional words, phrases, and images that could also go with that concept.

- Have pairs work in groups of four. Instruct pairs to analyze their work for parameters, "rules," qualifiers, or commonalities that they both utilized in their word sorts.

- Use the sorted words to write a constructed response to a focused question on their topic.

Content Area Connections

- Use Word Sort in math as a way for students to highlight not just words, but mathematical operations or formulas that are used for a given concept.

- Use this activity in English to analyze character types across a novel (e.g., dynamic, static, protagonist, or antagonist).

- Create a list of quotes from a historical figure. Have students sort the quotes into categories based on things such as theme, message, or historical period or event.

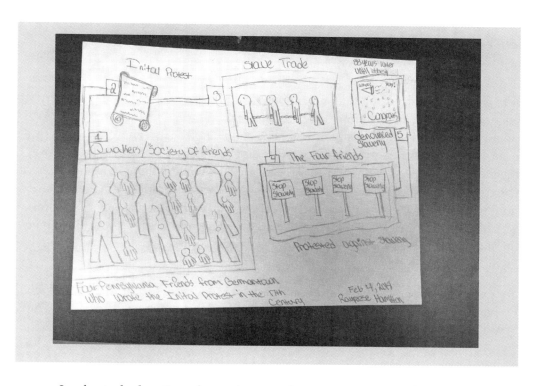

- In physical education classes, have students group exercises based on the targeted body area or muscle group.

- In health classes, have students group certain types of foods, healthy lifestyle choices, and exercises into categories.

- Sort artists based on the style, movement, and period of their works.

CHAPTER 1
Why Write Now?

CHAPTER 2
Parachute Writing

CHAPTER 3
Sum It All Up

CHAPTER 4
All the Right Words

CHAPTER 5
Digital Worlds

CHAPTER 6
Just the Facts

CHAPTER 7
Expecting the Unexpected

CHAPTER 1
Why Write Now?

CHAPTER 2
Parachute Writing

CHAPTER 3
Sum It All Up

CHAPTER 4
All the Right Words

CHAPTER 5
Digital Worlds

CHAPTER 6
Just the Facts

CHAPTER 7
Expecting the
Unexpected

WORD SPLASH

A large factor in improving student comprehension is based on activating prior knowledge and making connections between past experiences and new learning. Word Splash is a fantastic way for students to make connections between words and activate prior knowledge *before* reading a text or starting a lesson. This strategy helps "prime the pump," if you will, and get students ready for the content that is coming. Because it focuses on connections and prior experiences, students are able to use these connections to better improve their performance. It also allows them to consider the words in an isolated list but make connections based on what they already know. Plus, it gets them thinking about the text before they even see it so they are able to anticipate the topics of the text and possibly the purpose as well.

For example, when reading an excerpt on the peacock flower, from the book *Wicked Plants: The Weed That Killed Lincoln's Mother and Other Botanical Atrocities*, by Amy Stewart, I put the following words on the board:

peacock

tragic

lacy

poison

ornamental

flower

slavery

tropical

Students were instructed to pick two words that they thought went together and draft an explanation for their connections. Some examples students connected were the words *peacock* and *ornamental* since peacocks have very ornamental plumage. Others connected *slavery* and *tragic* due to the very nature of slavery. After reading the passage, students made new connections. They found that some of their original connections were the same, such as *slavery* and *tragic*, but others were different. For example, *ornamental* was paired with *flower* because of the ornamental foliage of the peacock flower. In this example, students were able to see that *ornamental* could be used in a very similar manner, but to describe two different items. While their original connections were not wrong, they found that many were altered after reading the excerpt.

Putting It to Work

1. Before assigning a passage of text for reading, create a list of words that accompany the text. It is important to include both new and familiar vocabulary words. You want to ensure that the list includes at least four words that the students know.

2. Have students select two words from the list that they think are connected.

3. Instruct students to write the words as well as a sentence explaining why they think the words are connected.

4. Have students share their words and connections with a partner.

5. Allow some students to share their work with the class.

6. Distribute copies of the selected text (or have them locate the text in their textbook or online), and have students read the text independently or in pairs.

7. After reading the text, have students go back to the words they initially connected. Instruct them to reevaluate their justification for the word pair connection based on the reading. If necessary, have students amend their connections.

8. Instruct students to think back to the text and pick two new words from the list that they feel are connected. Have students write a brief explanation of the connections.

9. Allow students time to share their new connections with their partners.

10. Select students to share their work with the class.

Quick Tip!

This book, along with Stewart's *Wicked Bugs: The Louse That Conquered Napoleon's Army and Other Diabolical Insects*, are fantastic resources for science and history classes. Most of the excerpts are about two pages long so they can easily be dropped into instructional time. Plus, they offer unique historical and scientific facts that can be used in conjunction with a variety of content standard sets.

When to Use It

- To complete a prereading engagement

- As a way for students to make connections between words

- As a collaborative group or partner activity

- To determine what type of experience or background knowledge students have with a given list of words

CHAPTER 1 Why Write Now?

CHAPTER 2 Parachute Writing

CHAPTER 3 Sum It All Up

CHAPTER 4 All the Right Words

CHAPTER 5 Digital Worlds

CHAPTER 6 Just the Facts

CHAPTER 7 Expecting the Unexpected

CHAPTER 1
Why Write Now?

CHAPTER 2
Parachute Writing

CHAPTER 3
Sum It All Up

CHAPTER 4
All the Right Words

CHAPTER 5
Digital Worlds

CHAPTER 6
Just the Facts

CHAPTER 7
Expecting the
Unexpected

Why It Works

- Because the words are provided, students are able to focus exclusively on those words and any connections they may have between the words.

- Word Splash is an informal and approachable strategy, not an extended written response.

- Word Splash allows students to make connections between types of words and describe similarities between different words.

- Students can explain their word connections with partners and the class.

Modifications

- Use images to create a Picture Splash instead of a Word Splash.

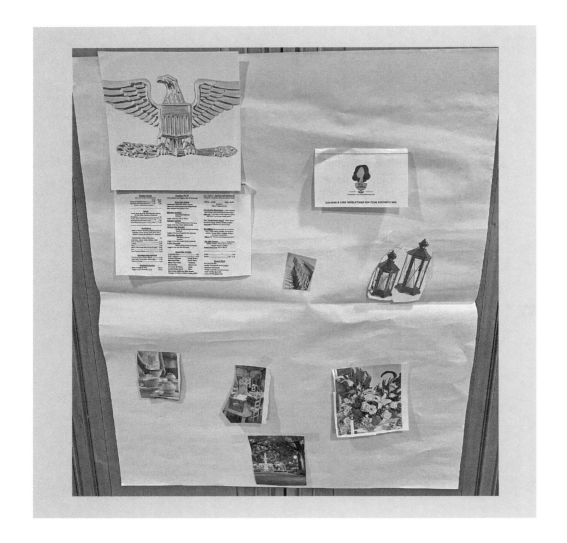

- Use a combination of words and images on the list provided to students.

- Have students choose one of the words on the list and connect it to a word that is not on the provided list and is self-selected by the student.

- Have students record their words on a paint strip and complete the activity using only the strip.

Extensions

- Have students add new words to be included in the Word Splash after they complete their reading.

- Provide students with sticker address labels and have them write connections on the labels, which they place next to the words.

- Use the words from the Word Splash to write a constructed response to a focused question or to summarize the text.

- Use the Word Splash words as a springboard into the Ransom Note Writing or Word Sort.

CHAPTER 1
Why Write Now?

CHAPTER 2
Parachute Writing

CHAPTER 3
Sum It All Up

CHAPTER 4
All the Right Words

CHAPTER 5
Digital Worlds

CHAPTER 6
Just the Facts

CHAPTER 7
Expecting the Unexpected

CHAPTER 1
Why Write Now?

CHAPTER 2
Parachute Writing

CHAPTER 3
Sum It All Up

CHAPTER 4
All the Right Words

CHAPTER 5
Digital Worlds

CHAPTER 6
Just the Facts

CHAPTER 7
Expecting the
Unexpected

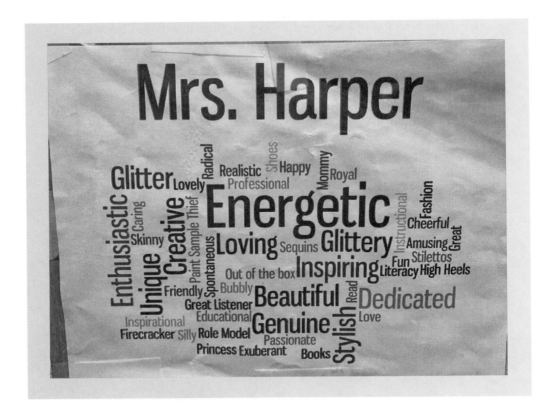

Content Area Connections

- Include formulas and math examples or computations in addition to words listed in the Word Splash.

- For novel studies in English, include characters and different traits.

- Include images of maps, historical figures, and important documents as additional selections on the word list.

- In science, use elements from the periodic table and compounds.

- In health or science, have students connect health conditions with symptoms or causes.

CHAPTER 1
Why Write Now?

CHAPTER 2
Parachute Writing

CHAPTER 3
Sum It All Up

CHAPTER 4
All the Right Words

CHAPTER 5
Digital Worlds

CHAPTER 6
Just the Facts

CHAPTER 7
Expecting the
Unexpected

Chapter 5

DIGITAL WORLDS

Strategies for Meeting Students Where They Are Already Hanging Out

Finding Rigor in the Digital World

When I work with teachers, they often tell stories about how their students struggle with academic literacy demands and the sophisticated skills demanded by content area reading and writing. Yet, daily I see that students are taking part in sophisticated literacy practices in their personal lives.

By now, you probably know that I am a huge proponent of real-world literacy. Just today, I was sitting next to a ninth grader who I watched skim and scan a number of stories and posts on Snapchat at a speed equivalent to that of a NASCAR driver. My guess is that this is pretty typical of many students who sift through a number of social media posts on a daily basis. Skimming and scanning are reading strategies that students must employ in the classroom, and they are skills that students are actively using on their own time, likely without even realizing it. My observation is similar to what Bartels (2017) described as "sophisticated composition strategies" (p. 91) when examining how his students utilized the tool Snapchat in their daily lives. Within this application, users make a number of sophisticated design decisions when creating one single "snap." Students determine the audience who will be receiving the "snap" (a close friend, acquaintance, family member, etc.), the distribution of the material (whether or not it will be shared with others aside from the original intended recipient), time and location, whether it is part of a "Snap Streak" (a continued conversation with the same recipient over the course of several days), the message or story, and more.

CHAPTER 1
Why Write Now?

CHAPTER 2
Parachute Writing

CHAPTER 3
Sum It All Up

CHAPTER 4
All the Right Words

CHAPTER 5
Digital Worlds

CHAPTER 6
Just the Facts

CHAPTER 7
Expecting the Unexpected

>>> *Social Media as Writing Practice*

Think about the last post you made on any social media site. Consider the following:

- What was the purpose of the post?

- Who did you consider as the audience?

- Did you include a photo with the post?

- How about a caption or hashtag?

- When posting, did you write it all at one time or make any revisions as you wrote?

- If anyone posted comments, how did you respond?

Within that one post, see the myriad literacy, and in particular, writing practices that were put into place? Yet social media isn't the only venue that these practices occur. Some of the same literacy practices pop up when people send texts, post reviews online, publish blog postings, or participate in other forms of digital communication.

Within this one social media platform, students are making multiple literacy decisions with posts that might only take a few seconds to compose and post online. Yet, are they consciously aware that these literacy decisions and practices are real-world examples of the same types of academic literacy demands the classroom requires? I am not so sure. In many ways, how the real world handles literacy is way cooler (yes, that doesn't sound academic, I know) than the way it is presented in the classroom. Sometimes, the answer lies in how we talk about skills, demands, and competencies in the classroom. Using language that is part of our students' worlds creates an environment that makes learning and success more attainable. In fact, Freire (1987) argued that "Words used in organizing a literacy program come from what I call the 'word universe' of people who are learning, expressing their actual language, their anxieties, fears, demands, and dreams. Words should be laden with the meaning of the people's existential experiences, and not of the teacher's experience" (p. 35).

How important this sentiment is in the classroom! Think about the tasks, assignments, material, and language used in a large portion of today's schools. For many, these experiences do not fully integrate what Freire (1987) argued for above: experiences, words, and the worlds of those we teach—not simply ones from those doing the teaching.

Making Meaningful Connections

While using familiar and relevant vocabulary is vital, it is equally important to connect academics to aspects of our students' lives in order to make learning more relevant. In today's digital age, it's difficult to ignore the multiple modes in which our students communicate and disseminate information. In many instances, students are utilizing higher-order thinking processes and sophisticated literacy practices that they may not consciously recognize. As a result, students may not see the connections between these real-world literacy practices and their academic ones.

One example of this is the skill of making inferences. Teachers know this is a difficult skill for students because it requires them to look beyond the text. Often students find this task daunting because the answer doesn't lie exclusively within the text itself. However, several months ago, I witnessed a car full of teenage girls, ages ten to sixteen, demonstrate their ability to make quite sophisticated inferences without even realizing it. While transporting my daughters and their friends to swim practice last spring, my ears perked up when I heard them discussing a boy from a prior swim meet who they saw, thought was "hot" (to quote them directly), but didn't catch his name. Fortunately, they knew this kid had dropped forty seconds in the mile, an event most swimmers don't even attempt. In about seven minutes, these girls had located their mystery guy and proceeded to proclaim that they knew he didn't have a girlfriend. How did they figure this out? Here's how:

- They located the swim meet on the meet results recording platform, Meet Mobile.

- They knew about how old he was, so they located the 1650-yard boys' event for participants fifteen and up.

- While looking at the participants, they found the one young man who dropped forty seconds from his entry time.

- Now they knew which team he swam for, the general location where he lived, and most importantly, his name.

- Using this information, they located all his social media accounts and scanned his posts.

After finding out this information, they informed me that he didn't have a girlfriend. How did they know? Here's what they told me:

- He never posts pictures of himself and the same girl.

- In his pictures, he is never "hugged up" on any of the girls, but rather is standing next to them in a friendly sort of way.

- There was no girlfriend mentioned in his bio, which they seemed to do a couple of close reads of.

- He didn't have a padlock icon next to his name which generally indicates that someone is "locked down" and in a relationship.

When I informed the girls that they had made an inference, they argued with me and told me they didn't, but rather just told me that they knew he didn't have a girlfriend.

CHAPTER 1
Why Write Now?

CHAPTER 2
Parachute Writing

CHAPTER 3
Sum it All Up

CHAPTER 4
All the Right Words

CHAPTER 5
Digital Worlds

CHAPTER 6
Just the Facts

CHAPTER 7
Expecting the Unexpected

CHAPTER 1
Why Write Now?

CHAPTER 2
Parachute Writing

CHAPTER 3
Sum It All Up

CHAPTER 4
All the Right Words

CHAPTER 5
Digital Worlds

CHAPTER 6
Just the Facts

CHAPTER 7
Expecting the Unexpected

I asked them the one question that they could not answer directly: "Where does it say specifically, 'I do not have a girlfriend'?" After a few minutes of discussion, I reminded them that they were using textual evidence from his social media page and what they had done was make an inference about this young man and his relationship status. Of course, I was thrilled that this occurred, not because of the nature of the topic, but because it was more evidence of the real-life literacy practices students engage in on a daily basis.

Why is something like this important? Because on a random Wednesday, with no academic task on the horizon, these young girls did what teachers often say is a struggle in the classroom. Think of the skills that the girls had to utilize and the strategies they employed to find the correct information. Here are just a few examples:

- Researched using appropriate search terms

- Eliminated unnecessary information

- Narrowed focus of information

- Read closely

- Skimmed and scanned text

- Used digital tools and platforms proficiently

This led me to wonder what it was about this task that made those sophisticated academic skills easier to tackle? These things made the difference:

- The content was relevant.

- The platforms were familiar (social media, Google searches, Meet Mobile, etc.).

- There was a reward associated with the task (learning the guy's name and background info).

- The material was of high interest and had specific real-life value.

- The task could be completed quickly.

When I began to think through this one exchange, it became evident once again that young people in many instances *do* possess the ability to complete sophisticated and complex literacy tasks; they just need to be reminded, or in many cases, told for the first time that they already know how to do the work. A fantastic way to support students with this kind of learning is to incorporate engagements that use digital tools and make connections to social media where students are already actively engaged and "hanging out." Increasingly, students are not only the consumers of information media; they are becoming the producers of it. This access to new digital literacies also involves the acquisition of a new visual vocabulary. Digital components such as emojis, GIFS, video clips, and other tools are quickly replacing traditional written communication (Hempel, 2014). Consider these statistics from the Pew Research Center (Meeker, 2014):

- Nearly 90% of middle and high school youth have access to a computer

- 95% of U.S. teens ages 13–17 have a Smartphone

- At least 75% of U.S. teens report using Instagram or Snapchat

- 85% of teens use YouTube

- 90% of teen cell phone owners also use texting to communicate

- On average, adolescents receive their first Smartphone at age 10

- Nearly 50% of all middle schoolers have a social media account by 8th grade

- 1.8 billion photographs are shared per day on social media (p. 62)

These statistics translate into spendable capital in the classroom when used in conjunction with content-rich, standards-based instruction. Plus, in today's classroom, forged by fluid distance, hybrid, and blended learning structures due to the COVID-19 pandemic, more and more students are proficient in software and internet information delivery platforms than ever. Offering students new opportunities to write their worlds provides engagements that motivate students and meet academic demands of the classroom. This merger of out-of-school literacy practices and academic literacy practices has been conceptualized as *third spaces* (Bhabha 1994; Elsden-Clifton 2006; Gutiérrez et al., 1999; Moje et al., 2004; Soja 1996), which Gutiérrez (2008) defined as what happens when "teacher and student scripts—the formal and informal, the official and unofficial spaces of the learning environment—intersect, creating the potential for authentic interaction and a shift in the social organization of learning and what counts as knowledge" (p. 152).

This intersection offers opportunities for students and teachers to build bridges between knowledge and discourse, as well as create new understandings that challenge and redesign academic content literacy and students' everyday lives (Barton, 2001; Morrell & Collatos, 2003; Seiler, 2001). Today's students can benefit from the reminder that the literacy they engage in daily can provide them with an added advantage and edge in the classroom. By bringing deliberate attention to these third spaces, teachers can offer students additional opportunities for success in the classroom.

With this in mind, teachers can begin to explore new ways to meet the literacy demands in the content classroom. Instead of a traditional response to literature, try Tweet the Text (page 158) or Instagram Ideas (page 140). Use Pinterest Paragraphs (page 145) or Hashtag Summaries (page 163) to write and rewrite compositions in the classroom. In this chapter, you'll find a variety of strategies that take their cues from the popular social media and digital literacy practices that students currently utilize.

CHAPTER 1 Why Write Now?

CHAPTER 2 Parachute Writing

CHAPTER 3 Sum It All Up

CHAPTER 4 All the Right Words

CHAPTER 5 Digital Worlds

CHAPTER 6 Just the Facts

CHAPTER 7 Expecting the Unexpected

CHAPTER 1
Why Write Now?

CHAPTER 2
Parachute Writing

CHAPTER 3
Sum It All Up

CHAPTER 4
All the Right Words

CHAPTER 5
Digital Worlds

CHAPTER 6
Just the Facts

CHAPTER 7
Expecting the Unexpected

INSTAGRAM IDEAS

At the writing of this book, Instagram is the second most engaged social network, with over one billion active monthly users. It serves as a popular photo and video sharing app, with at least 71 percent of users falling in the "below 35" age bracket. It is the most popular social media network among teenagers with 63 percent of all users logging in to the application at least once a day. While many utilize the network to keep up with friends and family, it is also used for e-commerce and is a source for current events and news.

Due to its popularity among teenagers and students' familiarity with the network, Instagram is a fantastic tool for the classroom when used appropriately. Plus, Instagram offers opportunities for students to take part in engagements that utilize visual literacy, something Metros (2008) defines as "the ability to decode and interpret visual messages and also to be able to encode and compose meaningful visual communication" (p. 102). When I began to think about Instagram as a possibility for teaching, I asked a sampling of teenagers about their purposes for using the platform. In my impromptu conversations, I noticed a trend in how teens decide to post something as a regular post or include it in their story. What I found was that a number of these kids were able to articulate that items that were part of their stories served as more extraneous details while those items that they posted were more important aspects of their lives. Without realizing it, they were taking part in differentiating the difference between a main idea or important detail, and a detail or item of lesser importance.

Instagram Ideas provide students with a contemporary method for presenting academic material that combines both written text and images. This strategy can be used to address thematic material, main ideas and details, or a pictorial summary. Think about it: When you post something on Instagram, you are using images to convey a message or meaning. These images, along with the accompanying text, provide the audience with a narrative, response, rebuttal, or anecdotal information. All these items have a purposeful place inside the classroom.

Putting It to Work

1. Determine the content you want students to create an Instagram post around, such as an overarching concept, vocabulary term, historical figure, or character from a novel.

2. Display examples of high-quality Instagram posts. As a class, generate a list of features that high-quality Instagram posts possess. These can be termed the *Instagram Essentials*. Sample questions to support this discussion include the following:

   - What does each post include?

   - How many words are used?

CHAPTER 1
Why Write Now?

CHAPTER 2
Parachute Writing

CHAPTER 3
Sum It All Up

CHAPTER 4
All the Right Words

CHAPTER 5
Digital Worlds

CHAPTER 6
Just the Facts

CHAPTER 7
Expecting the Unexpected

- How is the image related?
- Are there any tags?
- Are hashtags utilized? If yes, how are they used?

3. Select one Instagram post topic for the class to examine and complete together as a sample. Using the class list of quality Instagram features, have students work in pairs to create an Instagram post for that topic. Allow about ten minutes for this task. These posts can be created using paper and pencil or with an electronic template created using a tool such as Microsoft Publisher or something similar.

4. Select students to share their created posts with the class.

5. Provide students with a list of topics around which they can create new posts. This list could include academic terms, concepts, key events in history, or example math problems, for example.

6. Have students work individually or in pairs to select a concept and create an image and a post that explains their image.

7. Students should use the class list of quality Instagram features to assist them when creating their own posts.

8. Allow students to share with the class.

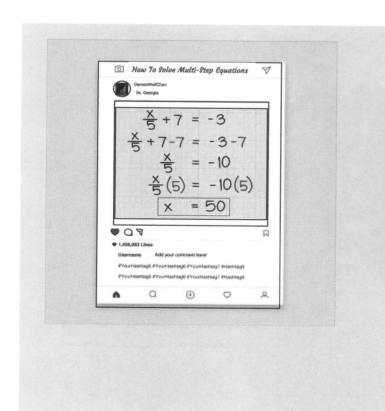

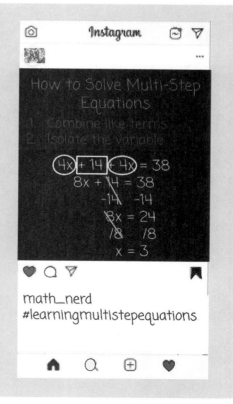

CHAPTER 1
Why Write Now?

CHAPTER 2
Parachute Writing

CHAPTER 3
Sum It All Up

CHAPTER 4
All the Right Words

CHAPTER 5
Digital Worlds

CHAPTER 6
Just the Facts

CHAPTER 7
Expecting the
Unexpected

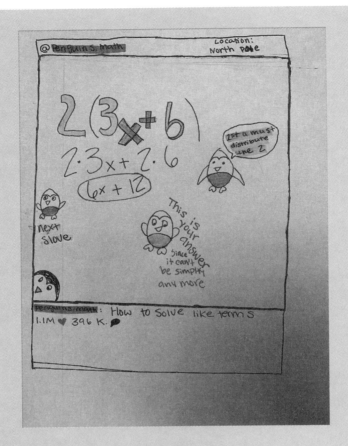

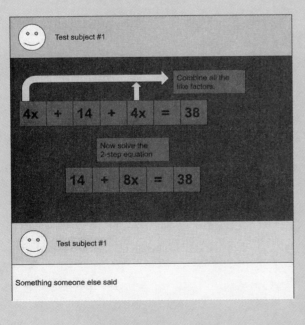

When to Use It

- To summarize material using social media

- As a way for students to link a visual image with a main idea

- As a real-world connection with social media

- As a brief written response

Why It Works

- It offers students a real-world connection to academic writing through social media.

- Instagram Ideas provides another layer of information through the use of pictures and images, which is especially helpful for struggling readers and writers.

- Instagram Ideas are an informal and approachable strategy, not an extended written response.

Modifications

- Instead of having students complete an Instagram Idea, have students create a Headline Summary/Main Idea using traditional newspapers as a model.

- Have students create the list of Instagram Essentials in pairs instead of as a whole class. To do this, provide each group with a set of Instagram posts. Have pairs record their observations and then have them share with the class to create a master list. Follow the remaining lesson steps as written.

- Use teacher-created Instagram Ideas and have students examine the model posts. Have students determine which ones they like best by affixing a heart sticker (or another shape) to the post and attaching a justification as to why they like the post using textual evidence.

Extensions

- Have students use address labels to translate any informal language in their posts into more formal academic language.

- Allow students to develop an Instagram story that serves as a hook for their post.

CHAPTER 1
Why Write Now?

CHAPTER 2
Parachute Writing

CHAPTER 3
Sum It All Up

CHAPTER 4
All the Right Words

CHAPTER 5
Digital Worlds

CHAPTER 6
Just the Facts

CHAPTER 7
Expecting the Unexpected

CHAPTER 1
Why Write Now?

CHAPTER 2
Parachute Writing

CHAPTER 3
Sum It All Up

CHAPTER 4
All the Right Words

CHAPTER 5
Digital Worlds

CHAPTER 6
Just the Facts

CHAPTER 7
Expecting the Unexpected

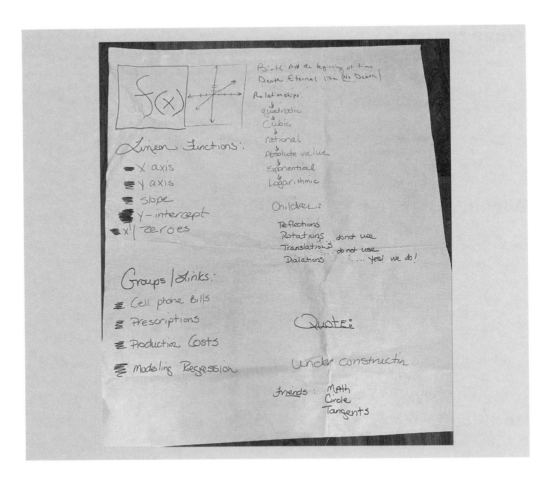

- As a Ticket in the Door, have students respond to a classmate's post with a heart sticker or sticky note, and have them explain why they "liked" the post.

- Connect Instagram Ideas to the Hashtags strategy (page 163) by having students take a Hashtag that they have created for a concept or topic and create an Instagram Idea to go with it.

Content Area Connections

- Use Instagram Ideas as a way for students to incorporate a math model or illustration to explain a math problem or concept.

- Have students complete an Instagram lab report by creating a post for each part of the lab report (materials, procedure, results, etc.).

- Have students create "Then and Now" Instagram posts for key inventions in history, social justice issues, or technological improvements or changes.

- Use Instagram posts as timelines when studying key time periods in history or when completing a novel study to trace the events of the work over an extended time.

CHAPTER 1
Why Write Now?

CHAPTER 2
Parachute Writing

CHAPTER 3
Sum It All Up

CHAPTER 4
All the Right Words

CHAPTER 5
Digital Worlds

CHAPTER 6
Just the Facts

CHAPTER 7
Expecting the
Unexpected

PINTEREST PARAGRAPHS

It is important that students learn how to organize information both in the context of writing as well as across other subjects, and even outside of school. I often think about ways that components of paragraphs exist in other forms that may be more contemporary and relatable to students. Pinterest is a great visual example of what a pictorial paragraph might look like. If you consider that paragraphs are a system of order that places like sentences in the same places, then Pinterest functions as a sort of image-based paragraph. Instead of calling their organizational blocks paragraphs, they are called *boards*. These boards house any "Pins" that belong in that category. Pins function as the sentences that make up the paragraphs. For example, if I am searching for ideas for my bathroom remodel, I name that board "Bathroom Remodel" and place all images and pins that are related to that topic on that board. Recipes and the latest fashion trends would not belong on the "Bathroom Remodel" board. This is very similar to how paragraphs are organized but in a more visual manner.

While this may be an unorthodox way to teach paragraph construction, it offers students another visual example of how to organize content in their writing. Because many students have difficulty organizing their writing into clear and coherent paragraphs, offering them another example of effective organization in the real world may aid students in creating better overall compositions.

How are images grouped?	
What are some possible names for the boards?	
Could any of the boards be broken down into sub-boards (sub categories)?	
How many images are included?	
How many groups or boards are used?	
What written descriptors, if any, are included?	

CHAPTER 1
Why Write Now?

CHAPTER 2
Parachute Writing

CHAPTER 3
Sum It All Up

CHAPTER 4
All the Right Words

CHAPTER 5
Digital Worlds

CHAPTER 6
Just the Facts

CHAPTER 7
Expecting the
Unexpected

Putting It to Work

1. Provide students with examples of Pinterest boards.

2. Have students make "Notice Notes" about what they observe on the pages. To support students with their observations, ask them specific questions such as the following:

   - How are images grouped?

   - What are some possible names for the boards?

   - Could any of the boards be broken down into subboards (or subcategories)?

   - How many images are included?

   - How many groups or boards are used?

   - What written descriptors, if any, are included?

3. Allow students time to share their Notice Notes with the class and add any ideas to their lists that their classmates shared, if necessary.

4. Divide students into collaborative groups or pairs.

5. Provide students with a new topic around which to create their own Pinterest board, using the class example and their Notice Notes as a guide.

6. Provide students with specific parameters for their boards. These might include the number of boards, number of images, or number of accompanying sentences to correspond with the boards.

7. Have students share with the class.

Quick Tip!

Have students use an internet application such as Canva.com, PicCollage, PicStitch, or Snappic to create their Pinterest page or create it old school with magazines and newspapers.

TRENCH WARFARE

A new strategy for war was trench warfare. This made WWI very deadly and very long. In trench warfare soldiers fought in deep ditches which helped them defended their position. Soldiers would fight in these wet, muddy, and cold ditches for sometimes months at a time. Due to the extreme conditions in the trenches, many soldiers on BOTH sides died of diseases. The empty patch of land between enemy trenches was called "no man's-land". This land was soon stripped of trees due to the explosions. Someone who went onto "no man's-land" was likely to be killed by the enemy.

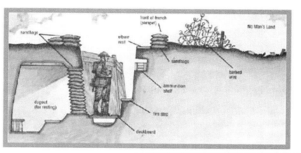

PIC·COLLAGE

CHAPTER 1
Why Write Now?

CHAPTER 2
Parachute Writing

CHAPTER 3
Sum It All Up

CHAPTER 4
All the Right Words

CHAPTER 5
Digital Worlds

CHAPTER 6
Just the Facts

CHAPTER 7
Expecting the Unexpected

CHAPTER 1
Why Write Now?

CHAPTER 2
Parachute Writing

CHAPTER 3
Sum It All Up

CHAPTER 4
All the Right Words

CHAPTER 5
Digital Worlds

CHAPTER 6
Just the Facts

CHAPTER 7
Expecting the
Unexpected

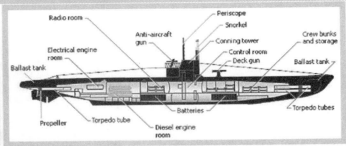

U-Boats / Submarines

Germans had submarines called U-boats during WWI. They used these submarines to shoot torpedos at Allied Powers' ships. Germans also attacked ships that belonged to NEUTRAL countries that were believed to be helping the Allied Powers. The Lusitania, a U.S. passenger ship, was attacked by a German submarine which led the U.S. into war.

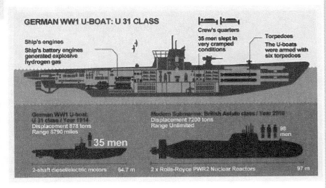

PIC·COLLAGE

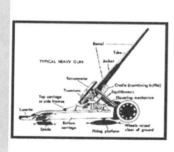

MACHINE AND ARTILLERY GUNS

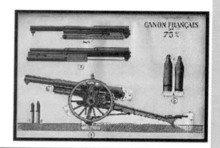

THE NEW MACHINE GUNS COULD FIRE 400 TO 600 BULLETS A MINUTE. GIANT ARTILLERY GUNS FIRED SHELLS OVER THE TRENCHES. THE SHELLS THEN EXPLODED AND SENT SPEEDING SCRAPS OF METAL ONTO THE SOLDIERS BELOW IN THE TRENCH.

PIC·COLLAGE

CHAPTER 1
Why Write Now?

CHAPTER 2
Parachute Writing

CHAPTER 3
Sum It All Up

CHAPTER 4
All the Right Words

CHAPTER 5
Digital Worlds

CHAPTER 6
Just the Facts

CHAPTER 7
Expecting the Unexpected

CHAPTER 1
Why Write Now?

CHAPTER 2
Parachute Writing

CHAPTER 3
Sum It All Up

CHAPTER 4
All the Right Words

CHAPTER 5
Digital Worlds

CHAPTER 6
Just the Facts

CHAPTER 7
Expecting the
Unexpected

When to Use It

- To classify information into groups

- To link a visual reminder with written text

- To introduce the visual conceptualization of organized writing

- As a real-world connection with social media

- To teach text structure and text features since headings and subheadings, images, and captions are employed

Why It Works

- It offers students a real-world connection to academic writing through social media.

- It provides another layer of information through the use of pictures and images, which is especially helpful for struggling readers and writers.

- Pinterest Paragraphs are artistic in nature and are less intimidating than a traditional paragraph or essay.

- It is a low-stakes writing assignment that can be built on every day with more information added as a unit progresses.

Modifications

- Divide the implementation of this strategy over two days. Day 1 includes the acquisition and organization of the images. Day 2 includes the drafting of the sentences that support the images.

- Provide students with the subcategories for their pages ahead of time so they can locate images that fall into those categories.

- For ELLs, have students name the boards in their native language and have a partner translate into English.

- When showing examples at the start of the lesson, omit the board names and have students create names for the boards based on the images and information that they see.

Extensions

- Have students use address labels to stick appropriate academic vocabulary onto their "boards."

- Use the Pinterest boards as a foundation for a lesson on transition sentences. Have students use transition words to link the contents together on each board.

- Have students make an addition to a classmate's board by adding another image and an accompanying statement.

- Use Pinterest boards as a sentence-building activity with primary students

CHAPTER 1
Why Write Now?

CHAPTER 2
Parachute Writing

CHAPTER 3
Sum It All Up

CHAPTER 4
All the Right Words

CHAPTER 5
Digital Worlds

CHAPTER 6
Just the Facts

CHAPTER 7
Expecting the Unexpected

CHAPTER 1
Why Write Now?

CHAPTER 2
Parachute Writing

CHAPTER 3
Sum It All Up

CHAPTER 4
All the Right Words

CHAPTER 5
Digital Worlds

CHAPTER 6
Just the Facts

CHAPTER 7
Expecting the
Unexpected

- Have students create a more modern List, Group, Label, Pin that incorporates Pinterest. With this extension, the strategy becomes List, Pin, Label, Share (page 168).

- Take an existing essay and have students develop a Pinterest page that corresponds with the essay using boards as visuals for the existing essay's paragraph.

Content Area Connections

- Use Pinterest Paragraphs in English to provide an overall summary of a novel or for a character analysis.

- Use Pinterest Paragraphs for students to group similar math concepts, formulas, or problem-solving strategies together and explain.

- Have students complete a Pinterest lab report in science. Instead of the traditional format, have them use boards and accompanying sentences to complete the lab report.

- In primary classes, use Pinterest pages for grouping certain types of words and sounds.

CHAPTER 1
Why Write Now?

CHAPTER 2
Parachute Writing

CHAPTER 3
Sum it All Up

CHAPTER 4
All the Right Words

CHAPTER 5
Digital Worlds

CHAPTER 6
Just the Facts

CHAPTER 7
Expecting the
Unexpected

PICTURE COLLAGE CONTENT

The creation of photo collages is a fantastic way for students to incorporate more than just images into their writings. In today's world, students must move seamlessly across platforms, both digital and nondigital, to create multimodal products that convey an intended message. Using a picture-based application, such as PicCollage, students can incorporate graphics, images, words, directional arrows, and more to develop a presentation that includes both visual and written content for a concept. While there are some similar components to the Pinterest Paragraphs strategy, creating a Picture Collage involves more than the classification of images or material into boards; it offers students the ability to utilize creative license with the content they are studying.

Visual literacy is necessary in today's classroom teaching and society as many standard sets (Common Core Standards, NCTE standards, ILA standards) include digital and visual literacy components. In order for students to be visually literate, they must learn to process both pictures and words (Burmark, 2008). Utilizing engagements such as the Picture Collage allows teachers to achieve authentic learning goals through the support of digital resources. Plus, effectively integrating visual literacy engagements can improve comprehension for English learners (Britsch, 2009). Picture Collages can be used as a unique way to journal in content area classrooms since they marry both words and pictures in a logical progression.

Putting It to Work

1. Ask students to recall what they know about collages. Remind them of engagements they may have taken part in during art classes.

2. Provide students with examples of PicCollage creations using a variety of layouts and templates.

3. Have students make Notice Notes about what they observe on the pages. To support students with their observations of the graphics or images, ask them specific questions such as the following:

   • What formats are used for each type of information presented?

   • How are images integrated into the design?

   • What types of descriptive words or academic terms are used in the examples?

   • Are any directional images (arrows, NSEW directions, coordinates, etc.) used? If so, what kinds?

CHAPTER 1
Why Write Now?

CHAPTER 2
Parachute Writing

CHAPTER 3
Sum It All Up

CHAPTER 4
All the Right Words

CHAPTER 5
Digital Worlds

CHAPTER 6
Just the Facts

CHAPTER 7
Expecting the Unexpected

- What words are included in the image?
- Are any words accompanied by definitions?

4. Allow students time to share their Notice Notes with the class and add any ideas to their lists that their classmates shared, if necessary.

5. Divide students into collaborative groups or pairs.

6. Provide students with a new topic around which to create their own Picture Collage, using the class examples and their Notice Notes as a guide. Discuss which types of templates work best with the assigned topic(s).

7. Have students brainstorm with their partners to determine which layout would best fit their topics.

8. Allow students time to locate images and the accompanying text for their Picture Collage.

9. Share with the class.

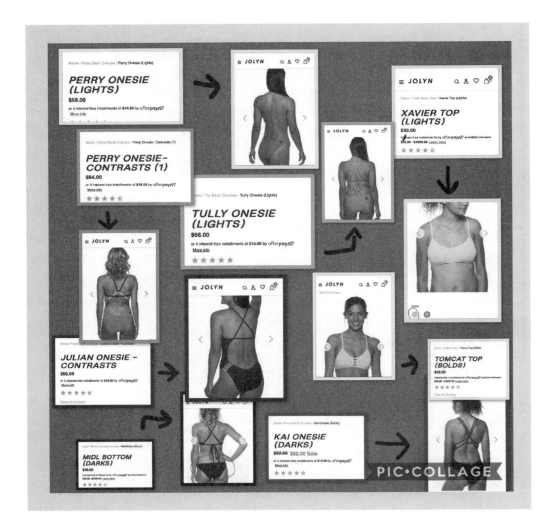

When to Use It

- As a way for students to link a visual cue or reminder with written text

- To create a product that offers students the ability to take creative license of their work

- As a real-world connection with social media

- To vary the product based on the goals and interests of the student

⚡ *Quick Tip!*

Other digital applications for this strategy include Glogster, Canva.com, and Infogram.com.

Why It Works

- It offers students a real-world connection to academic writing through social media.

- Picture Collage Content provides another layer of information through the use of pictures and images, which can be especially helpful for struggling readers and writers.

- Picture Collage Content is artistic in nature and less intimidating than a traditional paragraph or essay.

- It works well with content that includes a series of steps or utilizes an order of events.

- It is easily adapted to online learning delivery.

Modifications

- Divide the implementation of this strategy over two days: Day 1 includes the acquisition and organization of the images and Day 2 includes the drafting of the sentences that support the images.

- Provide students with specific material that should be included in the PicCollage. Have them use their creativity to uniquely present the information.

- Provide students with a specific template to use based on the material being taught.

- Allow students to use magazines and newspapers to cut out the images and do it old school. Use address labels for the directional texts and accompanying textual information.

CHAPTER 1
Why Write Now?

CHAPTER 2
Parachute Writing

CHAPTER 3
Sum It All Up

CHAPTER 4
All the Right Words

CHAPTER 5
Digital Worlds

CHAPTER 6
Just the Facts

CHAPTER 7
Expecting the Unexpected

CHAPTER 1
Why Write Now?

CHAPTER 2
Parachute Writing

CHAPTER 3
Sum It All Up

CHAPTER 4
All the Right Words

CHAPTER 5
Digital Worlds

CHAPTER 6
Just the Facts

CHAPTER 7
Expecting the
Unexpected

Extensions

- Have students use address labels or other text features to draw attention to academic vocabulary.

- Use the material created in Picture Collage Content as a springboard into Pinterest Paragraphs (page 145).

- Create a class book of student work that addresses a specific overarching topic or concept.

- Use Picture Collage as a model for a classroom presentation. Picture Collages can offer a quick way for students to present a larger classroom project in an abbreviated manner.

Content Area Connections

- Use Picture Collage Content as a way for students to trace the events in a novel, evolution of a character, or story elements.

- Have students trace the steps in a complex math problem, identify examples of mathematical content in their daily lives, or use when studying geometry or measurement.

- Invite students to complete a Picture Collage Content about their interests and personal lives as a beginning-of-the-year or semester "Getting to Know You," or a Pictorial Autobiography.

- In social studies, have students develop a Picture Collage of a historical figure or an event in history.

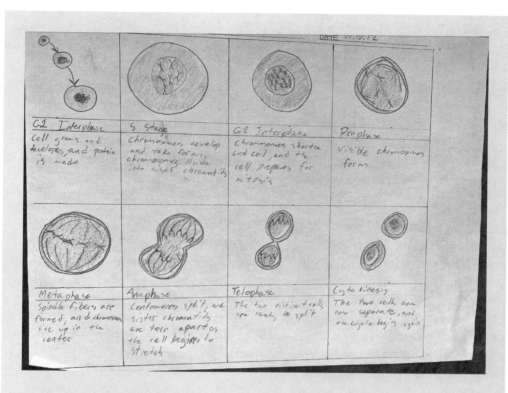

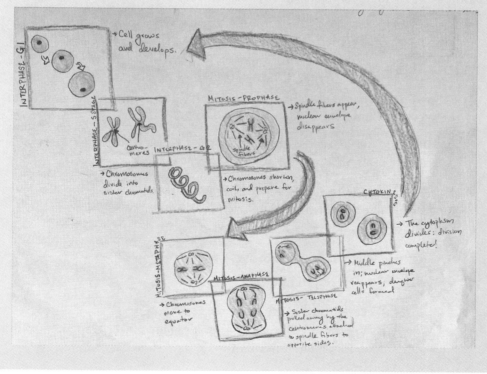

CHAPTER 1
Why Write Now?

CHAPTER 2
Parachute Writing

CHAPTER 3
Sum It All Up

CHAPTER 4
All the Right Words

CHAPTER 5
Digital Worlds

CHAPTER 6
Just the Facts

CHAPTER 7
Expecting the
Unexpected

CHAPTER 1
Why Write Now?

CHAPTER 2
Parachute Writing

CHAPTER 3
Sum It All Up

CHAPTER 4
All the Right Words

CHAPTER 5
Digital Worlds

CHAPTER 6
Just the Facts

CHAPTER 7
Expecting the
Unexpected

TWEET THE TEXT

It is possible that tweets might be one of the most useful social media posts in the classroom due to their versatility across instruction. Tweets can be used for a number of classroom engagements. Some examples include finding support for social justice arguments online, political and government policy, social and economic movements, and reflection and response. Plus, since the internet is full of these types of social media posts, it's extremely easy to locate ones to use in classroom instruction.

The use of tweets in classroom instruction is another easy everyday writing activity that can be used for several academic demands and standards. Responding to literature and other types of texts is a skill that is practiced across the content areas. Even in math, students must make notations regarding specific problems or solution strategies. Sometimes, responses to texts need to be lengthy, but in most instances, shortened, abbreviated responses can meet the needs of the content classroom. Most tweets tend to be abbreviated or shortened compositions. One way to incorporate a shortened, written response is by having students Tweet the Text. In this strategy, students take portions of their content text and respond to it using a series of tweets or texts. Students are encouraged to utilize social media abbreviations (IMO, BTW, FTFY, etc.) as well as hashtags when they complete these tweets so they mirror the same components seen in the real world.

Putting It to Work

1. Display a piece of text, such as a photograph, excerpt from a textbook, math problem, or even a short video clip.

2. Remind students of the length and content of typical tweets and texts. Show a couple of example texts and tweets as a reminder.

3. Have students complete tweet responses to the media displayed in step one on a sticky note. Tweet content will vary, but consider using some of the prompts below as starters.

   - How would you respond to this text, image, or quote?

   - What does it make you think of?

   - What is the author's message or intent?

   - What questions do you have after examining the piece? Depending on the nature of the lesson and time allotment, have students complete two to five sample tweets.

4. Once students have written their responses, have them display their responses next to the text.

5. Discuss their responses as a class.

6. Divide students into groups of three or four.

7. Distribute chart paper that has new text excerpts written or glued to the chart paper.

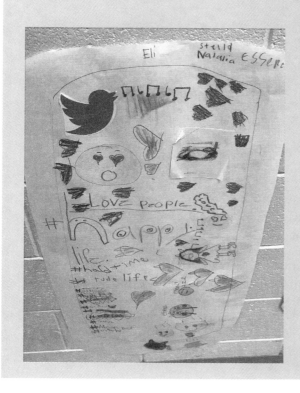

CHAPTER 1
Why Write Now?

CHAPTER 2
Parachute Writing

CHAPTER 3
Sum It All Up

CHAPTER 4
All the Right Words

CHAPTER 5
Digital Worlds

CHAPTER 6
Just the Facts

CHAPTER 7
Expecting the Unexpected

CHAPTER 1
Why Write Now?

CHAPTER 2
Parachute Writing

CHAPTER 3
Sum It All Up

CHAPTER 4
All the Right Words

CHAPTER 5
Digital Worlds

CHAPTER 6
Just the Facts

CHAPTER 7
Expecting the
Unexpected

8. Give students two to three minutes to examine the text and draft a tweet in response to the excerpts. Have students write their tweets on the chart paper next to the original text or piece.

9. If using different excerpts with each group, have students rotate to a new excerpt and repeat Steps 7 and 8. If the whole class is using the same excerpt, then have them share their top three tweets.

When to Use It

- To create a shortened response to literature or content material

- As a collaborative engagement for students

- To focus on the quality of a response but not necessarily the mechanics or sentence structure

- As a real-world connection with social media

Why It Works

- It offers students a real-world connection to academic writing through social media.

- It requires students to focus on a specific piece of content and then develop tweet responses around the sample text.

- Tweet the Text focuses on content and students' ability to utilize contemporary modes of communication rather than spelling, grammar, and formal sentence structure.

Modifications

- Have students choose the text they want to tweet about as a group.

- Provide students with sample tweets to get them started.

- Have students write their tweets on sticky notes. By doing this, you can pull the sticky notes off the chart paper and use them as tickets in the door for the following day's lesson.

Extensions

- Have students use address labels, sticky notes, or arrows to draw attention to specific elements of the text they are tweeting about.

A Ticket in the Door

Here is how to use this strategy as a Ticket in the Door. After the class is over, pull all the sticky notes from each chart paper. Post the chart papers in random spots around the room. On Day 2, distribute the original tweets as students walk in the door, but this time, give them a blank sticky note as well. Instruct students to find the text that the tweet is about and use their blank sticky note to explain how they knew where it belonged.

CHAPTER 1
Why Write Now?

CHAPTER 2
Parachute Writing

CHAPTER 3
Sum It All Up

CHAPTER 4
All the Right Words

CHAPTER 5
Digital Worlds

CHAPTER 6
Just the Facts

CHAPTER 7
Expecting the
Unexpected

CHAPTER 1
Why Write Now?

CHAPTER 2
Parachute Writing

CHAPTER 3
Sum It All Up

CHAPTER 4
All the Right Words

CHAPTER 5
Digital Worlds

CHAPTER 6
Just the Facts

CHAPTER 7
Expecting the
Unexpected

- Allow students to transfer one of their tweets to an Instagram post and incorporate an image with the tweet.

- Give students a note card and have them complete a Gallery Walk of all the tweeted texts. Have students record their favorite tweets from each sample on their notecard.

- Use this as a companion activity with the Hashtag strategy (page 163).

Content Area Connections

- Use Tweet the Text as a way to divide a science or history textbook chapter into chunks for quick review of the key concepts.

- Ask students to tweet about mathematics word problems, graphs, sections of their textbooks, or possible solutions.

- Have students tweet about a musical score, work of art, or current event in sports.

- Use tweets as a more current ticket out the door or exit slip prompt.

- Have students use address labels to construct their accompanying tweets when completing a math problem.

CHAPTER 1
Why Write Now?

CHAPTER 2
Parachute Writing

CHAPTER 3
Sum It All Up

CHAPTER 4
All the Right Words

CHAPTER 5
Digital Worlds

CHAPTER 6
Just the Facts

CHAPTER 7
Expecting the Unexpected

HASHTAG SUMMARIES

One way that teachers can address the skill of summarizing is by using social media influences. Because many students are fluent in the language of social media, Hashtag Summaries is an easy way to use students' social media capital to demonstrate their academic knowledge. I first came to this realization when walking through the hallways of my daughter's elementary school at the beginning of the school year. While looking at their student work, I noticed that many of the students included hashtags with their summertime selfies. Each student had drawn a picture of their summer activity on a template of a smartphone and had written a tweet about their summer fun. Hashtags such as #awesome, #charlesonfun, and #summertimefun were just a few I observed in this student work.

"I played all summer long. #awesome"

"I went to Charleston I stayed at Holiday Inn I went to the beach in Charleston I boogie boarding and then I went on a boat to Fort Sumter I went in a museum there then I went back I went on a battleship it was fun. #charleston fun"

CHAPTER 1
Why Write Now?

CHAPTER 2
Parachute Writing

CHAPTER 3
Sum It All Up

CHAPTER 4
All the Right Words

CHAPTER 5
Digital Worlds

CHAPTER 6
Just the Facts

CHAPTER 7
Expecting the Unexpected

While I am not certain that the elementary students truly understood what the hashtag meant, they knew enough about it to know that it functioned as a main idea. Each hashtag somehow related to the overarching main idea of their summertime selfie image and tweet. In other words, these students wrote about their summer escapades and then encapsulated it in a hashtag that functioned as a main idea.

My own second-grade son has recently taken to following up statements with a hashtag that basically captures what he has just stated in an abbreviated manner. His sisters think it is annoying, but I am delighted because once again, there is more evidence that young children are aware of this term AND know how to use it. I began to think about this. If students as young as second and third grade understand enough about hashtags to know that they could function as a main idea, why not use them more formally in instruction with older students? As a result, I began utilizing this idea to teach summarization and main idea. Because hashtags serve a real-world function in students' lives, many can identify with hashtags as a practical example of a main idea. Even if they don't tweet on a regular basis, students are exposed to this social media frenzy in their daily lives through television programming, advertisements, reading materials, and more. Using a construct that is well known to students makes creating a summary a little more attainable and reachable instead of the traditional academic role that can feel disconnected and disjointed from their daily lives.

> ## ≫ Celebrity Hashtag Conversations
>
> Jimmy Fallon has posted some hashtag conversations with himself and celebrities such as Justin Timberlake and Jonah Hill that poke fun at society's overuse of hashtags. It is easy to find video clips of these conversations with a quick Google search. But be sure to preview the clips to make sure they are appropriate for your students! It's easy enough to cut the clip early to avoid some bleeped inappropriate language.

Putting It to Work

1. Review a concept or idea that students have previously studied.

2. Make a list of that topic or concept's key points as generated by the class discussion.

3. Ask students to define the word *hashtag*. Record their definitions on a sheet of chart paper or on the board.

4. Using the student-generated lists, display six to ten possible hashtags that could be associated with the reviewed topic or concept.

5. Discuss which one(s) work(s) best and have students provide explanations of their recommendations.

6. Divide students into groups of three or four.

7. Distribute additional material for students to read or explore on their own (e.g., a section of a textbook, a chapter from a novel, a segment from a video lecture, or a film clip).

8. Instruct students to create an overarching hashtag that represents the overall message or main idea of the material and write it on a sheet of chart paper.

9. Have students share and defend their hashtags to the class.

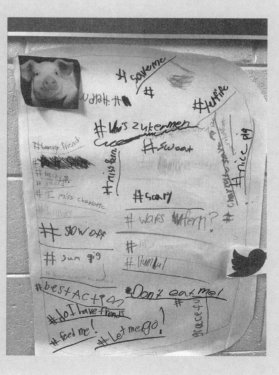

CHAPTER 1
Why Write Now?

CHAPTER 2
Parachute Writing

CHAPTER 3
Sum It All Up

CHAPTER 4
All the Right Words

CHAPTER 5
Digital Worlds

CHAPTER 6
Just the Facts

CHAPTER 7
Expecting the
Unexpected

CHAPTER 1
Why Write Now?

CHAPTER 2
Parachute Writing

CHAPTER 3
Sum It All Up

CHAPTER 4
All the Right Words

CHAPTER 5
Digital Worlds

CHAPTER 6
Just the Facts

CHAPTER 7
Expecting the
Unexpected

When to Use It

- To summarize material in a manner that feels less intimidating than traditional main idea writing

- As a ticket out the door

- As a culminating engagement after a unit of study, chapter, or concept

- As a real-world connection with social media

Why It Works

- It offers students a real-world connection to academic writing through social media.

- Hashtags are a familiar form of communication and a medium students encounter on a regular basis in the real world.

- They are abbreviated written responses.

Modifications

- Provide each group with a different text focused on the same topic or concept instead of using one main text for the entire class.

- Provide students with a list of possible hashtags that could be used and allow them to determine the best choice and explain.

- Provide students with a piece of text that utilizes headings and subheadings. Have students change the headings and subheadings to hashtags.

Extensions

- Have students use sticky notes to write their own tweets (140 characters or less) as a reflection on the material studied.

- Use Hashtag Summaries as a Ticket in the Door for the next day's lesson.

- Use Hashtag Summaries as a springboard for the Pizza Slice Summary strategy (page 63).

- Use Hashtag Summaries in conjunction with Pinterest Paragraphs or Picture Collages.

Content Area Connections

- Divide the content of a textbook chapter into sections and have students write Hashtag Summaries for each section.

- Use Hashtag Summaries as reminders or key points for solving certain types of math problems.

- Have students create Hashtag Summaries at the end of each chapter of a novel as a way to continually summarize the story.

- When studying historical figures, instead of having students write a traditional timeline or biography, ask students to create hashtag biographies or hashtag timelines. With this idea, students draft hashtags for a historical figure's major accomplishments or life events.

 Quick Tip!

It is important to use sticky notes. They are small pieces of "real estate," so even the most reluctant writer can write enough to fill up one sticky note.

CHAPTER 1
Why Write Now?

CHAPTER 2
Parachute Writing

CHAPTER 3
Sum It All Up

CHAPTER 4
All the Right Words

CHAPTER 5
Digital Worlds

CHAPTER 6
Just the Facts

CHAPTER 7
Expecting the Unexpected

CHAPTER 1
Why Write Now?

CHAPTER 2
Parachute Writing

CHAPTER 3
Sum It All Up

CHAPTER 4
All the Right Words

CHAPTER 5
Digital Worlds

CHAPTER 6
Just the Facts

CHAPTER 7
Expecting the
Unexpected

LIST, PIN, LABEL, SHARE

This is a great strategy for activating prior knowledge, brainstorming, and thinking about concept-specific vocabulary. Activating prior knowledge is key for improving comprehension and understanding of concepts. Providing students with engagements that allow students to call up background knowledge and information can improve a lesson's success. Sometimes, students aren't aware of the information that they already know can help them when learning a new concept. While they may not have specific knowledge of the new concept, they may possess *related* knowledge that can assist them when learning new material.

This strategy contains similarities between some social media platforms—in particular, the idea of a collecting platform such as Pinterest. While the actual activity still functions in the same manner, changing the names and drawing parallels between the classroom task and the real world allows students to see the authentic and real-world relevance. Plus, it is a low-stakes engagement that is informal in nature yet yields several benefits. It also is broken into specific parts, so it can easily be divided over a few days of teaching or can be conducted in one class period.

Putting It to Work

1. Provide students with a topic or concept that they will use during a brainstorming session.

2. Have them come up with as many words as possible that fall under the concept or category of material.

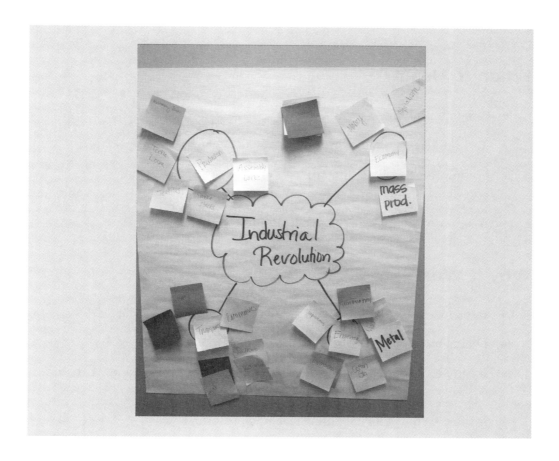

3. Have students arrange the words into categories.

4. Using an app such as PicCollage, students will group or "pin" the words into sections on their board. For example, if studying World War I, students might put all the words that describe fighting techniques together and all the words that list historical figures in another group. The PicCollage app has several different layouts for grouping text and images. Students can use a ready-made template or create their own.

 Quick Tip!

Provide sticky notes or small slips of paper for brainstorming. Or create an online document that can be shared and edited collaboratively using a program such as Google Docs, Etherpad, or Microsoft tools.

CHAPTER 1
Why Write Now?

CHAPTER 2
Parachute Writing

CHAPTER 3
Sum It All Up

CHAPTER 4
All the Right Words

CHAPTER 5
Digital Worlds

CHAPTER 6
Just the Facts

CHAPTER 7
Expecting the Unexpected

CHAPTER 1
Why Write Now?

CHAPTER 2
Parachute Writing

CHAPTER 3
Sum It All Up

CHAPTER 4
All the Right Words

CHAPTER 5
Digital Worlds

CHAPTER 6
Just the Facts

CHAPTER 7
Expecting the
Unexpected

5. Once students have pinned all the appropriate words in their corresponding groups, have students label their boards. This should be done in text that stands out so that the reader is aware that these labels function as headings.

6. Have students locate images that correspond with the words they have pinned on their board.

7. Allow students to share their finished boards by publishing them online or on the classroom webpage.

When to Use It

- As a brainstorming activity

- To complete a task that involves the use of digital tools

- To study topics where students have extensive experience and knowledge

- As a way to incorporate images in conjunction with content

Why It Works

- It is a low-stakes, informal assessment of students' knowledge.

- Digital tools are used to present the material.

- It can be completed quickly or utilized as an extended assessment over the course of several days.

- It works well in a digital online teaching platform.

Modifications

- Provide students with the list of words to group focused around a specific topic, rather than brainstorm words on their own.

- Have students use a set of images instead of words and then proceed according to the directions.

- Set a specific number of boards that the class must complete collaboratively. Divide the class into groups and assign a board to each group so that collaboratively, the class completes the page together.

Extensions

- Have students explain and justify why the images they included on their boards best represent the topic.

- Have students generate questions that might go with an image or board.

CHAPTER 1
Why Write Now?

CHAPTER 2
Parachute Writing

CHAPTER 3
Sum It All Up

CHAPTER 4
All the Right Words

CHAPTER 5
Digital Worlds

CHAPTER 6
Just the Facts

CHAPTER 7
Expecting the
Unexpected

CHAPTER 1
Why Write Now?

CHAPTER 2
Parachute Writing

CHAPTER 3
Sum It All Up

CHAPTER 4
All the Right Words

CHAPTER 5
Digital Worlds

CHAPTER 6
Just the Facts

CHAPTER 7
Expecting the
Unexpected

- Display the final products in the classroom. As a ticket in or out of the door, have students add a word and image to a classmate's board with a justification as to why that item was added.

- Have students use this activity as a springboard into the Pinterest Paragraphs (page 145) of Picture Collage (page 153) tasks.

Content Area Connections

- Have students create a corresponding key that translates the words into another language.

- Have students utilize images of important works of art instead of words.

- Have students create lists of synonyms or shades of meaning that they can use as a word bank to increase the quality of the vocabulary they use in their writing.

- Have students focus on different aspects of a character from a novel or historical time period. For example, board categories could be physical traits, character traits, important quotes, and specific actions.

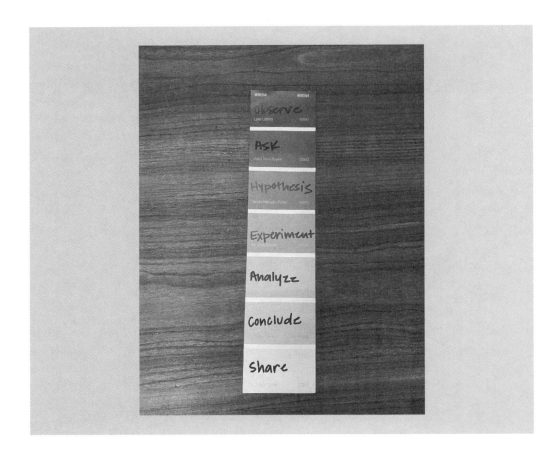

JUST THE FACTS

Strategies for Finding and Using Textual Evidence

. . . .

The Importance of Evidence

Utilizing and including evidence in writing is increasingly important in today's ELA *and* content classrooms because textual evidence plays a key role in the construction of arguments, justification of answers, constructed response elaboration, and more. The informational and argument genres make up a significant portion of student writing and often must include a variety of evidence from multiple sources with effective integration into their responses, arguments, and explanations. A solid grasp of how to locate and position textual evidence in writing should be a key component of instruction, including how to write direct quotations, summaries, and paraphrased passages. Plus, many careers require individuals to utilize some component of evidence-based writing or the genre of persuasion or argument. Providing students with opportunities to practice these skills allows them to address and refine writing skills that can be utilized in a variety of careers and settings.

Quantity and Quality Make a Difference

Teaching students about evidence involves a number of layers of instruction. Attention must be paid to the quantity of evidence, quality of evidence, how the evidence is positioned, the credibility of the evidence used, and more, but it can be hard for students to learn all of these nuances at once. Initially, students need to understand the need for quantity of evidence—what constitutes enough and how to locate it from a variety of sources. Once they have experience with locating and integrating evidence

CHAPTER 1
Why Write Now?

CHAPTER 2
Parachute Writing

CHAPTER 3
Sum It All Up

CHAPTER 4
All the Right Words

CHAPTER 5
Digital Worlds

CHAPTER 6
Just the Facts

CHAPTER 7
Expecting the
Unexpected

CHAPTER 1
Why Write Now?

CHAPTER 2
Parachute Writing

CHAPTER 3
Sum It All Up

CHAPTER 4
All the Right Words

CHAPTER 5
Digital Worlds

CHAPTER 6
Just the Facts

CHAPTER 7
Expecting the
Unexpected

from a variety of sources, special attention must be paid to the quality and credibility of evidence. By incorporating a variety of strategies that teach students how to utilize and position evidence, students are able to develop stronger academic literacies and arguments, practice critical thinking, and demonstrate a broader and greater depth of understanding of content materials (Takao & Kelly, 2003). In addition, crafting compositions that utilize textual evidence effectively involves much more than simply locating evidence and placing it in a composition. Students must master the skill of close reading, as they take part in directed, focused reading of texts to locate specific examples of textual evidence. Plus, annotation and citation are important subcomponents of textual evidence mastery, as many engagements begin with students annotating texts and require them to cite specific evidence from a variety of sources.

Students typically do well with visual reminders, so it's important to offer them the opportunity to link a strategy or skill to a specific visual or pictorial cue. I use the activator strategy Evidence Tug-of-War to give students a visual of what constitutes **quantity of evidence**. Once students understand the quantity of evidence, the focus moves on to what constitutes **quality of evidence** using the What's Missing activator strategy. Both activator strategies can be found on pages 175 and 177. Showing students what counts as enough evidence and what is considered quality of evidence through these visual activators is helpful because it gives students a visual reminder as a reference. However, for students to master the craft of evidence, this skill must be practiced consistently using a variety of topics and purposes for writing. The strategies in this chapter focus on the integration and effective implementation of textual evidence.

EVIDENCE TUG-OF-WAR ACTIVATOR STRATEGY

Evidence Tug-of-War is a great way to *show* students what an appropriate quantity of evidence looks like. It uses the visual of a tug-of-war to compare the textual evidence from two passages. This is a great activator to use as an introductory strategy with students or as a reinforcing strategy with students who have limited experiences writing these types of responses. (Note: Because this is an activator strategy, Modifications, Extensions, and Content Area Connections are not included because it can easily be integrated into a full class period lesson using another of the strategies in this chapter.)

⚡ Quick Tip!

Instead of buying your own, borrow a rope from the physical education teacher to use for this strategy.

Putting It to Work

1. Select two passages on the same topic but with different amounts of textual evidence. One should obviously include more textual evidence than the other.

2. Prior to the lesson, choose two different colored sets of notecards, one per passage, and write down the specific textual evidence for each passage.

3. Distribute the notecards, one per student. Some students may not receive a notecard depending on the class size.

4. Lay out a large tug-of-war rope. Have students stand with their "passage team" on the appropriate side of the rope as they would in a tug-of-war game.

5. Have each student read off their evidence from the card aloud to the class.

6. Ask the students in the audience which team they think would win the contest. Students should realize that the team with the most members or the most evidence would likely win.

When to Use It

- To provide initial understanding of the necessary quantity of text evidence

- To practice using evidence from more than one source

- When you want students to compare textual evidence from more than one source

CHAPTER 1
Why Write Now?

CHAPTER 2
Parachute Writing

CHAPTER 3
Sum It All Up

CHAPTER 4
All the Right Words

CHAPTER 5
Digital Worlds

CHAPTER 6
Just the Facts

CHAPTER 7
Expecting the Unexpected

CHAPTER 1
Why Write Now?

CHAPTER 2
Parachute Writing

CHAPTER 3
Sum It All Up

CHAPTER 4
All the Right Words

CHAPTER 5
Digital Worlds

CHAPTER 6
Just the Facts

CHAPTER 7
Expecting the
Unexpected

Why It Works

- It provides a visual anchor for students to understand the necessary quantity of text evidence.

- It is active and gets students out of their seats, which helps them remember the experience.

- It can be used with a variety of text types and topics, which makes it an effective activator for multiple content areas.

CHAPTER 1
Why Write Now?

CHAPTER 2
Parachute Writing

CHAPTER 3
Sum It All Up

CHAPTER 4
All the Right Words

CHAPTER 5
Digital Worlds

CHAPTER 6
Just the Facts

CHAPTER 7
Expecting the
Unexpected

WHAT'S MISSING ACTIVATOR STRATEGY

This activator strategy works well to show students what quality evidence *looks* like. It involves the use of puzzles, taking away different puzzle pieces to illustrate how some evidence is more important than others in understanding the whole picture. (Note: Because this is an activator strategy, Modifications, Extensions, and Content Area Connections are not included because they can easily be integrated into a full class-period lesson using another of the strategies in this chapter.)

Putting It to Work

1. Select three jigsaw puzzles that can be used for this activity. (Puzzles should range in the total number of pieces, from 50 pieces to 500, for example.)

2. Remove about ten to fifteen pieces from the first puzzle. Make certain that these pieces are obscure and don't include much specific detail, such as sky, water, grass, or flowers.

3. Remove about seven or eight pieces from the second puzzle. Find pieces that give more detail, but not too much, such as pieces of an animal's fur, part of a cape or clothing item, or a vehicle.

4. Remove one or two pieces from the last puzzle. These pieces should have a key piece of evidence, such as the face of a recognizable character in the puzzle.

5. Put the pieces from all three puzzles into a small plastic bag.

CHAPTER 1
Why Write Now?

CHAPTER 2
Parachute Writing

CHAPTER 3
Sum It All Up

CHAPTER 4
All the Right Words

CHAPTER 5
Digital Worlds

CHAPTER 6
Just the Facts

CHAPTER 7
Expecting the
Unexpected

6. Create a class set of similar bags so that you have enough for students to use when working in small groups.

7. Distribute a bag to each group.

8. Instruct students to divide the pieces into three piles based on which pieces they believe go together.

9. Once they have done this, instruct them to make a guess as to what they think each complete puzzle looks like based on the evidence they have in front of them. Students will most likely be able to accurately guess what the entire puzzle looks like with the one puzzle piece, representing one piece of evidence, that is most specific.

10. Discuss as a class the idea that even though you got more details and evidence from the other puzzle pieces, they weren't specific enough to make an accurate prediction about the entire puzzle.

11. Connect these visuals to quality evidence in writing. Show students examples of specific sentences and sentences that give obscure or vague details. Ask them to tell you if these are specific details (like the face puzzle piece) or less specific (like a blue sky puzzle piece).

When to Use It

- To illustrate how some evidence is more important than others

- To remind students of the importance of clear, specific, and quality evidence

- When you want students to have a visual image that they can easily connect to a piece of written textual evidence

Why It Works

- It provides a concrete example that students can easily remember.

- It provides a visual reminder of the difference between the quality of evidence and the quantity of evidence.

- It offers students an opportunity to collaborate with classmates.

CHAPTER 1
Why Write Now?

CHAPTER 2
Parachute Writing

CHAPTER 3
Sum It All Up

CHAPTER 4
All the Right Words

CHAPTER 5
Digital Worlds

CHAPTER 6
Just the Facts

CHAPTER 7
Expecting the Unexpected

MIX AND MATCH

Evaluating and responding to a prompt using evidence from multiple sources has become an increasingly prevalent task on standardized assessments and is one that is emphasized in a variety of state and national standards. Looking across sources can sometimes be overwhelming for students as multiple sources can be information overload. Sometimes, the tendency for students is to frontload a composition with a significant amount of evidence from only one of the sources and include limited evidence from the remaining sources. Other times, students may include information or evidence that came from one of the sources but doesn't really answer the question. How often have you taught students who think that if they pick a piece of textual evidence from a passage then they have automatically answered the question? One of the most common occurrences I saw as a middle grades teacher, and even now when working with teachers and students, is many students simply "drag and drop" evidence from a passage without always considering *what* the question is asking them. Using the Mix and Match strategy can address all these possible obstacles. Plus, it helps keep students organized due to the color-coded nature of the strategy.

Quick Tip!

You may choose to have students write down facts from each text with no direction. Or you may want to give them a focus for their evidence gathering, such as find evidence of the dangers of steroid use in this article.

Putting It to Work

1. Distribute different colored paint strips to students. Each source, text, or article they need to include in their writing should have its own color paint strip. (Students should have the same number of paint strips as they have articles.)

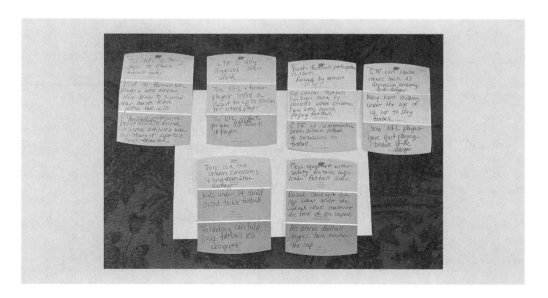

CHAPTER 1
Why Write Now?

CHAPTER 2
Parachute Writing

CHAPTER 3
Sum It All Up

CHAPTER 4
All the Right Words

CHAPTER 5
Digital Worlds

CHAPTER 6
Just the Facts

CHAPTER 7
Expecting the
Unexpected

2. Have students read the first text and list facts on one of the paint strips.

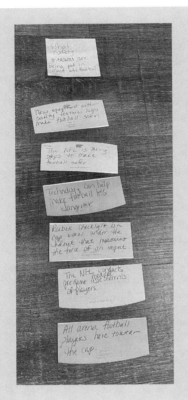

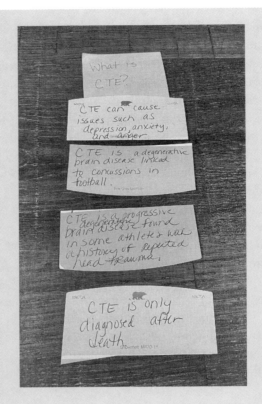

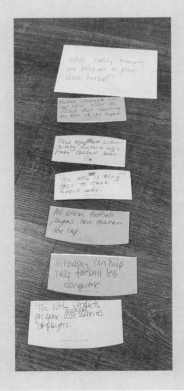

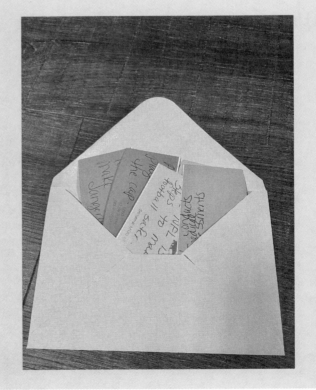

3. Have students repeat step two with the next article or source you want them to use.

4. Once students have located their evidence from each article, have students cut their paint strips into sections. Now students should have paint strip "cards" in front of them.

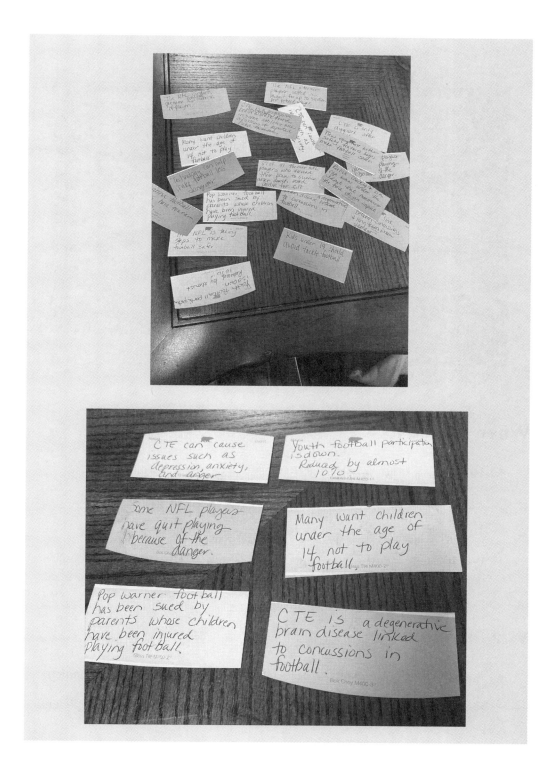

CHAPTER 1
Why Write Now?

CHAPTER 2
Parachute Writing

CHAPTER 3
Sum It All Up

CHAPTER 4
All the Right Words

CHAPTER 5
Digital Worlds

CHAPTER 6
Just the Facts

CHAPTER 7
Expecting the Unexpected

CHAPTER 1
Why Write Now?

CHAPTER 2
Parachute Writing

CHAPTER 3
Sum It All Up

CHAPTER 4
All the Right Words

CHAPTER 5
Digital Worlds

CHAPTER 6
Just the Facts

CHAPTER 7
Expecting the
Unexpected

5. Divide students into pairs and give them a notecard with the prompt they need to respond to using evidence from the different sources.

6. Have students mix and match their evidence to answer the prompt.

7. If desired, provide students with a new prompt that can be responded to with the same texts or evidence. This will help students understand how the same information can be used for different purposes.

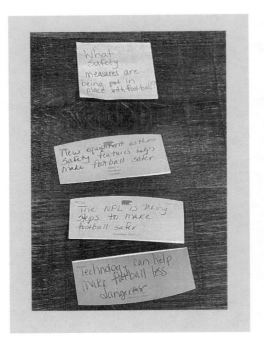
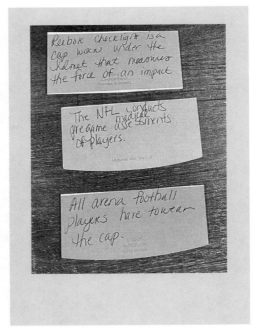

When to Use It

- To examine a variety of sources

- To craft a response that uses evidence from multiple texts

- To practice matching appropriate evidence to prompts

- When you are addressing a concept that is source rich, meaning students are going to be looking at multiple sources to learn about one concept or idea.

Why It Works

- It makes it easy for students to locate evidence that answers a specific question.

- It makes source citation more manageable due to the color-coding component.

- Students can sort the evidence and match the appropriate evidence to the correct question.

- It is a buildable lesson. You don't have to introduce all the sources in one day. Instead, you can start with one or two and add as the days and unit progress.

Modifications

- Instead of using paint strips, use different colored sticky notes or notecards to locate evidence from each article. Post different prompts on chart paper and have students stick the sticky notes or notecards that help answer the prompt onto the correct chart.

- Divide the class into groups and assign a different source to each group. With this modification, each student is only reading and locating evidence for one article, but together as a class, they are evaluating multiple articles on the same concept.

- Use video clips or images instead of traditional passages and excerpts from textbooks or literary works.

Extensions

- Use Mix and Match as a warm-up for a fully involved argument essay.

- Have students use the evidence they located from each individual article as content to use for a citation how-to lesson later on.

- Have students take their evidence and draft a constructed response answer using the evidence they located from the sources.

- Challenge students to find another source from different media to use in conjunction with the ones that were teacher-assigned.

> ### ⌖ Stop & Think
>
> Because each article is on a specific colored paint strip, citation is easy. You can coach students something like this: *"Did you use two yellow cards and one blue? Great! Now you know you need to cite Source 1 and Source 3 because Source 1 is yellow and Source 3 is blue."* Plus, if students only have two colors, but there are four texts they need to cite from, they know they need to look for evidence from the two articles (colors) they are missing. Coach like this: *"Only have red and purple? You are missing material from your yellow and blue sources."*

CHAPTER 1 Why Write Now?

CHAPTER 2 Parachute Writing

CHAPTER 3 Sum It All Up

CHAPTER 4 All the Right Words

CHAPTER 5 Digital Worlds

CHAPTER 6 Just the Facts

CHAPTER 7 Expecting the Unexpected

CHAPTER 1
Why Write Now?

CHAPTER 2
Parachute Writing

CHAPTER 3
Sum It All Up

CHAPTER 4
All the Right Words

CHAPTER 5
Digital Worlds

CHAPTER 6
Just the Facts

CHAPTER 7
Expecting the
Unexpected

Content Area Crossover

- Have students utilize different types of sources such as historical documentaries, primary sources, maps, speeches, and informational texts in history.

- Use science-based infographics, observational data, lab experiments, and textbook material as content for this strategy.

- Have students use multiple excerpts from the same novel to locate evidence when analyzing a character.

- Use this activity when teaching students how to conduct research using interviews. Instead of each paint strip focusing on a text excerpt, assign a paint strip to each interview subject. Use responses from different participants to help develop themes.

CHAPTER 1
Why Write Now?

CHAPTER 2
Parachute Writing

CHAPTER 3
Sum It All Up

CHAPTER 4
All the Right Words

CHAPTER 5
Digital Worlds

CHAPTER 6
Just the Facts

CHAPTER 7
Expecting the
Unexpected

CLOSE READING IMAGES

Close reading may look slightly different across the content areas, but it has been integrated into instruction in order to support students' explicit and deliberate reading of material to build deep understanding of a specific topic. Material selected for close reading is fairly dense and can include content that students have little background knowledge about. Often met with groans and long faces, close reading sometimes has a bad reputation in the classroom because it can *feel* super deliberate and tedious as students pore over a text looking for specific details or patterns. Plus, many times the material that they are asked to close read is not of high interest and some of the students do not have appropriate background knowledge about the material. Yet close reading doesn't have to be a tedious, boring process. It is one of the most important reading styles that we can instill in our students since as adults we use close reading all the time! Here are just a few ways that we use close reading on a regular basis:

- Reading a recipe

- Reading an instruction booklet to put something together

- Reading an owner's manual for a new piece of technical equipment

- Learning a new skill or hobby (e.g., photography)

- Reading a contract before we sign it (e.g., to buy a house or car, to take out a loan)

- Reading an insurance claim or doctor's bill

- Reading the instructions or drug interactions on medicine

By utilizing high-interest material that students have knowledge of, close reading becomes more approachable. And in today's increasingly visual world, another way to incorporate and address the skill of close reading is to utilize images, photographs, and video. Visual media offers students the opportunity to engage in critical reflection and analysis. As Rose (2016) states, "Taking an image seriously . . . involves thinking about how it positions you, its viewer, in relation to it" (p. 19). Utilizing images for close reading practice can assist students as they examine images for specific details, determine how the viewer is positioned, and critically examine the subject and material in the image.

This engagement is also a fantastic integration of multiple strategies and approaches. While standardized assessments will likely have material that might not be of high interest, because students

Close Reading Images offer opportunities to incorporate Visual Thinking Strategies (VTS), a curriculum designed to aid students in learning to read artwork (Yenawine, 2014). VTS encourages students to examine visual texts through critical questioning and examination. Further, when using video, such as movie clips or advertisements, students have the opportunity to not only analyze the visual message being presented but also consider how things such as camera angle, distance, lighting, and sound impact the meaning and message.

CHAPTER 1
Why Write Now?

CHAPTER 2
Parachute Writing

CHAPTER 3
Sum It All Up

CHAPTER 4
All the Right Words

CHAPTER 5
Digital Worlds

CHAPTER 6
Just the Facts

CHAPTER 7
Expecting the
Unexpected

have had experience with the strategy while using material that is relevant and engaging, it is likely that they will perform better on future close reading tasks.

Putting It to Work

1. Provide students with an image to closely read. This image may be directly related to a concept being studied or a random image you want students to focus on.

2. Give students a prompt or question as a focus for the image. Sample question stems are included below. The word in parenthesis is an example of how that question stem could be completed.

   - Find the real-world examples of _____ (*math*) in this image.
   - Make a list of all of the _____ (*inventions*) you notice in this image.
   - Find examples of _____ (*conflict*) in this image.
   - List the _____ (*social justice issues*) present in this image.
   - Locate the _____ (*geographic features*) in this image.

3. Have students share their findings with the class.

4. Provide students with a new image and a new prompt to use to analyze their image. This can be done individually, in pairs, or in small groups.

5. Have students share their work with the class.

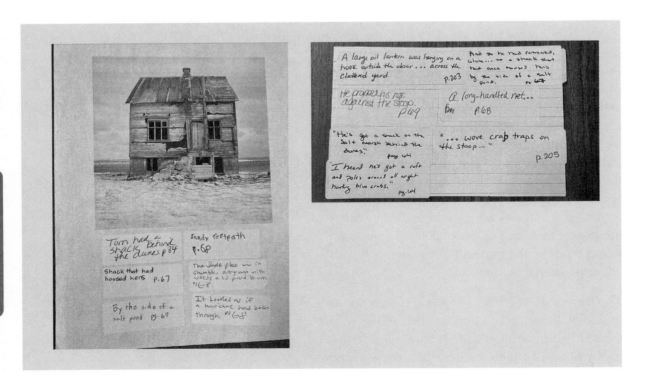

CHAPTER 1
Why Write Now?

CHAPTER 2
Parachute Writing

CHAPTER 3
Sum It All Up

CHAPTER 4
All the Right Words

CHAPTER 5
Digital Worlds

CHAPTER 6
Just the Facts

CHAPTER 7
Expecting the
Unexpected

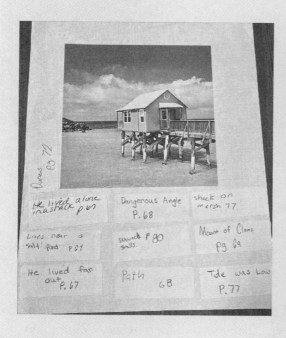

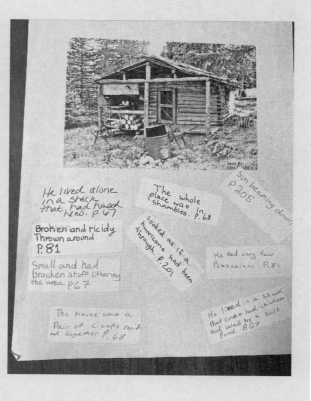

CHAPTER 1
Why Write Now?

CHAPTER 2
Parachute Writing

CHAPTER 3
Sum It All Up

CHAPTER 4
All the Right Words

CHAPTER 5
Digital Worlds

CHAPTER 6
Just the Facts

CHAPTER 7
Expecting the
Unexpected

When to Use It

- To link a visual representation with written text

- To introduce and reinforce the skill of close reading

- As an activator, exit slip, or picture break

- When you want to draw attention to figures, diagrams, and images that are used in conjunction with other texts

Why It Works

- Close Reading Images offer students a visual connection with close reading.

- They provide another layer of information through the use of pictures and images, which can be especially helpful for struggling readers and writers.

- Close Reading Images are quick and can be used as a low-stakes assignment such as a list or collection of words.

Modifications

- Have students use sticky note arrows to point out items on their images.

- Post multiple images on chart paper and have students conduct a Gallery Walk.

- Provide students with a list of possible descriptors or words that can be used for different images. Allow students to pick the ones that go with their images.

- Using the same image, give half of the class one prompt and the other half a different prompt. At the end of the lesson, display the image again and have students swap prompts for a ticket out the door.

- Develop a list of possible prompts or questions students can use with their images. Allow them to choose the one they want to focus on for their assigned image.

Extensions

- Use this activity as a springboard into the Paint Strip Partners strategy (page 210).

- Have students use their images to create boards for Pinterest Paragraphs (page 145).

- As a ticket in the door, have students make an additional observation about a classmate's image and add it to their work.

- Have students write additional prompts or questions that could be used with their image.

- Use Close Reading Photographs as a lead-in to the creation of a short movie clip where students write, direct, and film a short piece related to the content studied.

- After completing the lesson, save the images and written material. Use the written material for a new lesson where students have to try to match the written observations to the correct image.

Quick Tip!

You can have students all use the same image or distribute multiple images across the classroom all around the same topic or concept to get a wider variety of responses.

Content Area Connections

- Have students analyze a visual primary source and list the political messages, historical events, or issues that influenced it.

- Have students examine the possible examples of symbols in a work of art.

- Have students locate similar math concepts, formulas, or problem-solving strategies across a variety of example problems or images.

- Have students find examples of a specific science concept illustrated in an image (e.g., genetics or types of erosion).

- Have students describe an image using only figurative language or prepositional phrases.

CHAPTER 1
Why Write Now?

CHAPTER 2
Parachute Writing

CHAPTER 3
Sum It All Up

CHAPTER 4
All the Right Words

CHAPTER 5
Digital Worlds

CHAPTER 6
Just the Facts

CHAPTER 7
Expecting the Unexpected

CHAPTER 1
Why Write Now?

CHAPTER 2
Parachute Writing

CHAPTER 3
Sum It All Up

CHAPTER 4
All the Right Words

CHAPTER 5
Digital Worlds

CHAPTER 6
Just the Facts

CHAPTER 7
Expecting the
Unexpected

TEXT MAPPING

Text mapping is a great strategy that can be used for annotating a text, highlighting text features, and responding to texts. I first learned about text mapping when I stumbled upon the website http://www.textmapping.org/. Often textbooks and informational texts include several text features such as diagrams, charts, and graphs, along with content-rich vocabulary. In certain cases, students read in their textbooks and are asked to refer to a graph explained on prior pages. For some students, this causes confusion as the entire text is not in front of them at once. How often have you put something together with instructions that require you to refer to a diagram on page one? How about following a recipe that is written on the front and back of a page? Frustrating, isn't it? And you are an adult with significant experience reading informational texts. Now think about your students. They can get frustrated quickly. Text Mapping allows students to see the entire text at once so that they can refer to any diagrams, charts, or vocabulary right in front of them.

Here are some important tips to consider before implementing this strategy:

- Consider the spatial layout of your room. Do students have the room to spread articles out on the floor? If not, what types of workspaces are available?

- Determine how you want to group students. If you have found that there simply isn't room for all students to spread out their articles on the floor, you may consider having students work in pairs with their desks pulled together.

- How many pieces of text are you using? Is everyone reading the same article? Are you using multiple pieces of material? If so, this can impact the number of pairs or groups you use.

- Pay attention to the reading levels of the materials you are selecting. Can the students read and comprehend it on their own or with the assistance of a partner or group? Is it high-interest reading material? Is it related to what is already being studied and do students have adequate background knowledge to understand it?

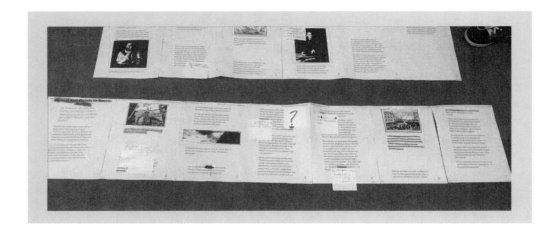

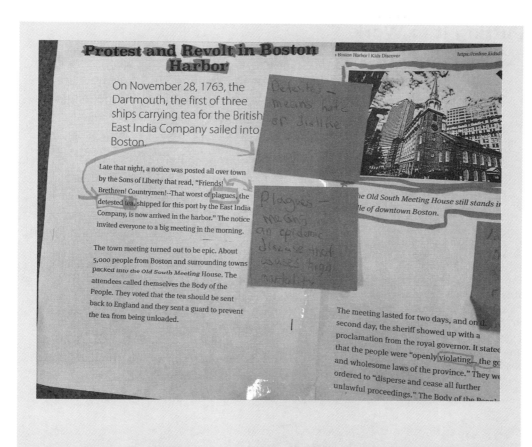

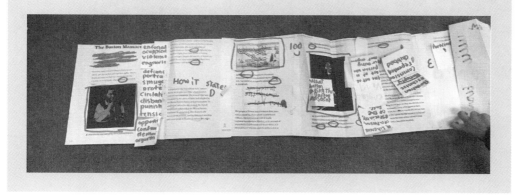

CHAPTER 1 Why Write Now?

CHAPTER 2 Parachute Writing

CHAPTER 3 Sum it All Up

CHAPTER 4 All the Right Words

CHAPTER 5 Digital Worlds

CHAPTER 6 Just the Facts

CHAPTER 7 Expecting the Unexpected

CHAPTER 1
Why Write Now?

CHAPTER 2
Parachute Writing

CHAPTER 3
Sum It All Up

CHAPTER 4
All the Right Words

CHAPTER 5
Digital Worlds

CHAPTER 6
Just the Facts

CHAPTER 7
Expecting the
Unexpected

Putting It to Work

1. Make copies of the text you want the students to read. The copies should be single sided since students will tape them together so that the entire article is put together in front of them. The text you select should be no longer than eight to ten pages, or else it's too much for students to put together and analyze in this format.

2. Pass out pencil boxes or plastic bags of the materials students will need to complete the activity. Possible materials include scissors, tape, highlighters, sticky notes, address labels, and colored pencils.

3. Have students tape the entire article together in a horizontal line.

4. Provide students with a list of tasks to complete along with the text.

5. Have students complete the tasks then share their work with the class.

Quick Tip!

Plan time for this activity directly related to the kind of task(s) you want students to complete. For example, if the objective is for students to highlight and notice specific text features, less time should be allotted than if students are expected to answer and draft questions about the reading.

Text Mapping Slip

Highlight the headings and subheadings.

Change the subheadings to hashtags.

Draw a box around any images, graphs, or figures.

Circle the bold words.

Draw an arrow from an image to the part in the text that describes it.

When to Use It

- To take a deep dive into informational texts

- To introduce or reinforce the skills of close reading, skimming and scanning, and highlighting text features

- To pay specific attention to the structure of a textbook or piece of text

- To practice finding specific evidence from a piece of text

Why It Works

- It allows students to see the entire text in front of them at once.

- Text Mapping can be used in a variety of settings because the tasks can be easily modified based on the lesson purpose or the readiness level of the students.

- It helps students pay specific attention to text features that often get overlooked.

- Text Mapping is often brief and consists mainly of annotations and responses to the text, so students are able to practice writing and responding to different genres in a quick, unique way.

Modifications

- Cut out the images and graphs included in the text and have students either draft or draw replacements or fill in the spots with the missing images that you cut out.

- Utilize prompts that focus on text features and structure to support struggling readers and writers.

- Provide English learners with address labels to translate key vocabulary into their native languages or to draw small visual representations of the words to support their understanding.

- Develop a list of possible prompts or tasks that can be completed with the text and have students choose the tasks they want to complete.

Extensions

- Use this activity to springboard into Hashtag Summaries (page 163).

- As a ticket in the door, have students answer a question based on the text that another group developed from their list of prompts.

- Have students create an Instagram Idea (page 140) that corresponds with their Text Mapping selection.

CHAPTER 1 Why Write Now?

CHAPTER 2 Parachute Writing

CHAPTER 3 Sum It All Up

CHAPTER 4 All the Right Words

CHAPTER 5 Digital Worlds

CHAPTER 6 Just the Facts

CHAPTER 7 Expecting the Unexpected

CHAPTER 1
Why Write Now?

CHAPTER 2
Parachute Writing

CHAPTER 3
Sum It All Up

CHAPTER 4
All the Right Words

CHAPTER 5
Digital Worlds

CHAPTER 6
Just the Facts

CHAPTER 7
Expecting the
Unexpected

- Use in conjunction with the Mix and Match strategy (page 179) when working across multiple sources.

Content Area Connections

- Use Text Mapping at the beginning of the year as a way to introduce students to the layout and structure of their math textbook.

- Use it in science when implementing complex, multiday labs that have a series of steps.

- Use Text Mapping to help students analyze written primary sources.

- When introducing a new genre of writing such as informational writing, use samples to draw attention to specific text features and components of the genre.

CHAPTER 1
Why Write Now?

CHAPTER 2
Parachute Writing

CHAPTER 3
Sum It All Up

CHAPTER 4
All the Right Words

CHAPTER 5
Digital Worlds

CHAPTER 6
Just the Facts

CHAPTER 7
Expecting the
Unexpected

✏️ WRITE AROUND THE TEXT

Write Around the Text utilizes a collaborative writing approach and is a great strategy to use with a variety of text types. Collaborative writing can offer a number of benefits in the classroom due to its cooperative nature and open-ended goals. In many instances, cooperative writing can provide students with the ability to write and respond with each other in a variety of settings for a number of purposes. Because students are creating a collaborative product, the individual contributions are much more manageable due to their abbreviated response lengths.

The flexibility of this strategy allows teachers to tailor the activity to best suit the class, time frame, and content. Plus, because students are divided into groups, this allows teachers to assign a variety of reading material centered around a specific theme. In addition, it is an easy way for teachers to vary the reading level of multiple pieces of texts for their students without drawing specific attention to the differences in reading proficiency that may exist among the students. Since everyone is reading around a centralized theme, class discussions are still beneficial and useful. And because multiple materials can be used, students can view a concept or event from multiple perspectives. In addition, this engagement works beautifully in the virtual classroom when using the breakout room feature in many web conferencing platforms.

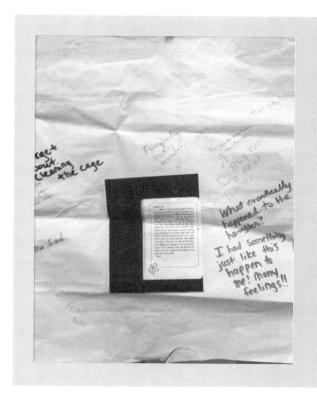
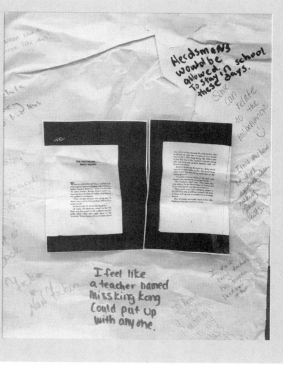

CHAPTER 1
Why Write Now?

CHAPTER 2
Parachute Writing

CHAPTER 3
Sum It All Up

CHAPTER 4
All the Right Words

CHAPTER 5
Digital Worlds

CHAPTER 6
Just the Facts

CHAPTER 7
Expecting the
Unexpected

Putting It to Work

1. Select an appropriate text for students to read. Select multiple texts if you want to divide students into groups based on their reading readiness levels.

2. Make a copy of the text(s) and paste it onto a large sheet of chart paper, one chart paper per group.

3. Divide students into groups and give each group one of the chart papers.

4. Instruct the students to read the text and then respond to it. These responses can take on a number of forms, such as thoughts, ideas, connections, or questions they have about the text. Students could even respond through a tweet or a hashtag.

5. Have students share with the class orally or by completing a Gallery Walk.

6. Students may need some "nudge questions" or sentence starters to get them going. Here are a few ideas:

   - The text reminds me of _____.
   - After reading, I wonder _____.
   - Make a text-to-self connection.
   - Draft a question that can accompany this text.
   - How does this text make you feel?
   - What happens next in this text?

When to Use It

- As a way to effectively move through the content of a textbook chapter
- To break a large piece of text into sections for student responses
- To collaboratively respond to an excerpt or specific piece of text
- When you want to utilize multiple types of text samples for a lesson

Why It Works

- It allows students to focus on a specific piece of text.
- It divides text into chunks that are more manageable for students to read and discuss.
- Write Around the Text allows students to read and discuss a piece of text with their peers.

- It can be extended or lengthened based on the nature of the content.

- Students receive text samples at their own reading level, which supports their individual reading development.

Modifications

- Invite students to develop the nudge questions to use when responding to their assigned texts.

- Give students different colored sticky notes to annotate and respond to different aspects of the text (e.g., blue: text-to-text connection, green: important vocabulary words, yellow: questions about the text, pink: a hashtag summarizing the text).

- Allow English learners to discuss orally their initial responses in their native language and then translate their responses to English.

- Have students draw a picture as an additional response to the text.

Extensions

- Use Write Around the Text as a way to introduce students to some of the tasks associated with the Text Mapping strategy. (page 190).

- Have students locate or create images and graphics to supplement their texts that don't include those text features.

- Allow students to find a companion text that could be used to support the main text or content being studied.

Content Area Connections

- Use Write Around the Text to introduce and integrate primary sources into instruction.

- Have students annotate diagrams of cells, anatomy figures, or other science content that involve identification and labeling.

- Ask students to respond and critique works of art.

- Use excerpts of literature for specific response questions, or use this to expose students to multiple examples of poetry.

CHAPTER 1
Why Write Now?

CHAPTER 2
Parachute Writing

CHAPTER 3
Sum It All Up

CHAPTER 4
All the Right Words

CHAPTER 5
Digital Worlds

CHAPTER 6
Just the Facts

CHAPTER 7
Expecting the Unexpected

CHAPTER 1
Why Write Now?

CHAPTER 2
Parachute Writing

CHAPTER 3
Sum It All Up

CHAPTER 4
All the Right Words

CHAPTER 5
Digital Worlds

CHAPTER 6
Just the Facts

CHAPTER 7
Expecting the
Unexpected

MURDER MYSTERIES

As a little girl, I often watched *Matlock* and *Murder, She Wrote* with my grand-mother when I spent the night at her house on the weekends. Similarly, my teenage daughter, Amelia, is fascinated with *Criminal Minds,* another show that utilizes real-world scenarios for collecting evidence when solving a crime. Although the plot of both shows that I watched as a child fascinated me, I didn't consider that the main characters of these television dramas were collecting evidence to build an argument regarding the possible suspect. Instead, I viewed them as individuals who located clues and then used those clues to make a claim or come to a conclusion regarding the culprit. However, the tactics these stars used in these shows are some of the same strategies that students use or *should* use when acquiring evidence and making a claim.

By incorporating the use of mysteries or crime investigations into instruction, we are providing students with a specific purpose around which to practice specific skills that they often find tedious or difficult. Plus, solving a mystery or conducting an investigation is an engaging way to incorporate the instruction of close reading, textual evidence, and making a claim. By examining "crime science evidence," students can collect and position evidence to solve a variety of crimes and mysteries.

The easiest way to incorporate this idea into the classroom is to utilize a book compilation of crime scene puzzles or murder mysteries. Some of my favorites are *Crime and Puzzlement: 24 Solve-Them-Yourself Picture Mysteries* by Lawrence Treat (2003) (there are multiple volumes in this series), *You Be the Jury: Courtroom Collection* by Marvin Miller (2000), and *Two-Minute Mysteries* by Donald J. Sobol (1991). Or you can create your own crime scene lesson using images, props, and written clues and evidence.

If you are developing your own crime scene, you will need to create a narrative account of what happened. This doesn't need to be long—about a paragraph or two will do. In the narrative account, make sure you:

- Provide a brief backstory of the event. A sample is included below.

- Include either an image or drawing of the crime scene, or use props in the classroom to create an actual crime scene.

- Include the names of the characters who took part in the event.

- Give the students any details needed to assist them with examining the evidence.

Here is a sample narrative backstory.

Dr. Page was planning to attend the awards dinner of his beloved colleague, Dr. Gambrell. After work, he came home, changed into his tux (the event was black tie), and proceeded to head out the door. Unfortunately, Dr. Page never made it to the dinner. He was discovered by his housekeeper, Ms. Gayle, who had returned to get the sweater that she left when cleaning Dr. Page's home earlier that day. According to Ms. Gayle, Dr. Page was startled when she entered the home and fell down the stairs. "I feel terrible. He must have tripped and hit his head."

Similarly, when creating your own physical crime scene or illustration, take into account the following:

- Who are your suspects?

- What is the setting?

- How does this image or physical crime scene correspond with your narrative account?

- What physical objects do you need to include in the crime scene?

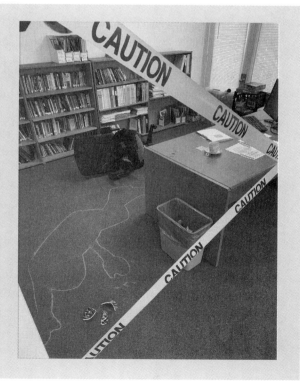

CHAPTER 1
Why Write Now?

CHAPTER 2
Parachute Writing

CHAPTER 3
Sum It All Up

CHAPTER 4
All the Right Words

CHAPTER 5
Digital Worlds

CHAPTER 6
Just the Facts

CHAPTER 7
Expecting the Unexpected

CHAPTER 1
Why Write Now?

CHAPTER 2
Parachute Writing

CHAPTER 3
Sum It All Up

CHAPTER 4
All the Right Words

CHAPTER 5
Digital Worlds

CHAPTER 6
Just the Facts

CHAPTER 7
Expecting the
Unexpected

Putting It to Work

1. Create a crime scene in the class using props for the students to examine.

2. Divide students into groups of three or four.

3. Include information on notecards that list all the physical evidence in the scene.

4. Provide students with a narrative account of the crime scene.

5. Use a list of guided questions for the students to consider when examining the evidence. These questions should be specific to the crime scene scenario and will vary. Examples could include the following:

   - Do you think the victim was alone in the room?
   - Was the door forced open or already unlocked?
   - Did anyone eat the food on the table?

6. Have students identify a suspect and use textual evidence from the notecards and the narrative account of the scene to support their claim. Students should be able to answer the following questions for each crime or murder mystery:

   - Who committed the crime?
   - What was the motive?
   - What weapon was used? (may not be applicable to all scenarios)
   - When did the crime take place?
   - Where did the crime take place?

7. Have groups share with the class.

When to Use It

- To practice the skills of close reading and the acquisition of textual evidence

- To engage students with skills they often find boring or difficult

- To examine multiple sources or pieces of evidence and make a claim based on information from more than one source

Why It Works

- It utilizes pictorial evidence and written accounts.

- Guiding questions help students determine what matters and the details they should attend to.

- The Murder Mysteries strategy provides a real-world connection to an academic task.

- Murder Mysteries are high interest and engaging.

Modifications

- Provide students with an image of the crime scene and have them draft a possible explanation or account of the scene.

- Use an image of a fender bender and have students determine who they think is at fault based on the physical evidence and eyewitness accounts.

- Give students other possible pieces of evidence that might belong in the crime scene. Have them determine which evidence belongs where and justify their choices.

Extensions

- Have students create their own crime scenes based on an event in history, current event, or selection of text from a book.

- Have students draft possible interview questions to ask potential suspects.

- Provide a set of crime scene images and a set of eyewitness accounts and have students match the appropriate account to the correct crime scene image.

Content Area Connections

- Incorporate clues that require students to complete mathematical computations.

- Present historical unsolved mysteries such as the Lost Colony of Roanoke or the vanished crew of the *Mary Celeste*. Or check out Jane Yolen's children's book series that addresses unsolved historical mysteries!

- Have students research specific laws and punishments or fines and determine which laws were violated in the given crime and what the maximum fine or penalty is.

CHAPTER 1 Why Write Now?

CHAPTER 2 Parachute Writing

CHAPTER 3 Sum It All Up

CHAPTER 4 All the Right Words

CHAPTER 5 Digital Worlds

CHAPTER 6 Just the Facts

CHAPTER 7 Expecting the Unexpected

CHAPTER 1
Why Write Now?

CHAPTER 2
Parachute Writing

CHAPTER 3
Sum It All Up

CHAPTER 4
All the Right Words

CHAPTER 5
Digital Worlds

CHAPTER 6
Just the Facts

CHAPTER 7
Expecting the
Unexpected

CONTINUUM DEBATE 2.0

Crafting an oral argument is a valuable skill that students in all grade levels and content areas need to master. Time to practice their orator skills is time well spent, as many students will be required to speak in front of others as part of their academic demands as well as in their future careers. Plus, you never know when you might actively need to call on your argumentative competencies, even as a young person. For example, as my oldest daughter approached high school, she began to craft a PowerPoint presentation arguing reasons why she should be able to leave her private middle school for the public high school in our zoning area. This presentation that she crafted required her to use both her written skills *and* her oral presentation skills as she presented her case to her father and me.

I have successfully used continuum debates with many students over the years. I included the strategy in my first book, but since its release, I have continued to modify and enhance the use of continuum debates. Thus, I present here Continuum Debate 2.0!

When using Continuum Debate 2.0, students use textual evidence to craft their argument. When the arguments are shared, students are able to hear their classmate's argument and also play an active role in the response to that argument. This is an extremely important skill as it serves as practice for evaluating arguments, something that is heavily emphasized in many states' standards. Being able to determine the strong and weak spots in someone's argument can also help students as they craft their own.

 Quick Tip!

If you are concerned that students will not have enough background information from the text(s) you choose with this strategy, try one of the other strategies in this book that help activate prior knowledge first, such as Quick Writes (page 24).

I have found that choosing polarizing historical figures or events makes this strategy extremely engaging for students. Current events also serve as great starter topics for continuum debates because they are real-world relevant. However, it is important to make certain the students have enough background information about the topic and relevant texts to draw their evidence from so that they can clearly articulate their argument.

Putting It to Work

1. Choose a topic that is debatable and defensible but also is one that students have adequate background knowledge about and relevant texts to support their arguments.

2. Provide students with a small 3" x 5" notecard.

3. Have students determine which side they want to debate. In most cases, this is a *for* or *against* choice, a *this* or *that* choice, or something similar.

4. Once students have determined their stance, remind them of their purpose.

5. Have students draft their argument on the provided notecard, using specific text evidence to support their stance. Allow about 20 to 25 minutes for students to draft these statements.

Quick Tip!

While I recommend allowing students the opportunity to choose their side, it is also acceptable (if students have enough background on both sides) to assign a side to them. This can ensure that you have a balance of material to use for both opposing sides.

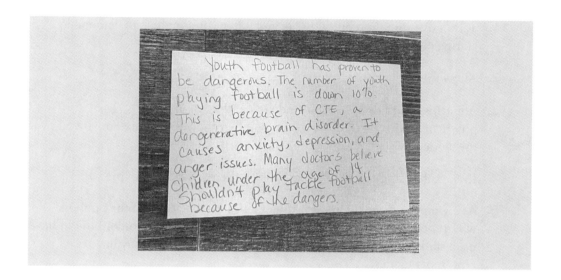

6. Using masking or painter's tape, tape a line on the floor of your classroom.

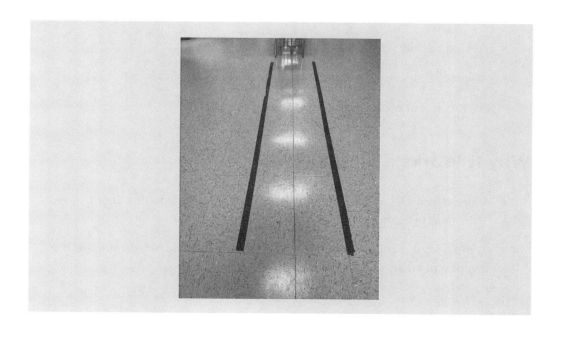

CHAPTER 1
Why Write Now?

CHAPTER 2
Parachute Writing

CHAPTER 3
Sum it All Up

CHAPTER 4
All the Right Words

CHAPTER 5
Digital Worlds

CHAPTER 6
Just the Facts

CHAPTER 7
Expecting the Unexpected

CHAPTER 1
Why Write Now?

CHAPTER 2
Parachute Writing

CHAPTER 3
Sum It All Up

CHAPTER 4
All the Right Words

CHAPTER 5
Digital Worlds

CHAPTER 6
Just the Facts

CHAPTER 7
Expecting the
Unexpected

7. Choose two students with opposing views to come and share their arguments. These students are called the anchors.

8. Have one student stand on one end of the line and the other stand at the opposite end.

9. Give each student about a minute to state their argument.

10. Once both have done so, ask for a couple of volunteers to come and place themselves on the line between the two students based on how convinced they were by the students' arguments.

11. Take a five-minute rebuttal break and allow your anchors to elaborate, clarify, or add to their argument.

12. Allow the anchors to re-present their arguments to the class.

13. After this rebuttal, have each student standing on the line physically move themself based on whether they were more convinced by the student.

14. Invite other students to come and place themselves on the line.

15. As a wrap-up, have the class list the tactics used by each of the anchors when they presented their arguments. For example, one student might have used statistics to solidify their argument while the other may have used emotional tactics.

When to Use It

- To practice the craft of oral debate

- As a conclusion or wrap-up of a concept or unit

- To practice locating text evidence for a debatable topic

- As a review of previously taught content

Why It Works

- Continuum Debate 2.0 gives students the opportunity to talk about a topic with their classmates.

- It provides the opportunity for students to use text evidence to support the crafting of an argument.

- The written component is brief and emphasis is placed on the oral debate itself.

- It offers students an opportunity to critique an argument.

Modifications

- Have students complete the engagement with partners and draft their arguments collaboratively.

- Instead of having students come stand on the line based on their personal opinion, have students come up with additional evidence that could support one of the sides of the argument. Have students place their evidence along the line based on which side it supports and then rank the evidence in order from strongest to weakest.

- Provide students with ready-made arguments for your anchors and have students gather evidence from their readings to incorporate in the sample. Then follow the directions as written.

- Allow students to use notecards to bullet their information instead of requiring them to write it in paragraph format initially.

Extensions

- Use Continuum Debate 2.0 in conjunction with the What's the Word (page 117) strategy.

- Have students use Continuum Debate 2.0 as an extension for the Attack or Defend Writing strategy (page 33).

- Have students analyze the language they are using in their arguments to ensure that they are employing appropriate, high-level academic vocabulary.

- Use the Mix and Match strategy (page 179) for students to add more evidence to their arguments.

Content Area Connections

- Have students debate government policy, war tactics, or social and economic issues.

CHAPTER 1 Why Write Now?

CHAPTER 2 Parachute Writing

CHAPTER 3 Sum It All Up

CHAPTER 4 All the Right Words

CHAPTER 5 Digital Worlds

CHAPTER 6 Just the Facts

CHAPTER 7 Expecting the Unexpected

CHAPTER 1
Why Write Now?

CHAPTER 2
Parachute Writing

CHAPTER 3
Sum It All Up

CHAPTER 4
All the Right Words

CHAPTER 5
Digital Worlds

CHAPTER 6
Just the Facts

CHAPTER 7
Expecting the
Unexpected

- For complex math problems that can be solved using multiple methods or approaches, have students debate which approach is best to employ.

- Have students debate health and sports topics including steroid use, college recruitment tactics, or weight-training regimes.

- In ELA classes, have students debate a character's actions or motives in a literary work.

CHAPTER 1
Why Write Now?

CHAPTER 2
Parachute Writing

CHAPTER 3
Sum It All Up

CHAPTER 4
All the Right Words

CHAPTER 5
Digital Worlds

CHAPTER 6
Just the Facts

CHAPTER 7
Expecting the
Unexpected

TWO TRUTHS AND A LIE

In today's world of fake news, it is more important than ever for students to be able to critically read a piece of text and analyze the content. Depending on people's biases, background, or past experiences, two people can read the same text and come up with very different conclusions. The strategy of Two Truths and a Lie helps students specifically look at what the text says to practice discerning fact from fiction.

This strategy can also help our students when taking assessments. We often show students how to identify ways that test makers draft questions to purposely trick them and misidentify facts. This strategy helps students practice identifying false statements by teaching them *how* to write questions that can trick their classmates.

Putting It to Work

1. Select a text that focuses on a current topic or unit of study. Read the selected text as a class.

2. Provide students with examples of truths and lies about the topic or concept, directly related to what was read in the text.

3. Have students use text evidence to explain what made the statements either true or false.

4. Share their statements with the class.

5. Create an anchor chart or list of phrases to use for drafting the statements, such as *except*, *always*, *all*, *never*, and *sometimes*.

6. Give students a new text on a similar topic for collaborative practice.

7. Divide students into pairs or small groups. Instruct students to draft two accurate statements (truths) and one false statement (lie) about the concept using evidence from the text.

8. Have students share their statements with the class and allow the class time to determine which statements are truths and which are lies. Instruct students to give text evidence as to why a statement is accurate or inaccurate.

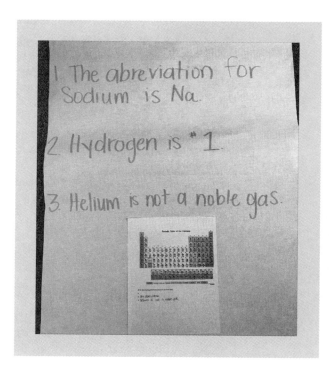

CHAPTER 1
Why Write Now?

CHAPTER 2
Parachute Writing

CHAPTER 3
Sum It All Up

CHAPTER 4
All the Right Words

CHAPTER 5
Digital Worlds

CHAPTER 6
Just the Facts

CHAPTER 7
Expecting the
Unexpected

When to Use It

- To focus on specific details of a topic or concept

- As a way to teach students how to think and write like a test writer

- To see what students have learned from reading a text

- As an end-of-unit assessment to measure student learning

- To utilize as a different form of assessment

Why It Works

- It allows students to use inaccurate or misinformation in a more positive manner.

- It helps students practice close reading skills when drafting statements that include subtle nuances that make them either inaccurate or accurate.

- Two Truths and a Lie address the skill of writing with specificity.

- It can be used as a ticket in the door, an exit slip, or as another quick writing task that can be inserted into a variety of lessons.

Modifications

- Provide students with premade truths and lies that they need to sort into the appropriate category.

- Distribute certain colored sticky notes or notecards, which correspond to either a lie or a truth. Based on the color card the students receive, they draft either a lie or a truth.

- Provide students with accurate statements about the concept that they have to alter to make false.

- Have students construct multiple lies and one truth and follow the instructions as written.

Extensions

- Use the prior day's truths or lies as tickets in the door. Display two pieces of chart paper in the room with the headings "Truths" and "Lies." Distribute the truths and lies from the prior day, one to each student as well as a blank notecard, as they walk in the door. Have the students place their provided statement on the appropriate chart paper along with an explanation as to why it is true or false on the blank notecard.

- Have students use their truths and lies to draft sample test questions to include on assessments.

- Have students revisit prior truths and lies to revise based on new information acquired.

Content Area Connections

- Use historical photographs and primary sources as the basis to create the truths and lies.

- Use images of habitats, environmental policies, and cells to complete this engagement.

- Use maps of specific regions, infographics, or other informational texts for close reads as the basis to create the truths and lies.

- Use math problems and have students draft statements that correspond to the problems.

- Use infographics or other figures from across content areas as sample texts for this engagement.

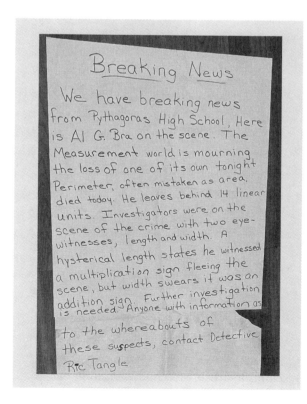

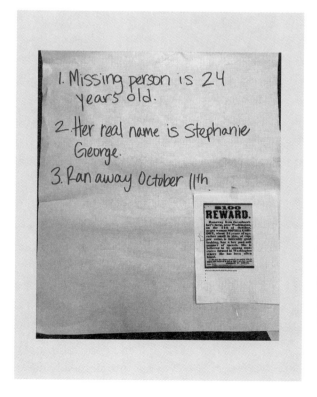

CHAPTER 1 Why Write Now?

CHAPTER 2 Parachute Writing

CHAPTER 3 Sum It All Up

CHAPTER 4 All the Right Words

CHAPTER 5 Digital Worlds

CHAPTER 6 Just the Facts

CHAPTER 7 Expecting the Unexpected

CHAPTER 1
Why Write Now?

CHAPTER 2
Parachute Writing

CHAPTER 3
Sum It All Up

CHAPTER 4
All the Right Words

CHAPTER 5
Digital Worlds

CHAPTER 6
Just the Facts

CHAPTER 7
Expecting the
Unexpected

PAINT STRIP PARTNERS

When a piece of writing involves explaining multiple steps, it is easy for students to forget all the steps included. This style of writing is often used in math and science when students explain mathematical or scientific processes or analyses they used to complete a process or problem. Paint Strip Partners assist students in breaking a task into smaller chunks and then writing an explanation of each part of the task. It is a great strategy to use when you want students to look at a task through different perspectives or lenses, and it is especially helpful when addressing problems that involve a series of steps or processes. Paint Strip Partners also allow students to view specific sections of a process when writing their explanation, which makes writing the larger composition much easier. Plus you can also modify this assignment so that students can collaborate with a partner and add other components such as a justification section or a questions section that accompanies it.

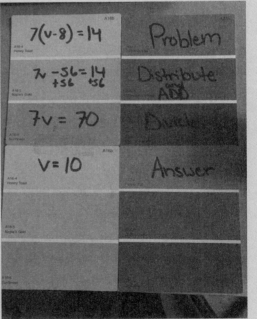

Putting It to Work

1. Select a concept, problem, or topic that is multistep in nature (e.g., problem-solving process, scientific process for an experiment, battle-plan sequence).

CHAPTER 1
Why Write Now?

CHAPTER 2
Parachute Writing

CHAPTER 3
Sum It All Up

CHAPTER 4
All the Right Words

CHAPTER 5
Digital Worlds

CHAPTER 6
Just the Facts

CHAPTER 7
Expecting the
Unexpected

2. Distribute a paint strip to each student and have them briefly write out the steps of the selected problem, sequence, or process.

3. Divide students into pairs and have them share the steps with their partner.

4. Distribute a second paint strip to each student.

5. Model how to take the brief explanation of a step and write a more detailed explanation in complete sentences on the same corresponding section of the second paint strip.

6. Have students take their series of steps, notes, or computations and use their other paint strips to write the explanation of each individual step.

7. Allow students time to share with their partners.

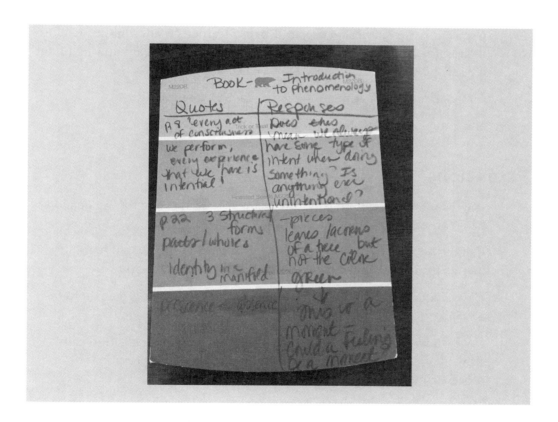

When to Use It

- As a way to first take notes and then explain

- To complete an activity and then explain the thinking

- To build on previous lessons (over the course of a few days) and complete a more comprehensive product

- As a springboard into constructed responses

CHAPTER 1
Why Write Now?

CHAPTER 2
Parachute Writing

CHAPTER 3
Sum It All Up

CHAPTER 4
All the Right Words

CHAPTER 5
Digital Worlds

CHAPTER 6
Just the Facts

CHAPTER 7
Expecting the
Unexpected

Why It Works

- Paint Strip Partners break a task into manageable chunks.

- They break down information into chunks by creating a list of facts or processes (in math) and then incorporating the explanation component.

- They can be extended or lengthened based on the nature of the content.

Modifications

- Have students complete this activity over two days:
  - Day 1: Students take notes or complete the computations.
  - Day 2: Students write their complete explanations.

- Use Paint Strip Partners to support English learners by allowing them to use their home language on the first strip and then translating it into English on the second strip.

- Allow students to draw pictures to explain their steps or thinking.

- Use Paint Strip Partners as a review or reteaching tool.

Extensions

- Have students use a third paint strip to write a justification (or explanation of why) for each step.

- Cut the original paint strips into individual blocks and have students put them back in the correct order to match their full explanations.

- Have students add a graphic or image to accompany their explanations (e.g., a graph or labeled diagram).

- Have students partner up to explain their paint strips. Using a third paint strip, their partner should summarize their classmate's explanations or process on their new paint strip.

Content Area Connections

- Have students write direct quotes from a text or novel on one paint strip and then a paraphrased version on the other paint strip.

- Have students complete the computations for a math problem on one paint strip and then explain the process or their mathematical thinking for each step on a second paint strip.

- Have students list the main events from a historical time period or war on one paint strip and then explain the historical significance on the second paint strip.

- Have students make a list of specific periods in art and include a description of each period on one paint strip and list specific works that are part of each period on the second paint strip.

- To support character building or bullying prevention, have students list specific behaviors or scenarios on one paint strip and then write possible solutions or approaches to the scenario on the second paint strip.

CHAPTER 1
Why Write Now?

CHAPTER 2
Parachute Writing

CHAPTER 3
Sum It All Up

CHAPTER 4
All the Right Words

CHAPTER 5
Digital Worlds

CHAPTER 6
Just the Facts

CHAPTER 7
Expecting the Unexpected

CHAPTER 1
Why Write Now?

CHAPTER 2
Parachute Writing

CHAPTER 3
Sum It All Up

CHAPTER 4
All the Right Words

CHAPTER 5
Digital Worlds

CHAPTER 6
Just the Facts

CHAPTER 7
Expecting the
Unexpected

EXPECTING THE UNEXPECTED

Answers to Your Most Common Questions

Every experienced teacher knows that even with the best instructional strategies, materials, administrative support, and parental involvement, sometimes things simply fall flat with their students. In fact, from my experience, it is often when I expect a lesson or strategy to go off without a hitch that the wheels come off. I remember planning fantastic lessons that I thought would take all period, but in reality were done in twenty minutes, leaving me to scramble to fill the remaining block of time. Similarly, I planned quick engagements that I thought my students would be able to complete in ten or fifteen minutes but ended up lasting all period putting me behind schedule. And then there are the technology problems—websites that work beautifully when tested by one teacher but can't handle the traffic of thirty students at once, live documents that don't load or edit in a timely manner, and the list goes on. And don't even get me started on the challenges of teaching online, face-to-face, or hybrid during a pandemic! These challenges are not unique to me or to any teacher. In fact, we all have experienced lessons that simply didn't go as planned. The important thing to remember is that no matter how far off the rails the lesson goes, you have to get the train on the track again and press forward.

Throughout this book I have provided some ideas and strategies for the writing classroom that I have found to be effective and engaging; however, I would be remiss to say that there won't be challenges at some point. And although I can't promise that you will reach every student every time, or that every strategy will work with every class, if you are flexible enough and are willing to "fail forward," I can assure you that writing lessons across the content areas can be successful.

CHAPTER 1
Why Write Now?

CHAPTER 2
Parachute Writing

CHAPTER 3
Sum It All Up

CHAPTER 4
All the Right Words

CHAPTER 5
Digital Worlds

CHAPTER 6
Just the Facts

CHAPTER 7
Expecting the
Unexpected

So, what can you do when challenges present themselves? How can you expect the unexpected? This chapter will offer some tips and suggestions that may help you get through the challenges of writing across the content areas and are centered around questions that I often receive when working with teachers across the country. No matter where I am, it seems that many teachers are facing the same challenges and have similar concerns.

What Do I Do About Students Who Aren't Motivated?

One challenge that teachers often face is student motivation. How do we get students to *want* to engage with the material and learn what is being taught? This seems to be a question on teachers' minds no matter where they teach or what grade level they work with. From kindergarten teachers who have students who don't want to draw an illustration to go with their sentences to high school teachers who have students who don't really want to write that essay, getting students motivated to complete their academic tasks can sometimes be difficult.

Lack of motivation can often be attributed to the fact that students may not see the relevance between their academic and personal lives. Remember the section about "third spaces" in Chapter 5? That merger of home and academic practices can offer students the connection that is missing and can improve student motivation. Too often, student interest and ideas are not the driving force behind the planning of instruction and curriculum, especially when it comes to tasks that involve written composition. Although we know there is a significant connection between motivation, student interest, and learning, this is not always possible in every academic setting. Think of it less as a complete overhaul of everything you are primed to teach and more as little tweaks here and there. It would be unrealistic to expect you to completely overhaul everything you do and use material that every student finds interesting. Instead, think of how you can infuse what you are already teaching with high-interest, motivational material. For example, when it comes to teaching informational text structure, it would be beneficial to integrate informational texts that capitalize on student interests instead of simply using the material that came with the textbook. Simply adding a few new sources or strategies can make a world of difference in student performance. Plus, varying the *types* of material (video clips, music, images, primary sources, etc.) can also aid in capturing and keeping student interest.

Recently, within a sixth-grade lesson on informational text structure and the credibility of sources, I used a variety of nonfiction texts about the dangers of football. My bell ringer activity was an infographic that provided statistical information about football and concussions. For the work period, I utilized several articles that addressed similar topics. One article addressed the health dangers that result from repeated concussions, one addressed parental concerns and the decline in youth football participation, and the third addressed a legal battle resulting from a player's health issues obtained while playing football. Because I knew that the students were interested in this topic, they were more engaged and motivated. Plus, because I used more than one article, I was able to find texts that were on a variety of reading levels so that more students would be able to understand the material. In addition, each of the text samples was formatted in a different way. One was heavy with written text, one utilized a variety of text features including text boxes and parenthetical information, and the other included more photographs and captions. Plus, the infographic was similar to many of the charts and figures often utilized in science and math textbooks due to its spatial layout and inclusion of statistical information.

For students who struggled with the reading of the text, the article that included additional photographs allowed them to rely on those visual images to help cement meaning and understanding. Because all the samples were informational texts, but all looked different, it allowed students to see how a specific genre of writing may be formatted in different ways, yet maintain some common features.

While locating material that is interesting and more engaging does take time and effort, it is likely that this will increase motivation. But how do you know what students are interested in? Just ask! Recently I was speaking with a high school teacher about whether his students use Instagram or tweet frequently. He responded, "How should I know?" Friends, you must ask. How long and how much effort does it really take to ask what your students are interested in? Greeting students as they come into class, asking about their weekends, and commenting on items you know they like (movies, television, music, etc.) can provide you with nuggets of information that can be helpful in classroom instruction.

In my experience, I found that I bought more goodwill with my students simply by just being interested in them. Not just interested in who they were as students, but who they were as people. When students know you are interested in them and are willing to make connections, many of them will perform better. One of my very favorite students was a talented basketball and football player, who as an eighth grader, barely read on a third-grade level. Because I knew how much sports meant to this student, every time I read about one of his games in the paper where his name was mentioned, I cut it out and either gave it to him in class or mailed it to him once he went to high school. Plus, whenever possible, I brought in texts about sports, asked him questions about basketball when I did not understand something, and celebrated his accomplishments, big or small. This resulted in outstanding performance in my class and increased his motivation. In fact, it was not unusual to hear other teachers remark that they could not get him to do anything in their classes, so how did he perform so well in mine?

The secret is there is no secret. All I did was work to get to know the student and do my best to incorporate materials that capitalized on his interests. Now, I am not saying that I was always able to successfully reach every student. I know that there were ones who I missed. However, I'd like to think that because I worked to get to know my students, I was able to reach some who otherwise would have fallen through the cracks had I utilized traditional materials and teaching methods. (And just an update on this student, I recently ran into him in downtown Atlanta over a decade after having him in my class. Can you guess what he told me? "You sent me my basketball stuff in the mail!")

CHAPTER 1
Why Write Now?

CHAPTER 2
Parachute Writing

CHAPTER 3
Sum It All Up

CHAPTER 4
All the Right Words

CHAPTER 5
Digital Worlds

CHAPTER 6
Just the Facts

CHAPTER 7
Expecting the Unexpected

CHAPTER 1
Why Write Now?

CHAPTER 2
Parachute Writing

CHAPTER 3
Sum It All Up

CHAPTER 4
All the Right Words

CHAPTER 5
Digital Worlds

CHAPTER 6
Just the Facts

CHAPTER 7
Expecting the
Unexpected

However, knowing students entails more than simply knowing what they like or what they are interested in. It also involves knowing what attitudes they harbor about certain subjects, skills, and concepts. Many students already have very cemented beliefs about certain concepts as well as firmly rooted beliefs about what they do well and what they don't. Knowing these can also aid in determining the best avenues for exploration in the content classroom. Plus, getting to know your students isn't exclusive to a certain grade level or age. Even now in my teaching at the graduate level, I still send students notes and cards in the mail and make sure that I get to know them both as students and individuals.

What About Students Who Are Reading and Writing Below Grade Level?

When I taught middle school, roughly 90 percent of my students read below grade level and did not pass the state assessment in writing. By middle and high school, many struggling readers have mastered "fake reading" and are pros at playing the game of school reading. We've all done it, myself included. I will never forget one of my first PhD classes where we were required to read *The Metaphysical Club* by Louis Menand. For two solid weeks, I was convinced my professor assigned that book just so we would get frustrated and know how our students felt when they were learning to read. I quickly found out that was NOT her intention, but no matter how hard I tried, I could not comprehend that book. So, what did I do? I went to class and listened to what she said and what some of my colleagues said. Then I made one well-placed comment that was a combination of all of those comments and it worked. I fake read my way through that book and I am here to tell you, our students are doing the very same thing.

Now, why do students fake read? Sometimes it's because the material they have been given is too difficult for them to read. Other times, they may be able to decode the words, but the comprehension isn't there. One way to address this challenge is to differentiate reading and writing tasks. While you may use the textbook as a resource, bring in additional text materials that are written at a variety of reading levels and are in a variety of formats. Not all materials need to be formatted in the same manner. In fact, students need to see that some types of writing are structured differently, include different text features, and utilize specific traits that all combine to create a unique composition.

There are great resources online where you can get access to leveled reading passages. Here are just a few:

- Newsela (www.newsela.com)

- Reading Is Fundamental (lower reading levels only) (www.rif.org)

- Read Works (www.readworks.org)

- Common Lit (www.commonlt.org)

- Smithsonian Tween Tribune (www.tweentribune.com)

Meeting students where they are is something that can help students get to the final product. Often teachers bombard students with vocabulary they don't understand, passages they can't read independently, written language that is highly sophisticated, and tasks that multistep complex pieces. I argue for meeting students where they are FIRST, and then we can work on getting them to the ultimate goal.

How Can I Make a Large Task More Manageable?

Another reason students sometimes lack motivation and drive is that for some the entire task may seem too difficult to complete. Many students shut down when they hear they will be completing a research paper, not because they can't do it but because the overall task seems too large with too many moving parts. However, by breaking that task into a series of smaller tasks, students can complete the final product simply by finishing all the smaller pieces that go together to make up the culminating assignment. Plus, when teachers break up especially large and difficult tasks and grade these as they go, for students who may not turn in the final product, they at least receive grades for the smaller tasks completed along the way. This can help address another motivation sinker: the inability to recover from a major failing grade.

How often have you had students who missed a major final project, failed an exam that carried a significant amount of weight, or had excessive absences and never seemed to be able to catch up on everything they missed? This happens every day. When students fail a major assignment, or even worse, receive a zero for something they did not turn in, many of them are aware that their grade cannot recover and, therefore, lose any motivation or drive to put forth much effort in the future.

Not all assignments lend themselves to being broken into smaller tasks. Some are already small and manageable. However, for those that require students to synthesize information from a variety of sources and create a portrait of a large phenomenon, breaking tasks like these into smaller ones can have multiple benefits.

Students also work better when they have a vested interest in the process and the product. This is why, whenever possible, students should be included in the design and development of projects, readings, and engagements. Yes, many would argue that this simply is not possible; the curriculum is mandated, reading lists chosen, and so on. However, allowing students to have input can be as simple as having them assist in generating topics for writing. For example, when I taught persuasive writing, I always had my students assist me in generating ideas for topics we could write about. This worked well because their ideas tended to be centered on current issues in their schools or lives.

To increase motivation in students, I suggest implementing these ideas frequently:

- Develop engagements that capitalize on student interest.

- Break tasks into manageable chunks that students can master.

- Allow student input into assignments when possible.

- Differentiate reading materials where possible.

- Get to know your students as people first and students second.

CHAPTER 1
Why Write Now?

CHAPTER 2
Parachute Writing

CHAPTER 3
Sum It All Up

CHAPTER 4
All the Right Words

CHAPTER 5
Digital Worlds

CHAPTER 6
Just the Facts

CHAPTER 7
Expecting the Unexpected

CHAPTER 1
Why Write Now?

CHAPTER 2
Parachute Writing

CHAPTER 3
Sum It All Up

CHAPTER 4
All the Right Words

CHAPTER 5
Digital Worlds

CHAPTER 6
Just the Facts

CHAPTER 7
Expecting the
Unexpected

What About Time? There Isn't Enough of It

Time seems to be every teacher's greatest challenge. There just does not seem to be enough time in the day to do everything that is needed, and now we have to add writing to our laundry list of things to do. Plus, add to that the fact that in many instances, typical instructional schedules are disrupted for a number of reasons that further reduce the amount of prime instructional time available.

Yet if you think about the writing strategies that we've discussed in this book, many of them are quick, five-to-ten-minute engagements that can be used in conjunction with what you are already teaching. Not sure students understand what you just went over? Try a Drop Draft. Unsure of what students know up front about a given concept or subject? Try Survival Words. Need a bell ringer that serves as a springboard into your lesson for the day? Try a Quick Write. Instead of attempting to incorporate a fully involved writing engagement in your class for the first time ever, try one of the quick strategies. This way, if you find that it doesn't jive with the class or unit, you've only spent five minutes on it, not five days.

Many of these strategies are also not meant to end up as a final, polished product. This means that if they don't end up completely done, that is perfectly fine. Here's another added benefit: You don't have to grade all of them. If you remember, much of what we are using writing for in the content areas is to process material, think through items, and deepen understanding. This means that you don't always have to grade it. Now, of course, you certainly can grade it, but I would be remiss if I didn't make one plea. When grading, think of the goal of the writing engagement. You aren't interested in how *well* they construct a sentence per se, you are interested in the overarching goals of the assignment. How well do they understand the content? Did they answer the question(s)? Did they provide enough textual evidence? Grade for characteristics and qualities such as those and tread lightly on the grammar, spelling, and construction front. Nothing makes a kid shut down faster than to have their paper slashed with red marks calling attention to every single mechanical error. There is a time and place to focus on mechanics and structure; it just isn't always right now.

What About Behavior Challenges?

We've all had challenging classes, students who struggle with behavior, or students who routinely cause disruptions. Sometimes, there are social or emotional causes for this type of behavior. However, sometimes, students act up because they simply are bored and are not engaged or interested in the material. Let me give you one example.

Last semester, I implemented literacy escape rooms in several classes at local middle schools in my area. When I went to one particular school, the instructional coach and teacher were hesitant to conduct one of the escape rooms in a particular class. This particular class was rather large (30+ students) and had some substantial behavior challenges. Instead, they wanted to implement them only in the gifted sections for the seventh-grade classes. After some convincing, they agreed to let me go into all the

CHAPTER 1
Why Write Now?

CHAPTER 2
Parachute Writing

CHAPTER 3
Sum It All Up

CHAPTER 4
All the Right Words

CHAPTER 5
Digital Worlds

CHAPTER 6
Just the Facts

CHAPTER 7
Expecting the
Unexpected

classes and try them out. Let me tell you, the class that performed the best was NOT the gifted one! In fact, that class did the worst! The class that performed the best was the one labeled as "below average" and "a behavior problem class."

During that particular escape room, where students had to solve a series of puzzles revealing codes that opened multiple locks, one group was so engaged that one of the students lost her hair (seriously she had a fake ponytail that fell out) and they kept working. I found the hair on the floor and asked the class if anyone lost anything. One girl patted her head, snatched up the ponytail, put it in her bag, and kept solving the puzzles. And believe it or not, that young lady's group won!

Now I know that some behavior challenges are not easily remedied, but I have found that teachers can reduce and actually eliminate some behavior problems simply by doing the following:

- Know who your students are and what strengths they possess.

- Use high-interest engagements.

- Allow students to be mobile and move around. (Think about the strategies in this book that allow for this: Text Mapping and Summary Sweeps to name a couple.)

- Provide time for student feedback and discussion.

- Remain flexible.

What If the Resources Needed Aren't Available?

In some cases, teachers are stuck with the textbooks, curriculum, and other resources that they have access to. Because curriculum programs are so expensive, teachers often have to utilize the materials that have been purchased for several years. Plus, there are significant inequities regarding resources across schools. Some have access to numerous trade books (children and young adult books), while others have libraries with outdated materials. In my experience, the quality of literature and the number of resources available can vary among schools in the very same county. In fact, last year I visited two schools that are roughly five miles apart in the same district. The difference in the availability of materials was startling. One media center was predominantly filled with outdated materials, with few titles that addressed contemporary topics. The other media center was full of new contemporary literature, new class novel sets, and professional literature for faculty. Part of this discrepancy is due to the fact that some schools have specific monies and allocated funds that can be used to purchase materials such as supplemental texts, full subscriptions to online article repositories, and more, whereas others don't. Regardless of the school budget allocations, I found when I was a classroom teacher, if I kept a working list of titles I would like to have, I usually had an opportunity to give input to the media specialist and administration when supplementary titles were purchased.

CHAPTER 1
Why Write Now?

CHAPTER 2
Parachute Writing

CHAPTER 3
Sum It All Up

CHAPTER 4
All the Right Words

CHAPTER 5
Digital Worlds

CHAPTER 6
Just the Facts

CHAPTER 7
Expecting the
Unexpected

As a content area teacher, you can also suggest that new curriculum programs and textbooks are supplemented with various trade books on a number of reading levels. This can help ensure that students are exposed to a variety of reading levels, text types, and interests. In some schools, I have worked with content-area teachers to create crates of supplemental content texts organized by grade level and topic that can be used by faculty. This way, when a teacher starts a unit on World War I, for example, there is a crate of supplemental texts that can be checked out and used during the teaching. This saves time as teachers don't have to spend their planning periods perusing library shelves for supplemental texts.

In some cases, teachers just need to take inventory of what supplies, texts, and items are available. Check with the media specialist, bookkeeper, and grade-level chairs to determine what materials are available. If possible, enlist district curriculum personnel for information regarding resources that are available districtwide. For example, districts may have software licenses and other subscriptions or resources that are available for all teachers in the county. This is a great beginning-of-the-year activity that can help teachers plan their year. For example, if you know that you have access to back issues of *National Geographic* from your media center, you may begin to incorporate these in some form or fashion in your classes. (Think about the Word Splash or List, Group, Label, Pin strategies.)

For rather small items, like sticky notes and notecards, these could be easily integrated into your supply list you send home at the beginning of the year. Instead of requiring students to have five folders, maybe they only need three folders, so you can add two packs of sticky notes to the list instead. For additional resources such as books, manipulatives, and other materials, many local and state affiliates of national organizations like the International Literacy Association and the National Council of Teachers of English offer mini-grants. In some communities, companies offer small grants that could also be used for these types of materials as well.

Stop & Think

You may have more resources available to you than you think. Just last semester, I was in a high school media center speaking with the media specialist about the books and resources available for the school. She told me about all the new books she had purchased for the school in addition to some software subscriptions and class magazines. When I went back to the classrooms to work with the teachers, none of them were aware of these materials. Additionally, during my workshops, I always mention books that can be used for a variety of literacy lessons. On several occasions, teachers have told me that they didn't have the titles I mentioned, but when I went to their media center, I was able to find many of them. It is important to ask your media specialist or your district leaders what resources are available. You may discover things you didn't know that you had access to!

What About the Existing Curriculum?

Making these strategies work within existing curriculum programs isn't as difficult or overwhelming as it may seem. In fact, so many of the strategies addressed in this book can be used to teach multiple skills. Even with the strictest, most scripted curriculum program, you can drop a strategy in as a new way to teach the content. Plus, the versatility of these strategies makes them a cinch to incorporate regardless of the curriculum standards used by districts.

One of the easiest ways to begin implementing new material along with the components that are required teaching is to get familiar with the standards and curriculum plans provided. By knowing what is expected, it is much easier to determine exactly what strategies you can incorporate as well. For example, you could use Survival Words with a variety of topics. The Summary Sweep can be utilized when you require students to conduct any kind of summary. Quick Writes can be incorporated anywhere. Newsela or a similar online source of leveled reading content may be a supplemental resource you use to help your struggling readers. If you start with the framework that must be used and the items that are nonnegotiable, you can fill in all the rest with high-interest, engaging activities and still be able to demonstrate that you are using the mandated curriculum program.

You Can Do This!

Even if incorporating literacy engagements in your content class is new to you, rest assured that you can successfully integrate quality reading and writing engagements into your teaching. By making strategic choices about when and what you plan to utilize in your teaching, you'll find that your students are able to engage with the material at a deeper level. Plus, when you start small and have successes with small engagements, it makes those extended, more complex writing tasks much more manageable. Remember, no matter where or what you teach, the time to write is NOW!

CHAPTER 1
Why Write Now?

CHAPTER 2
Parachute Writing

CHAPTER 3
Sum It All Up

CHAPTER 4
All the Right Words

CHAPTER 5
Digital Worlds

CHAPTER 6
Just the Facts

CHAPTER 7
Expecting the Unexpected

APPENDICES
TABLE OF CONTENTS

APPENDIX A

Quick Reference Guide

. . . .

Notice Notes for Strategies

Notice Notes for Pinterest Paragraphs

- How are images grouped?

- What are some possible names for the boards?

- Could any of the boards be broken down into subboards (subcategories)?

- How many images are included?

- How many groups or boards are used?

- What written descriptors, if any, are included?

Notice Notes for Picture Collage Content

- What formats are used for each type of information presented?

- How are images integrated into the design?

- What types of descriptive words or academic terms are used in the examples?

- Are any directional images (arrows, NSEW directions, coordinates, etc.) used? If so, what kinds?

- What words are included in the image?

- Are any words accompanied by definitions?

Sample Prompts

Tweet the Text Sample Prompts

- How would you respond to this text, image, or quote?

- What does it make you think of?

- What is the author's message or intent?

- What questions do you have after examining the piece?

Write Around the Text Sample Prompts

- The text reminds me of _____.

- After reading I wonder _____.

- Make a text-to-self connection.

- Draft a question that can accompany this text.

- How does this text make you feel?

- What happens next in this text?

Quick Write Nudge Questions

- *This piece made me think of _____.*

- *I wondered _____.*

- Borrow a line from the text and put your own spin on it.

- Take the same event but write from a different point of view and/or perspective.

- Draw a picture that best captures the mood of this piece.

- Write a list of words that describe the image (if using an image).

Text Mapping Slips

General Text Mapping Slip

1. Highlight the title and subtitles.

2. Put a box around the graphics, side bars, and illustrations.

3. Choose a word from the text. Use an address label to write the definition. Stick it on the text near the word.

4. Change the subheadings to hashtags.

5. Create a question for the selection of text. Write the question on a post-it or notecard. Draw an arrow to the place in the text that answers the question.

Focusing on Text Features Slip

1. Highlight the title and subtitles.

2. Put a box around the graphics, images side bars, and illustrations.

3. Circle any captions.

4. Change the subheadings to hashtags.

5. Highlight any bold printed words.

Focusing on Comprehension Text Map Slip

1. Choose an image in the text. Write a new caption to accompany it.

2. Choose a word from the text. Use an address label to write the definition. Stick it on the text near the word.

3. Change the subheadings to hashtags or questions.

4. Create a question for the selection of text. Write the question on a sticky note or notecard. Draw an arrow to the place in the text that answers the question.

5. Find a website that could be used for more information on this topic. Write the web address on an address label and stick in on the text.

6. Replace one of the images, diagrams, or figures with your own image.

Neighborhood Map Guiding Questions

- Who is in the story?

- Where did it occur?

- What time of day was it?

- When did it happen?

- What was the main event?

APPENDIX B

Student Resources

Say What?

They Say	I Say

Pizza Slice Summary

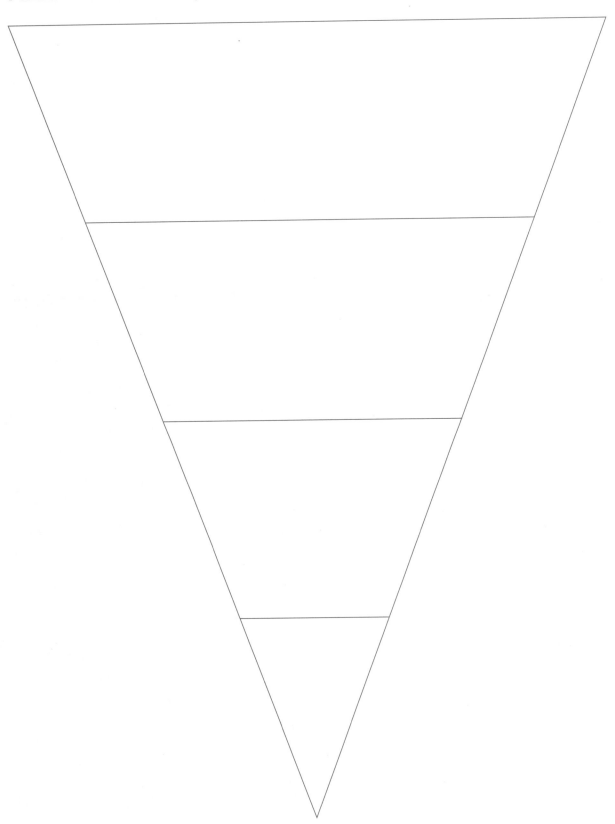

Survival Words

Directions: Write the provided words in the Word List column. Use the key below to rate yourself on your knowledge of each word. Include any extra comments in the third column, if needed.

Word List	Rate Yourself	Comments

Key

A: I know what this word means, and I use it.

B: I know what this word means, but I do not use it.

C: I have seen the word, but I am not sure what it means.

D: I have no idea what this word means.

Figure This Reference Guide

Idiom	Onomatopoeia	Alliteration
• A group of words whose meaning isn't understood from their literal meaning Example: *The detective's interrogation of the suspect was simply an acid test.*	• The formation of a word from a sound associated with what is named Example: *Bing! Bang! Boom! Blast! Bombs lit up over the horizon.*	• The repetition of the same letter or sound at the beginning of adjacent or closely connected words. Example: *Five famous foxes ate six slender serpents for seven days straight. How many serpents were swallowed?*
Hyperbole	**Simile**	**Metaphor**
• An exaggeration that can't possibly be true Example: *My geometry teacher gave us a million problems to do.*	• A comparison of items using the words *like* or *as* Example: *Martin Luther King sang like a bird, his songs of dreams and equality soaring overall.*	• A comparison of two unlike things that says one is like the other Example: *Ray Lewis stood at the line, a stone wall before those in front of him.*
Allusion	**Oxymoron**	**Pun**
• A reference to a famous person, place, or event Example: *The novel Dumplin is a real Cinderella story.*	• A phrase that uses two words that appear to contradict each other, but make sense overall Example: *That interception was pretty bad.*	• A play on words Example: *He threw sodium chloride at me! That's a salt!*

Murder Mystery/Crime Scene Analysis

When examining your murder mystery or crime scene, consider the following:

- Who are the individuals at the scene or who are involved?

- What is the setting?

- Are there any possible murder weapons present? What are they?

- What time of day is it?

- Are there any items that are out of place? If so, what are they?

- Trace any movement in the crime scene. For example, can you tell if one of the individuals has moved from their current location? Are there items that have been displaced?

- Read the narrative account of the crime scene. Match the physical evidence to the information in the narrative.

- Construct a timeline of the events the occurred in the scene. Which events occurred first? Which ones occurred last?

Two Truths and a Lie

Use this chart as you develop your truths and lies.

Truths	Lies

Choose one lie and rewrite it so it now it becomes a truth.

Choose one truth and rewrite it so now it becomes a lie.

Paint Strip Partners

Steps in the Process

Explanations of the Process

Generic Paint Strip 1

Generic Paint Strip 2

REFERENCES

Ahearn, L. M. (2017). *Living language: An introduction to linguistic anthropology*. Wiley.

August, D., Carlo, M., Dressler, C., & Snow, C. (2005). The critical role of vocabulary development for English language learners. *Learning Disabilities Research & Practice, 20*(1), 50–57.

Bartels, J. (2017). Snapchat and the sophistication of multimodal composition. *English Journal, 106*(5), 90–92.

Barton, D. (2001). Directions for literacy research: Analysing language and social practices in a textually mediated world. *Language and Education 15*(2), 92–104.

Bawarshi, A. S. (2003). *Genre and the invention of the writer: Reconsidering the place of invention in composition*. University Press of Colorado. https://doi.org/10.2307/j.ctt46nxp6

Beck, I. L., McKeown, M. G., & Kucan, L. (2013). *Bringing words to life: Robust vocabulary instruction*. Guilford Press.

Beck, I. L., Perfetti, C. A., & McKeown, M. G. (1982). Effects of long-term vocabulary instruction on lexical access and reading comprehension. *Journal of Educational Psychology, 74*(4), 506.

Bhabha, H. K. (1994). Frontlines/Borderposts. In A. Bammer (Ed.), *Displacements: Cultural identities in question*. (pp. 269–272). Indiana University Press.

Bhabha, H. K. (1994). *The location of culture*. Routledge.

Bloomberg News. (2012, September 12). Report: U.S. teens report decline in writing skills. *Houston Chronicle*. https://www.houstonchronicle.com/news/nation-world/article/Report-U-S-teens-show-decline-in-writing-skills-3866501.php

Britsch, S. (2009). ESOL educators and the experience of visual literacy. *Tesol Quarterly, 43*(4), 710–721.

Brown, L. (2014). *Depressed, repressed, obsessed*. California Bookstore Day.

Burmark, L. (2008). Visual literacy: What you get is what you see. In D. Fisher & N. Frey (Eds.), *Teaching visual literacy: Using comic books, graphic novels, anime, cartoons, and more to develop comprehension and thinking skills*. (pp. 5–25). Corwin.

Chung, S. F. (2012). Research-based vocabulary instruction for English language learners. *Reading Matrix: An International Online Journal, 12*(2), 105–120.

Conley, D. T. (2005). *College knowledge: What it really takes for students to succeed and what we can do to get them ready*. Jossey-Bass.

Conley, D. T. (2007). The challenge of college readiness. *Educational Leadership, 64*(7), 23–29.

Cullen, M. (2020). *The costs of poor business writing (Statistics, examples, and case studies).* https://www.instructionalsolutions.com/blog/costs-poor-business-writing

Demographics of Social Media Users and Adoption in the United States. (n.d.). Pew Research Group. https://www.pewresearch.org/internet/fact-sheet/social-media/

Dieterich, D. (1977). The decline in student's writing skills: An ERIC/RCS interview. *College English, 38*(5), 466–472.

Elsden-Clifton, J. (2006). Exploring the spaces of art education. In R. Jeffery, W. Shilton, and P. Jeffery (Eds.), *Australian Association for Research in Education 2005 Conference Papers,* 1–11. http://www.aare.edu.au/05pap/els05012.pdf

Fletcher, R. (2007). *How to write your life story.* Collins.

Freire, P., & Macedo, D. (1987). *Literacy: Reading the word and the world.* Praeger.

Graham, S., & Perin, D. (2006, Oct. 9). *Writing next: Effective strategies to improve writing of adolescents in middle and high schools.* Alliance for Excellent Education. https://all4ed.org/reports-factsheets/writing-next-effective-strategies-to-improve-writing-of-adolescents-in-middle-and-high-schools/

Graham, S., & Perin, D. (2007). A meta-analysis of writing instruction for adolescent students. *Journal of Educational Psychology, 99*(3), 445–476. https://bridgestolearning2009.pbworks.com/f/graham%26perin07.pdf

Graves, M. F. (2007). Vocabulary instruction in the middle grades. *Voices from the Middle, 15*(1), 13–19.

Gutiérrez, K. D. (2008). Developing a sociocritical literacy in the third space. *Reading Research Quarterly, 43*(2), 148–164.

Gutiérrez, K. D., Baquedano-López, P., & Tejeda, C. (1999). Rethinking diversity: Hybridity and hybrid language practices in the third space. *Mind, Culture, and Activity, 6*(4), 286–303.

Heard, G. (1999). *Heart maps: Helping students create and craft authentic writing.* Heinemann.

Hempel M. (2014). *Ecoliteracy: Knowledge is not enough.* In Worldwatch Institute, State of the World. Island Press. https://doi.org/10.5822/978-1-61091-542-7_4

Langer, J. A., & Applebee, A. N. (1987). *How writing shapes thinking: A study of teaching and learning.* National Council of Teachers of English. https://wac.colostate.edu/docs/books/langer_applebee/langer_applebee.pdf

McKeown, M. G., Beck, I. L., Omanson, R. C., & Perfetti, C. A. (1983). The effects of long-term vocabulary instruction on reading comprehension: A replication. *Journal of Reading Behavior, 15*(1), 3–18.

Meeker, M. (2014). *Internet Trends Report 2014.* Kleiner Perkins. https://www.kleinerperkins.com/perspectives/internet-trends-report-2018/

Metros, S. E. (2008). The educator's role in preparing visually literate learners. *Theory into Practice, 47*(2), 102–109.

Miller, M. (2000). *You be the jury: Courtroom collection.* Scholastic.

Moje, E. B., Ciechanowski, K. M., Kramer, K., Ellis, L., Carrillo, R., & Collazo, T. (2004). Working toward third space in content area literacy: An examination of everyday funds of knowledge and discourse. *Reading Research Quarterly, 39*(1), 38–70.

Morrell, E., & Collatos, A. (2003). Toward a critical teacher pedagogy: Utilizing student sociologists as teacher educators. *Social Justice 29*(4), 60–71.

National Center for Education. (2018). *Digest of education statistics: 2018*. https://nces.ed.gov/programs/digest/d18/

National Center for Education Statistics. (2011). *Writing 2011: National assessment of educational progress grades 8 and 12*. National Center for Education Statistics, Institute of Education Sciences, U.S. Department of Education.

National Commission on Writing for America's Schools and Colleges. (2004, September). *Writing: A ticket to work . . . or a ticket out*. National Writing Project. https://archive.nwp.org/cs/public/print/resource/2540

National Council of Teachers of English. (2018). *Understanding and teaching writing: Guiding principles. Position Statement*. https://ncte.org/statement/teachingcomposition/

National Reading Panel. (2000). *Teaching children to read: An evidence-based assessment of the scientific research literature on reading and its implications for reading instruction: Reports of the subgroups*. National Institute of Child Health and Human Development, National Institutes of Health. https://www.nichd.nih.gov/sites/default/files/publications/pubs/nrp/Documents/report.pdf

National Writing Project. (2021). https://sites.google.com/nwp.org/c3wp/home

Pope, J. (2005, July). Report highlights cost of poor writing. *Boston Globe*. http://archive.boston.com/news/nation/articles/2005/07/04/report_highlights_cost_of_poor_writing/

Pulfrey, C., Buchs, C., & Butera, F. (2011). Why grades engender performance-avoidance goals: The mediating role of autonomous motivation. *Journal of Educational Psychology, 103*(3), 683–700. https://doi.org/10.1037/a0023911

Rose, G. (2016). *Visual methodologies: An introduction to researching with visual materials*. Sage.

Santelises, S. B. (2015). *Checking in: Do classroom assignments reflect today's higher standards?* Education Trust. https://edtrust.org/resource/classroomassignments/

Schinske, J., & Tanner, K. (2014). Teaching more by grading less (or differently). *CBE Life Sciences Education, 13*(2), 159–166. https://doi.org/10.1187/cbe.cbe-14-03-0054

Seiler, G., Tobin, K., & Sokolic, J. (2001). Design, technology, and science: Sites for learning, resistance, and social reproduction in urban schools. *Journal of Research in Science Teaching, 38*(7), 746–767.

Sheils, M. (1975). Why Johnny can't write. *Newsweek*, 58–63.

Shor, I., & Freire, P. (1987). *A pedagogy for liberation: Dialogues on transforming education*. Greenwood.

Sobol, D. J. (1991). *Two-minute mysteries*. Turtleback Books.

Soja, E. W. (1996). *Thirdspace: Journeys to Los Angeles and other real-and-imagined places*. Blackwell.

Swaminathan, V., Page, K. L., & Gürhan-Canli, Z. (2007). "My" brand or "our" brand: The effects of brand relationship dimensions and self-construal on brand evaluations. *Journal of Consumer Research, 34*(2), 248–259.

Takao, A. Y., & Kelly, G. J. (2003). Assessment of evidence in university students' scientific writing. *Science & Education, 12*(4), 341–363.

Treat, L. (2003). *Crime and puzzlement: 24 solve-them-yourself picture mysteries*. David R. Godine.

Westin, S. (2013). Social media eroding skills? *Philadelphia Inquirer*. https://www
.inquirer.com/philly/firsttake/20130406_Students_worry_that_social_media_erodes_basic_
skills.html

Yenawine, P. (2014). *Visual thinking strategies: Using art to deepen learning across school
disciplines*. Harvard Education Press.

Zinsser, W. (2001). *On writing well* (25th anniversary ed.). Harper Resource.

INDEX

Because...
ALL TEACHERS ARE LEADERS

DOMINIQUE SMITH, DOUGLAS FISHER, NANCY FREY

Take an active approach toward disrupting the negative effects of labels and assumptions that interfere with student learning.

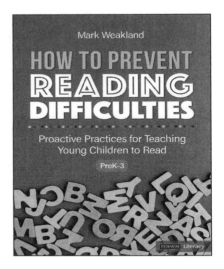

MARK WEAKLAND

Build on decades of evidence and years of experience to understand how the brain learns to read and how to apply that understanding to Tier 1 instruction.

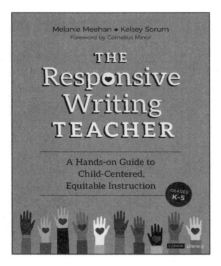

MELANIE MEEHAN, KELSEY SORUM

Learn how to adapt curriculum to meet the needs of the whole child. Each chapter offers intentional steps for responsive instruction across four domains: academic, linguistic, cultural, and social-emotional.

MATTHEW JOHNSON

Learn classroom-tested solutions that not only alleviate the feedback-burnout cycle but also lead to significant growth for students.

To order your copies, visit corwin.com/literacy

At Corwin Literacy we have put together a collection of just-in-time, classroom-tested, practical resources from trusted experts that allow you to quickly find the information you need when you need it.

DOUGLAS FISHER, NANCY FREY, NICOLE LAW

Using a structured, three-pronged approach—skill, will, and thrill—students experience reading as a purposeful act with this new comprehensive model of reading instruction.

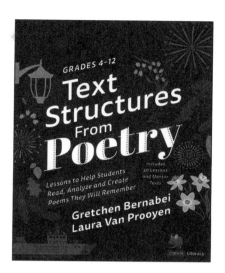

**GRETCHEN BERNABEI,
LAURA VAN PROOYEN**

Teach your students about poetry using the magic of poems themselves, and lead the way to a rewarding love of poetry for teachers and students alike.

LAURA ROBB, DAVID L. HARRISON

Present 24 powerful reading lessons using original poems and short texts that interest your students and encourage them to think deeply.

MOLLY NESS

Examine your use of time in the classroom in order to make more space for literacy and 40 innovative activities designed to replace seatwork.

CORWIN

A SAGE Publishing Company

Helping educators make the greatest impact

CORWIN HAS ONE MISSION: to enhance education through intentional professional learning.

We build long-term relationships with our authors, educators, clients, and associations who partner with us to develop and continuously improve the best evidence-based practices that establish and support lifelong learning.